"With de[...] the
authors c[...] [...]as-
sionate ac[...] [...]o's
health car[...] [...]o care about care,
and about [...] [...]gether to confront and limit violence."

Pat Armstrong, York University, and **Hugh Armstrong**, Carleton University, editors of *The Privatization of Care: The Case of Nursing Homes*

"Around the world, health care workers have been applauded for their tireless work during the pandemic. And yet as Keith and Brophy reveal in this powerful exposé, alongside these public displays of gratitude runs a hidden epidemic of violence—one that goes unchallenged by those with the power to prevent it. Harrowing, infuriating, and so important, this book could not be more timely. It should be on every policy maker's desk."

Caroline Criado Perez, author of *Invisible Women: Exposing Data Bias in a World Designed for Men*

"The pandemic highlighted the value and sacrifices of health care workers, but didn't answer them in terms of protections and clear support. This book is a reminder that the violence perpetrated against health care workers long predates the pandemic and will remain after the pandemic, unless there is a solidarity response."

Sam Gindin, co-author of *The Making of Global Capitalism: The Political Economy Of American Empire*

"Passionate. Dispassionate. Letting health care workers speak for themselves about the violence they face, Keith and Brophy's anger is palpable. Cool analysis of the many factors leading to this suffering leads them to identify a system that exploits workers and takes advantage of the vulnerabilities spawned by gender, racial, and migration status discriminations. A must-read for activists and theorists."

Harry Glasbeek, author of *Capitalism: A Crime Story*

"*Code White* does a great job not only analyzing and describing workplace violence in health care, but looks at why the problem exists, while offering a comprehensive approach to prevention. It should be essential reading for health care workers and their allies interested in acting to end this modern workplace scourge."

Michael B. Lax, MD MPH, medical director, Occupational Health Clinical Center, State University of New York Upstate Medical University

"If you want to understand why there is a critical shortage of front-line health care workers, read this book. It's all there—terrible violence and racist harassment from clients, victim-blaming and shaming from supervisors, indifference from management, and no help at all from government occupational health and safety authorities. You would almost think that these majority-female workers were considered to be expendable. As an ergonomist, I was especially interested in the environmental and design defects Keith and Brophy document: alarms that don't work or are confusing, dangerous objects on psychiatric wards, flaws in procedures. And a way of planning work that isolates workers from one another. An important call to action from longtime defenders of working people."

Karen Messing, Ph.D., professeure émérite, Université du Québec à Montréal

"Violence at work is a symptom. If workers are not appreciated, if there are too few staff, and if workloads are too high, you create a tinderbox of resentment, with staff on the receiving end. This groundbreaking publication reveals how unions are exposing the root causes of violence at work and shows conclusively that trade union organization is a surefire cure."

Rory O'Neill, editor, *Hazards* magazine

"A riveting and devastating account of the neglected toll of violence in health care. Told through the voices of health care workers, *Code White* describes the root causes of this epidemic and offers both an urgent plea and a blueprint to end it."

Stephanie Premji, associate professor, School of Labour Studies, McMaster University

"It is not "part of the job" for health care workers to put up with violence in the workplace. *Code White* exposes the extent of the ongoing violence against health care workers in Canada. The book provides an in-depth look into how our health care system has reached a point where staff do not feel safe or supported."

Dale Rajacich, professor emeritus, Faculty of Nursing, University of Windsor

"Keith and Brophy bring to light an under-recognized workplace hazard faced by all health care workers: violence. With the number of "code whites" seemingly increasing, this trend needs to be recognized, understood, and ameliorated. This book is a step to that end."

Abe Reinhartz, MD, Humber River Hospital

"We have long known that women—especially racialized women—make up the majority of health care workers and that acts of violence committed against them are ubiquitous and under-reported. It took Keith and Brophy's study and analysis to put real faces to those who are living with this workplace reality and to pull back the curtain on the depth of sexism and racism there. With compassion and their trademark lens of feminist analysis and social justice, they conclude with a blueprint of clear, reasonable solutions—solutions whose time has never been more critical."

Anne Rochon Ford, co-lead, Nail Salon Workers Project

"*Code White* is an indictment of our health care system's failure to address workplace violence as told through the powerful voices of victims who feel unprotected, unsupported, and silenced. Detailing the prevalence and root causes of violence in health care settings, including staff shortages, the authors call for violence prevention, as well as a fundamental shift in workplace culture to reject all forms of violence at work. As the authors make clear, the long-standing failure of governments and employers to act on this issue has devastating consequences for the entire health system, reducing safety for everyone, including patients, residents, and clients."

Linda Silas, president, Canadian Federation of Nurses Unions

"A must-read for health care workers and for everyone who wants to understand why our health care system is failing to meet our needs and how it has become designed to strip health care workers of their dignity, health, and safety. Keith and Brophy have given us the opportunity to understand the experience of working within the madness of a system that demands that health care function like a business that prioritizes budgetary efficiencies instead of community health."

Craig Slatin, professor emeritus, University of
Massachusetts Lowell, editor of *New Solutions:
A Journal of Environmental and Occupational Health Policy*

"*Code White* provides an excellent and important analysis of a disturbing issue that affects health care workers not only in Canada, but elsewhere in the world. Both authors have a long and very distinguished history of carefully and meticulously investigating Canadian and global occupational health and safety problems, related structural issues and then working out effective solutions to those problems through actions by organized labour and others. This approach shines through in the book, with its deep understanding of the political and economic as well as technical roots of the violence that affect health care workers. I commend *Code White* to readers, researchers, governments, and labour organizations everywhere."

Andrew Watterson, occupational health and safety
researcher, Stirling University, Scotland

CODE WHITE

Sounding the Alarm on Violence against Health Care Workers

Margaret M. Keith and James T. Brophy

Foreword by Michael Hurley

Between the Lines
Toronto

First published in 2021 by
Between the Lines
401 Richmond Street West, Studio 281
Toronto, Ontario, M5V 3A8, Canada
1-800-718-7201 · www.btlbooks.com

Library and Archives Canada Cataloguing in Publication

Title: Code white : sounding the alarm on violence against healthcare workers / Margaret M. Keith and James T. Brophy.
Names: Keith, Margaret M., author. | Brophy, James T., author.
Description: Includes bibliographical references and index.
Identifiers: Canadiana (print) 20210242310 | Canadiana (ebook) 20210242426 | ISBN 9781771135658 (softcover) | ISBN 9781771135665 (EPUB) | ISBN 9781771135672 (PDF)
Subjects: LCSH: Medical personnel—Violence against—Canada. | LCSH: Medical personnel—Health and hygiene—Canada. | LCSH: Violence in the workplace—Canada.
Classification: LCC R727.2 .K45 2021 | DDC 362.1068/4—dc23

Text and cover design by DEEVE

Printed in Canada

We acknowledge for their financial support of our publishing activities: the Government of Canada; the Canada Council for the Arts; and the Government of Ontario through the Ontario Arts Council, the Ontario Book Publishers Tax Credit program, and Ontario Creates.

*To our mothers, Eleanor C. Keith and Evelyn M. Brophy,
whose love, kindness, acceptance, and goodness shaped us
and inspired our life-long commitment to social justice.*

Contents

Foreword

COVID-19 brought health care workers onto the front pages. They were lauded as front-line heroes soldiering on, inadequately protected and with a high rate of infection and death in underfunded, understaffed hospitals, long-term care and retirement homes, and homecare. But if health care workers are soldiers in the war against the pandemic, what are their normal working conditions?

Long before the COVID-19 crisis began, health care staff, whom we rely on in our most vulnerable moments, were facing a workplace crisis of their own. This book pulls back the curtain on the shrouded epidemic of violence against health care workers.

Dianne Paulin was brutally beaten by a patient in the forensic psychiatry unit at her hospital. The door to his room locked automatically behind her and a design flaw prevented it from reopening from the inside. She suffered, including from ongoing gripping anxiety. Long after this incident, when code whites were sounded, Dianne would hide under a desk, terrified. She was not supported by her employer or by workers' compensation and was ultimately discarded, like a broken chair. Recently, after years of grinding poverty, she won her appeal for permanent benefits.

Scott Sharp was thrown through a wall at his hospital's emergency room by a patient high on crystal meth, who assaulted several staff that night. His spine was badly injured. The man who did that to him spat in his face when he met Scott in his wheelchair on the street months later. Although he was charged, this man was not held accountable by the courts for the assault.

Scott lost his house after being repeatedly cut off workers' compensation benefits and came very near to ending his life, in despair of ever being able to work or to help support his family again. Eventually, after years of surgeries and physiotherapy, he returned to full-time work at the hospital.

Dianne and Scott have suffered terribly, and they are just two of tens of thousands of Ontario health care workers who have been assaulted physically, sexually, racially, or verbally in the last few years. A river of suffering.

Polling of hospital workers and long-term care workers done by OCHU-CUPE in Ontario shows eye-popping levels of assaults of all kinds and a toxic environment for women in these workplaces.

The *Globe and Mail* produced a powerful series on the violence that is directed against women in Canadian society. It found that violence is rampant and that racialized and Indigenous women are particularly vulnerable. The victim is usually blamed. The police rarely press charges. The courts fail most victims.

Power, who has it and who doesn't, lurks in the background of this discussion.

In female-dominated working environments like health care (85 per cent of the workforce is female), society's attitudes towards violence against women, and about power and who has it, are not stopped at the door. In fact, these attitudes are invited in and given a prominent seat at the table.

Health care workers are denied basic civil liberties like the right to strike and the right to refuse unsafe work. Removing these rights has been key to ensuring that the workforce is less powerful, more vulnerable, and more open to exploitation.

Work is increasingly part-time, including 50 per cent of hospital work and 60 per cent of long-term care jobs. Part-time workers are dependent on the good will of supervisors for work and for the quality of their assignments. Full-time employees are dependent on that good will too, for the quality of their work assignments and for any unscheduled time off.

It is less expensive to employ people full-time, the costings that we have been given in bargaining tell us, but employers prefer part-time work because it leaves the workers more vulnerable and less powerful.

Ontario's hospitals have the fewest beds and staff to population anywhere in the world with a developed economy. Ontario's long-term care capacity and staffing is the second-lowest in Canada. This shortfall in capacity and staffing collides with the phenomenon of a rapidly aging and growing population.

This power over the workforce is used to deliver quality health care through wave after wave of austerity and downsizing. Health care management compensates for the shortfall in staffing and capacity by bullying and coercing its primarily female caregivers to treat greater and greater volumes of very sick patients and residents without complaint. The outspoken are often harassed, disciplined, and sometimes fired *pour encourager les autres.*

Three brave and outspoken women activists that I worked with on the violence studies that inform this book were fired. In one of these cases, a nurse was fired after being quoted in a media release saying that there is a problem with violence against nurses in Ontario. It took two years to have her reinstated through arbitration.

Patients are consumers and they have rights. Health care workers are servants under law without very many rights at all. Somehow the premise that everyone in society is equal has gotten completely lost in this working environment. I am hopeful that the spirited generation entering health care work now will overthrow the feudal notion that they are not as valuable as the people that they care for.

Who could tell this story and situate it in a context where the magnitude of the violence happening to health care workers can be understood, using the lenses of gender and race and class?

I have had the privilege to work with Dr. James Brophy and Dr. Margaret Keith for over forty years on occupational health and safety issues. I was immediately drawn to their humanity and analysis, and courage and activism. They have never been afraid to challenge government, employers, or unions. In telling the truth over their working lifetimes, they been a beacon of hope for health and safety activists whose movement was co-opted and neutralized in the 1980s.

The landmark work that the authors, Dr. Pat Armstrong, and others have done on violence pries open a locked door on power and gender and class relations in the health care sector. Let us rip that door from its hinges now and fight with them to transform working life in this sector.

Michael Hurley
President, Ontario Council of Hospital Unions-CUPE

Preface

We, Margaret and James, have been working together for four decades in the fields of occupational and environmental health. We met at a meeting about asbestos in the workplace and soon became spouses and research partners. We have raised four amazing children who, along with their own partners, have become our closest friends and confidants, and we now savour the joys of our growing flock of grandchildren and great-grandchildren. But having such a bounty of offspring brings with it a proportionate measure of concern about the world they are inheriting. It drives us to keep working towards a society that is more equitable and just.

We have been influenced by many inspiring social movements over the years, beginning with the civil rights, anti-war, labour, anti-nuclear, anti-poverty, feminist, AIDS, LBGTQ+, environmental, and climate change movements, and more recently by such courageous struggles against injustice as #MeToo, Black Lives Matter, Idle No More, and youth climate justice movements. Our focus, however, remains primarily on occupational health. We have seen over and over throughout the years that there is a very unequal relationship between employers and employees and that gains in health and safety never seem to come without a struggle on the part of those at risk. We unapologetically consider ourselves to be advocacy researchers. Our research always has a component of advocacy built into it, designed to provide those with less power additional resources with which to struggle for needed improvements.

The health care system that our parents' generation fought for, that we were so proud of, and that we depend upon is in tatters. We remember what it was like to be a patient or a family member of someone who was admitted to hospital in the 1970s and 1980s, before defunding began to erode timely care. In 1983, we took our son and daughter into the emergency department (a.k.a. emergency room or ER) after they had collided during a gymnastics stunt on our front lawn. Our daughter had a large open gash on her leg where it had met with our son's front teeth. His lip was severely split and bleeding. We were escorted directly to triage, then into an examining room where the children were assessed and their wounds cleaned. Shortly thereafter, a doctor came in and administered a local anaesthetic and stitches to each of them. We were all back home within two hours, although there would be several follow-up visits to the plastic surgeon—again with no significant wait time for the initial consults and treatment.

In more recent years we have watched health care staff throughout their shifts, run off their feet, exhausted, and doing their best to be supportive and attentive. We listened anxiously as a frustrated patient in the next room angrily shouted "Nurse! Nurse!" over and over again while the nurse finished taking our elderly family member's vitals. We watched with trepidation as security personnel and nurses fought to restrain an out-of-control ER patient on the gurney right next to a family member who was having a cardiac episode. And during hospitalization for a personal medical procedure, we witnessed a male roommate threaten to punch the nurse who was tending to him.

The days of comfort care, universal access to quality care, and trust in the medical care system are gone. Underfunding, understaffing, and the steady inching into privatization are eroding our precious universal health care system. We have too often found ourselves among the frightened and desperate people, waiting for hours in the ER, waiting days for a bed, or waiting months for surgery to alleviate our pain—or waiting, waiting, for the call bell to be answered.

Our society is different now too. Patients are different. There are new diseases. People are living longer, getting sicker. Drug addiction, particularly to opioids, is on the rise and there are too few supports in place to address the crisis. Services for people with mental health needs are under-resourced and many are left without timely treatment. We are all suffering from the decay of our health care system. Health care staff are suffering too. After they finish their shifts, they're left burnt out, carrying work-related physical and psychological injuries home with them. Then the next day, they have to go back and face overwork, sometimes hostile or aggressive patients, and frequently unsupportive supervisors all over again.

Health care workers—from doctors and nurses to cleaning staff—experience some of the highest rates of violence and sexual harassment of any occupational group, but they suffer in silence because they are barred from talking about it. As a result, for the most part, violence against health care staff remains a shameful secret.

This book is the result of collaborative work with Michael Hurley, president of the Ontario Council of Hospital Unions–Canadian Union of Public Employees (OCHU-CUPE), with whom we have worked for many years around various issues related to the risks and exploitation experienced by health care workers. He has opened our eyes to injustices we were unaware even existed. Although we have been working in occupational health for decades, the enormity of the issue of violence against health care staff had escaped our notice, which lends to our premise that this problem, with few exceptions, has been systematically hidden from the public.

Our research took place in Ontario, and much of the data we provide in this book is Ontario- or Canada-based. We have learned, however, that this is an international problem that urgently requires not only provincial and national action, but global action as well.

We completed our research on violence and most of the writing for this book just months before the COVID-19 pandemic reached Ontario in March 2020. The problems we had learned about only became worse when it hit. Hospital and long-term care workers had been facing serious challenges before the pandemic. Already overworked, burnt out, and demoralized, they now found themselves in the midst of a full-blown occupational health crisis in a system that did not have the resilience or resources to meet the greatly increased needs of patients, residents, or the people who care for them. We have added an afterword to describe a study we undertook with health care workers who talked to us about their experiences during the early months of the pandemic. They told us they felt exploited, unsupported, and unprotected—which is a kind of violence in itself.

It is our fervent hope that this book opens the doors of our health care institutions wide enough that we can hear the voices— the pleas—of those who care for us when we are sick and weak and unable to look after ourselves. We know that ending violence against health care workers is not going to have a simple on/off light-switch solution and the road ahead is fraught with difficulties that threaten to dissuade engagement. But we can't ignore this issue any longer, just as we can't ignore domestic assault, discrimination, harassment, or sexual assault. Violence against health care staff is a human rights issue that we are all being challenged now to address.

A note about the stories we share in this book

Three research studies that we conducted with health care workers are at the core of this book. The studies were previously published by Sage Publications in *New Solutions: A Journal of Environmental and Occupational Health Policy* and in a book chapter published by Between the Lines.[1] Because they have been systematically silenced, we have included, as much as possible, the voices of the health care workers themselves. They are the true experts. Some passages have been marginally edited for clarity or to protect the identity of the participants.

We have used various terms related to gender, sexuality, and racial identity. We are mindful that our understandings of the experiences of individuals in various groups are varied and that they are not homogeneous.

The passion and vehemence that we heard are not necessarily conveyed in the transcribed narratives; some interviewees were clearly crying, others were audibly angry. Some interviews had to be temporarily paused while the interviewees collected themselves emotionally.

Acknowledgements

We are grateful to Linda Clayborne and Heather Neiser, our invaluable research assistants. We thank Sharon Richer and Megan Yeadon, who managed myriad logistical and administrative tasks; Doug Allan, who provided important background information; and the Research Ethics Boards at the University of Stirling and the University of Windsor for their thoughtful review of the study protocols. We are also grateful to Andrew Watterson, who provided mentorship and encouragement; to Craig Slatin, for his expert advice, insights, and editing of the research articles cited herein; to Mary McArthur and Jane McArthur, who provided advice regarding methodical approaches and analysis; to Laura McArthur and John McArthur, for their loving, ongoing support; to our friends and family for keeping us going through some ups and downs; to our copy editor Tilman Lewis, and to the staff of Between the Lines, including managing editor Amanda Crocker, Devin Clancy, Dave Gray-Donald, and Karina Palmitesta.

We offer this heartfelt thank you to the brave, selfless, and visionary health care workers we have had the honour and privilege to meet through our work, some of whom are named in this book while others remain anonymous: *Our hats are off to you. Together, with your will, your power, and your compassion for each other, you can move mountains. Indeed, you always have. We wish you health, safety, contentment, and a work environment free of violence.*

Part One

Exposing a Hidden Epidemic

1.

Drawing Back the Curtain

"Then he started pounding on me"

On the morning of August 24, 2011, Dianne Paulin, an experienced psychiatric nurse in North Bay, Ontario, began her shift on the forensic unit (the unit that deals with patients found not criminally responsible, or NCR) at the local psychiatric hospital. She learned that a new patient, a man in his early twenties with a complex mental health diagnosis, had been admitted the night before. Her supervisor told her the new admission was to be her prime patient. Dianne reviewed his chart and noted that he was young and strong, about six foot two, weighing 260 pounds. And he had a history of violence. Her new patient had been placed in a seclusion room upon admission because he was extremely agitated. He had assaulted two police officers who had been called when he had attacked someone in the group home where he was living. As Dianne later learned, her patient had been removed from his family home and placed in the group home in the first place because he had physically assaulted his father and had been sexually aggressive with his mother.

When Dianne opened the door to the seclusion room, she observed right away that the patient was heavily soiled with urine and feces. He was mumbling and was visibly upset. She relieved the nurse who been attending to him and set out to establish a rapport with her new patient. Dianne had years of experience working with psychiatric patients and was confident in her ability to develop a respectful working relationship with even the most difficult cases. She was sure she would be able to manage him, and as it turned out, she was able to convince him that he should take a shower, get changed, and have something to eat. Sure enough, her patient was soon stable enough to be moved to a private room.

A psychotic patient who is prone to violence can be just a hair-trigger away from snapping. That is precisely what happened when Dianne went to check on him later that day. She relieved the nurse who was sitting with him and found her patient on his bed crying. When she asked what was wrong, he said he wanted to use the phone. She calmly explained that he could use it as soon as the other staff returned from their dinner breaks. He began demanding the phone and she repeated that he would have to wait a little while. He quickly turned from unhappy to irate. He jumped up from the bed, yelling something unintelligible, and grabbed a chair. Dianne turned to leave the room but found that the door had closed behind her. Then he unleashed his fury.

> I was barricaded behind the door with the chair hard against me.
> He pounded me on my head, my face, and on my shoulders. He was yelling and screaming while he punched me. And a patient who was on the other side of the door started yelling and screaming.

A code white was called, letting other staff know that someone needed help with a violent incident. After what seemed an eternity, staff did arrive, but they were blocked from entering the room. Injured but desperate, Dianne pushed back against the chair with all her strength in order for her rescuers to get the door open. The patient immediately turned and swung at the first person who rushed into the room. As more staff came in, he began to settle down and was ultimately calmed enough to walk to the seclusion room. In shock, Dianne was not immediately aware of how extensive her injuries were. She told us she remembers finding it difficult to walk and her co-workers having to help her to the nursing station. There she broke down.

> I started crying and shaking, and crying and shaking, and crying. Are you hurt? I don't know. I don't know if I'm hurt. I don't know. I just got hit all over. Am I hurt? Well, yeah, I'm hurt here, here, everything hurts, I don't know. Then, because I was shaking too much to walk, they took me in a wheelchair to the emergency department.

This brutal incident would change the course of Dianne's life.

What do we mean by violence?

Dianne's story of her horrific experience is a clear example of violence in the health care workplace. We heard many shocking stories of physical violence like this one. But we also heard stories of health care workers experiencing verbal abuse, hostile behaviour, hate speech, and sexual harassment, all of which are acts of violence against health care workers. Elizabeth Stanko, who has comprehensively studied violence against women in society, says violence is "any form of behaviour by an individual that intentionally threatens to do or does physical, sexual or psychological harm to others or themselves."[1]

Workplace violence is really an expression of societal violence, except that in the world outside of work, there are agencies and institutions in place that are intended to help to prevent violence, support victims, and bring the perpetrators to justice. As Colin Lambert, former CUPE national director of health and safety, once said:

> We've got to stop saying, when people cross over the threshold of their workplace, they lose the same rights they have outside . . . That

right should not be taken away from workers simply because they step over that magical line of workplace versus public place.[2]

While there is no uniform definition for workplace violence, experts who study it generally agree that it includes all kinds of abuse including "homicide, assault, threats, mobbing and bullying; in effect, all behaviour that humiliates, degrades or damages a person's well-being, value and dignity."[3] The American Academy of Experts in Traumatic Stress includes "near misses" and "fear of assault or witnessing an assault on a co-worker" in its definition.[4]

Violence that takes place in hospitals and long-term care facilities is generally reactive, such as spontaneously lashing out at a convenient target, often an immediate caregiver. It is usually referred to as "responsive behaviour" in psychiatric and dementia care facilities, taking into account the conditions or stimuli that might trigger it.

As the doors open into the ER, societal dysfunction spills in. Patients and their family members may not be at their best when they are seeking emergency care. Patients may be in pain, feeling weak, ill, and vulnerable, or experiencing anxiety. Family members may be fearful for and protective of the patients. They are entering a system that is often overtaxed and less responsive to their immediate needs than they would expect it to be. Add into the mix society's deeply entrenched sexist and racist attitudes, and the health care staff—most of whom are women, and many of whom are racialized or recent immigrants—become prime targets.

That is not to say that men working in health care do not experience violence on the job. Predominantly female workforces tend not to receive the occupational health attention or protections enjoyed in industries employing mostly men.[5] As a result, all front-line health care workers—in other words, workers of any gender dealing directly with patients and family members—are more prone to abuse. Studies have found that nurses, aides, and personal support workers (PSWs) are most at risk because they are more hands-on and, being lower in the medical hierarchy, may be viewed as easier targets. Physicians, however, are also vulnerable, especially those dealing with ER or mental health patients. Cleaners, dietary and clerical staff, and allied workers such as lab assistants and therapists, are not immune to violence either.

Once in the emergency room, Dianne was examined, given painkillers, X-rayed, and observed. After three hours she was told she should go home and rest. She did manage to sleep. The next morning, Dianne got up and the pain hit with a vengeance. Her face was swollen and bruised. Her head throbbed and her neck and shoulders ached. And so did her legs. She was shocked to see how black and blue they were. "How could that be," she wondered. His powerful blows had struck her head and upper body. Then she remembered the chair. He had pushed it so hard against her, it had left deep, painful bruising. She didn't yet know that this would be the beginning of the long unravelling of her personal and professional life.

We first met Dianne at a conference on violence in the health care system, six years after the assault had happened. While many of the health care workers we spoke with were reluctant to be identified, Dianne had decided she had nothing to lose by telling others about what had happened to her. Shaking, her voice quivering, she stood bravely in front of a large group of nurses, PSWs, aides, maintenance staff, and other allied workers and talked about the attack and about her injuries. She talked about the litany of callous disregard and abuse that came afterwards from her employer and the compensation board. She described how the indifference and even contempt she experienced from her employer and the compensation system in the aftermath of the attack compounded the harm from the original injuries and left her traumatized and, ultimately, impoverished. The delegates, and the two of us, were moved to tears.

A whispered epidemic

Violence against health care staff is not something most of us think about very often. Unless you have witnessed it yourself or have a close friend or family member who works in health care, you are not likely to have heard much about the issue. Our research into violence, which we will describe in the coming chapters, was a collaborative effort initiated by OCHU-CUPE, which represents registered practical nurses (RPNs), PSWs, and dietary, housekeeping, and other health care staff.

Increasingly concerned about reports of violence against its members, in 2016 OCHU-CUPE organized a conference in Kingston, Ontario, where RPNs from across Ontario could come together to discuss violence in their workplaces. An impromptu survey revealed that every one of the 150 nurses in attendance had personally experienced violence on the job. One of the participating nurses, Sue McIntyre, spoke briefly to the other conference attendees about the problem of violence against nurses and was later quoted in a media release. After the conference, she returned to work at the North Bay Regional Health Centre and was called into a meeting with her employer, who then fired her for speaking publicly about her concerns.[6] It took two years and cost her union half a million dollars in arbitration and legal fees to get her successfully reinstated. Her firing, although overturned, seems to have accomplished its likely purpose. It sent a message to health care workers across the province that they had better keep quiet.

We have spoken with over a hundred health care workers as part of our formal research and at least that many again informally. Almost universally, we heard how frustrating it is not to be able to talk openly about the problem. We were overwhelmed and humbled by the countless expressions of gratitude we heard for our efforts to get the story out. Some conversations took place as part of routine interactions with staff we encountered during our own medical appointments. When asked what we do for living, we would regularly disclose that we were researching the issue of violence against health care staff. That almost always resulted in reactions such as, "Oh, thank goodness!" or "Is that ever needed!" before they proceeded, usually unbidden, to tell us their own stories.

A technician at a sleep clinic told us about the sexual harassment she regularly experienced, often by being "invited" into bed by her overnight clients. She said it disgusted her, but she felt helpless to do anything about it. She had already left a job at another clinic because she felt there were not enough safeguards in place to protect her if a client were to become physically aggressive. A hospital pre-admission intake staff person, whose office was in a rather isolated location in the building, told us she often felt uneasy meeting with patients alone, but said she has felt somewhat safer since she and her co-workers were issued personal alarms. An ER triage nurse talked about the irate or threatening patients she frequently encountered. She said, "You can't believe what goes on in here! Thank goodness you're doing this. People need to know." Many people, including casual acquaintances and even journalists who interviewed us about our research, told us about friends or family who work in health care and who encounter violence on a regular basis.

A nurse who was looking after one of our own family members—we'll call her Amelia—told us she had been kicked in the face by an acute care patient and was still dealing with impaired vision and emotional trauma eleven months after. She described the incident.

> It was three o'clock in the afternoon. One of my patients became delirious. He was being wordy, but not aggressive. He pulled out his IV and there was blood everywhere, so I needed to clean him up. When I was changing his bed, he kicked me in the head. I was dazed. I walked out of the room holding my face. I was sent to the ER, where I waited three and a half hours for an X-ray. Then I drove myself home with a painful headache and a black eye.

Although she had been cleared to return to work, Amelia took several days off because she still was not feeling right. She had a relentless headache and was throwing up. A follow-up neurological assessment determined she had suffered a concussion. She told us she posted a picture of herself, her face black and blue and her eye swollen, on her personal Facebook page with the comment

"This is the face of a nurse." She soon received a call from Human Resources (HR) saying the hospital was not happy about her post, even though she had not identified where she worked or any details of the assault. She took the post down, begrudgingly, to protect herself from possible negative repercussions. She said with a little smile that by the time she complied her post had been shared thousands of times, no doubt to the chagrin of her employer, who clearly hoped to keep her injury under wraps. Her injuries, so far, have prevented her from returning to her position in acute care.

Voices of health care workers

In 2017, Michael Hurley, president of OCHU-CUPE, met with a number of victims of health care violence and recorded their stories, which were published anonymously to protect the participants from Sue's fate, in a booklet called *Voices: Hospital Workers Talk about Violence*.[7] The collection was a clear indictment of a health care system that purports to care and yet, according to those interviewed, leaves its employees unprotected and unsupported.

One of the nurses Michael interviewed—we'll call her Megan—described an assault that left her fearing for her life.

> He just lost it.
>
> There were two of us in the area at the time. It was hard to keep him calm, even with [de-escalation techniques]. He started knocking over the furniture. I remember I had a hold of him at one time—and I remember him throwing furniture. . . .
>
> And then some other staff came in. We got him to the ground but only after my co-worker almost went through the glass window. He got cut up pretty bad and he was full of blood and we were still dealing with this patient. And then the patient had a hold of my right hand and I was down and he flipped me over right on top of him. . . .
>
> The staff called a Code White but the team couldn't get on the unit. The doors had malfunctioned. Alarms were malfunc-

tioning. . . . Even the managers couldn't get in. Nobody had a key that could work. So it was just us—the staff on the floor trying to contain the other patients and the patient who was acting out. And I remember all through it I had blood all over me and I wasn't even sure who it was from. Was it me? Was it a patient? Somebody was hurt! . . .

And he had a hold of my wrist SO hard. He had it wrapped around a chair and he was trying to throw the chair. One of the staff finally got my hand free. But the patient was very strong. . . . It was just wild. . . .

And the panic you feel—with not being able to control somebody. We had to wait for other people, and people were still getting hurt. He was really psychotic and we just couldn't get control of him. And I don't know how long it went on. It just seemed like forever. And I don't remember anything past the point where they put the patient in seclusion. I don't know where I was or what I was doing. . . . I just remember smelling blood everywhere. . . .

There was so much blood. It turned out to have been from my co-worker. . . . Because he had a cut here, and down here, and his whole face was purple. And they couldn't even get him to an ambulance because nobody could get through the doors! The doors were all locked and they couldn't be opened. And to see a co-worker get beaten up like that! I can still remember the top that I had on—it was a white top—and I remember when everybody did manage to get on the floor, they said, "Oh my god, you're full of blood!" . . .

Some of the nurses helped me take my clothes off . . . and they checked me to make sure it wasn't me. And I was just in shock—I couldn't believe what had just happened. . . . To this day, when I go to that floor, I get so upset, I don't want to be there. But I realize it wasn't the patient; it was the actual incident that had such a traumatic effect on me . . . the fear of being in something like that. You never know if you're going to come out alive! Later on my co-worker and I talked about it. And he said, "Thank god it was you with me, and not somebody else. I could be dead and I wouldn't see my children again." That really did bother me.

The evidence is there, if we look for it

We have been working in occupational health since the 1980s, but the issue of violence against health care staff isn't something we heard much about until we were asked to run this study. After all, it's not exactly an issue that's widely discussed or reported on in the media. There was one significant exception. Because we were working and living in Windsor, Ontario, we were well aware of the 2005 murder at the local Hôtel-Dieu Hospital of a thirty-six-year-old nurse and single mother, Lori Dupont. She was brutally stabbed in the chest at work by a co-worker, a doctor with whom she had had a relationship.

Most serious injuries of health care workers due to violence, however, are not caused by co-workers. In an interview with the *Windsor Star* a decade after Lori Dupont was killed, Linda Haslam-Stroud, president of the Ontario Nurses Association, said that, while there have been other cases of nurses being stalked or harassed by physicians, "most of the violence issues . . . are patient or visitor related."[8] In other words, the majority of violent incidents would be categorized by the *Occupational Health and Safety Act* as Type II violence, which, by definition, is perpetrated by a "client at the workplace who becomes violent towards a worker or another client."[9]

When we started to explore the problem of violence, and because we had heard so little about it, we expected to find that not much research had been done. We were mistaken. In 2017, we conducted a search of published articles on Medline, an online database of medical and scientific research papers, and discovered a copious amount of research going back decades. We found out that in 1983 the World Health Organization (WHO) had proclaimed that physical assaults on staff by patients was a significant problem.[10] When we updated the search in May 2019, we found that over a thousand articles on "workplace violence hospital" or "workplace violence against nurses" had appeared in international peer-reviewed academic journals in the previous twenty years. These articles had titles like "Physical assault, physical threat, and verbal abuse perpetrated against hospital workers by patients in six U.S. hospitals"; "Human dignity and professional reputation under threat: Iranian nurses' experiences of workplace violence"; "Violence against doctors and nurses in hospitals in Turkey"; "Understanding the rise of Yineo in China: a commentary on the little-known phenomenon of health care violence"; and "Workplace violence towards workers in emergency departments of Palestinian hospitals." Violence against health care staff was clearly a global problem that had already been well documented and analyzed.

Laura Stokowski, a registered nurse, clinical editor for Medscape, and author of "Step away from that nurse! Violence in healthcare continues unabated," says that "a disheartening trend evident in the healthcare literature is that violence against nurses appears to be a growing problem globally."[11] The International Council of Nurses reported, "Nurses are the health care workers most at risk, with female nurses considered the most vulnerable."[12] While many of the published studies are limited to violence against nurses, others do include doctors, hospital aides, paramedics, and other patient care workers.[13] According to researchers who have explored violence against doctors worldwide, most incidents are perpetrated by "patients with low impulse control, psychiatric disorders, emergency cases, or under the influence of alcohol/drugs [who] may be unable to deal with emotionally distressing situations."[14]

Almost every research article we reviewed outlines causes of violence against staff and suggests strategies for preventing it. In other words, experts know what needs to be done. Increased staffing, more security, and training top the list. But the measures that have been repeatedly recommended for two decades are not being put into place, at least not to the degree they are needed. Consider the title of a 2014 article that was published in the *Journal of Emergency Nursing*: "Nothing changes, nobody cares: understanding the experience of emergency nurses physically or verbally assaulted while providing care."

Under-reported, ubiquitous, and persistent

Despite these studies, however, we don't have an accurate count of the number of violent incidents. Many of the studies' authors argue that widespread under-reporting means that data on the prevalence of violence against health care staff grossly underestimates the number of incidences.[15] According to a U.S. study published in the *New England Journal of Medicine*, "Health care workplace violence is an underreported, ubiquitous, and persistent problem that has been tolerated and largely ignored."[16] The study found that health care workers required time off work due to violence four times more often than from other causes of injury. It also identified that the most frequent victims were nurses and nursing aides. Patient caregivers in ERs, psychiatric units, and dementia units were found to be particularly at risk.

We know less about violence against home care personnel, who were not specifically included in our research. We do know that most home care is done by PSWs employed by private agencies and that workers are averse to reporting for fear of losing their jobs. According to Laura Bulmer, a registered nurse (RN) and professor in the PSW program at George Brown College, PSWs working in home care "are at a high risk for violence and receive lots of verbal abuse, like racial, sexist and homophobic slurs. But they are hesitant to report."[17]

Looking at the statistics that are available on violence in all kinds of workplaces, out of all occupational groups, it turns out that health care workers bear the greatest risk of workplace violence.[18] In 2017, the Canadian Federation of Nurses Unions (CFNU) reported that 61 per cent of RNs surveyed experienced serious workplace violence, in contrast to 15 per cent in other industries.[19]

The U.S. Occupational Safety and Health Administration (OSHA) says health care workers are four times more likely to be assaulted than those working in private industry.[20] In the last ten years, incidents of violence increased by 52 per cent among health care and social assistance workers in the U.S.[21]

Statistics released by the Ontario Workplace Safety and Insurance Board (WSIB) show that, "in 2014, lost-time injuries due to workplace violence in the health care sector greatly outnumbered those in other sectors surveyed."[22] More recent data show that Ontario's education workers are now comparable to health care workers in the number of violence-related claims.[23] Although the incidence of violence against women working in health care, particularly verbal abuse and harassment, is shown to be greater than for men,[24] a study found that men are twice as likely to have lost-time claims for assault. One of the researchers explained that the difference "may be that acts of aggression experienced by men are more likely to result in severe injuries that require emergency department treatment."[25]

Canadian data show that violence-related lost-time injuries for front-line health care workers increased 66 per cent between 2006 and 2015, three times the rate of increase for police and correctional service officers combined.[26]

Hospital violence by the numbers

In September 2017, OCHU-CUPE commissioned a province-wide poll of the union's health care worker members to investigate the prevalence of violence perpetrated against hospital staff by patients. A total of 1,976 health care workers responded to the telephone survey, providing results with a high level of statistical confidence. According to the poll:

- 68 per cent of RPNs and PSWs had experienced at least one incident in the past year of physical violence, such as pushing, hitting, or having things thrown at them; 20 per cent had experienced at least nine such assaults
- 83 per cent of RPNs and PSWs had experienced non-physical violence, such as abusive language, name-calling, or threatening gestures; 20 per cent had experienced at least nine incidents

- 42 per cent of RPNs and PSWs had experienced sexual harassment or assault
- 26 per cent had lost time from work due to workplace violence
- Despite the high number of violent incidents cited, only 57 per cent of respondents said they had filed any formal reports[27]

Extrapolating from the results, we calculated that altogether the survey participants had experienced at least 10,078 incidents of violence against them during the previous year. The results indicated there were approximately 2,577 or more incidents of physical violence; 1,632 or more incidents of sexual violence; and at least 6,220 incidents of non-physical or verbal violence. There were clearly injuries—at least 1,136 instances of lost time related to violence. The poll also revealed that there has been serious under-reporting. Out of the thousands of incidents cited, the poll indicates that formal reports were filed for only about 12 per cent of them.[28]

In 2012, the Ontario Nurses Association, whose members are primarily RNs, carried out a survey on workplace violence. It found that 54 per cent had experienced physical violence, 85 per cent verbal abuse, and 19 per cent sexual violence or abuse.[29]

According to a 2017 editorial in the *Canadian Medical Association Journal*, physicians also bear significant risks. A survey of 720 primary care physicians found that almost a third had been victims of aggressive behaviour in the previous month.[30]

Although violence against health care workers is still a subject most of us never hear about, the media have gotten a hold of a few dramatic stories. Maybe you have seen some of the headlines: "Windsor Regional Hospital nurse recovering after a horrible workplace choking"; "Labour ministry investigating after nurse, security guard assaulted at Southlake"; "Attack leaves Moncton nurse with head trauma, broken nose"; "Pregnant nurse attacked by patient a week after safety concerns dismissed"; "Grace Hospital nurse attacked in meth-fuelled incident."

In September 2019, under the headline "Male patient charged after B.C. nurse badly beaten on the job," the CBC reported that police in British Columbia had arrested a patient who had brutally assaulted a nurse at the Abbotsford Regional Hospital. The sixty-two-year-old patient was undergoing dialysis treatment when he attacked the nurse providing his care. He hit her in the face with a hand weight, fracturing her cheekbone, breaking part of her jaw, and displacing some of her teeth. She required immediate surgery and suffered a suspected concussion. According to the nurses' union president, "the injuries are so severe, it's not clear when, or if, the nurse will be able to return to work."[31]

"My head went through a steel rack and into the wall"

The media knew nothing, however, about the 2015 attack on patient support worker Scott Sharp, at the Guelph General Hospital. Scott, a tall, handsome man and father to four children, who describes himself as a jock, worked as a Shakespearean actor in Stratford, Ontario, before pursuing a career in health care. At age forty-two, Scott was seriously injured during an assault by a patient and spent the next year in a wheelchair. His injuries were so debilitating, his spine so damaged, that he wasn't able to return to his job. Scott's nightmare began on January 3, 2015.

> I was put on night shift for a reason, because it's a skeleton crew, and I'm 250 pounds and six foot four. And the bars don't let out at two in the afternoon; they let out at two in the morning . . . I went into work that night not expecting that my life would change forever.
> I could hear a patient being verbally aggressive and that was usually a clue as to what my night was going to turn out to be like. After several hours went by, this same patient started becoming physically aggressive. As health care workers, we all realize that the very last resort is restraining a patient. We'll only do that if our safety is in jeopardy or if the patient's safety is in jeopardy. In this case it was both. I was with a very competent team. We had, unfortunately, had to do this many, many times. We went in to restrain this individual and he broke free and struck two nurses. He hit one of them so hard

he broke her clavicle. The other one sustained neurological damage. And then he struck me. My feet went underneath the gurney. My backside hit the floor and my head went through a steel rack and into the wall.

After the patient was restrained, Scott's co-workers turned their attention to him, recognizing he was seriously hurt.

Seeing how much pain I was in, they admitted me right away. The CT scan showed I needed to have emergency surgery. And I spent at least three months in the hospital, but that isn't where my real problem started. My real problems started when I got out of the hospital.

Scott would go on to face serious medical challenges, demoralizing conflict with the compensation system, and devastating economic hardship.

Long-term care violence by the numbers

Believe it or not, one of the most dangerous health care environments to work in is long-term care. In January 2019, OCHU-CUPE commissioned another poll, this time for Ontario long-term care staff. A total of 1,223 people responded, again providing results with a high level of statistical confidence. Of them, 85 per cent were women, 13 per cent were men, and 2 per cent were unspecified; 49 per cent self-identified as Indigenous, racialized, recent immigrant, or visible minority.

- 89 per cent of PSWs and 88 per cent of RPNs experience physical violence on the job; 62 per cent and 51 per cent, respectively, at least once a week
- 72 per cent of PSWs and 67 per cent of RPNs experience non-physical violence, such as abusive language, name-calling, or threatening gestures

- 65 per cent of female staff have experienced sexual harassment, and 44 per cent have experienced sexual assault
- 69 per cent of those identifying as Indigenous, racialized, recent immigrant, or visible minority indicated they have experienced related abuse
- 92 per cent said they believe that additional staffing would help to prevent violence
- Only 47 per cent said they ever filed formal incident reports

How is all of this abuse affecting the mental health of long-term care staff? Of respondents, 71 per cent were in the upper half of the range in terms of stress, anxiety, and depression related to their working conditions and violence, and 65 per cent have considered quitting their jobs. It should be of considerable concern to the general public that 75 per cent believe they are unable to provide adequate care due to their workload and low staffing levels.[32]

Candace Rennick, secretary-treasurer of CUPE Ontario and a former PSW, said, "These results paint a grim picture of a scandalously unsafe environment. We should not believe that this culture cannot be changed. Violence should never be seen as part of the job."[33]

The polling results would be no surprise to Dr. Pat Armstrong and her colleagues at York University, who have carried out multiple comprehensive studies on violence in long-term care. In a study looking at long-term care in Canada and Scandinavia, they found that 90 per cent of Canadian caregivers had experienced "physical violence from residents or their relatives and 43 percent reported physical violence on a daily basis." This next finding really caught our attention. When compared to their Scandinavian counterparts, Canadian staff were six times more likely to experience physical assault.[34]

The issue of violence becomes complicated in the context of long-term care, where many of the perpetrators are cognitively challenged. The Ontario Long Term Care Association (OLTCA) says that aggressive actions or so-called responsive behaviours are often the result of a resident reacting to "triggers in their environment." OLTCA claims that "aggression implies malicious intent, and this is rarely the case."[35] But regardless of whether there is intent to cause harm and whether offenders have full understanding of the consequences of their actions, assaulted staff can nevertheless be as negatively affected as if the assaults were deliberate.

"I was screaming at the top of my lungs"

It was in a long-term care facility that Lara was sexually assaulted. She had been working for twelve years as a PSW, providing hands-on care, attending to the daily basic needs of a dozen or so residents per shift. Her work involved waking, dressing, transporting, feeding, toileting, bathing, and generally handling all aspects of personal daily life. When we asked if she had ever experienced violence, she told us a story that left us shaken. One of Lara's residents was a man with mild dementia. He was in his fifties and very strong. It was his shower day and she was alone in a tub room with him. He seemed pleasant and co-operative—when suddenly he turned on her.

> I was given no warning that he could be a potential danger to me. I had assisted him in removing his clothing and was about to seat him on the shower chair when he grabbed me by my smock and threw me against the wall, with my lower back jammed into the towel bar. I was physically immobilized for several minutes. He was pushing me into the towel bar repeatedly. As soon as the assault started, I pulled the emergency bell. I was wearing a loose smock and nursing pants. He pressed his hand forcefully into my vagina to the point where I felt his fingers penetrate through my clothing.

Lara began sobbing and took a few minutes to wipe her eyes and compose herself before continuing to describe the nightmare.

I pushed him away. My immediate thought when I pushed him away was regret, because I was terrified that I was going to make him unstable and he would fall, and it would mean that I had hurt him. [*tearful pause*] After pushing him away he came back at me again, grabbed my breast and was actually able to pull my breast out of my brassiere. He twisted it so hard that his handprint was on my breast for three and a half weeks. I was screaming at the top of my lungs. Finally—and this had been going on for approximately ten to fifteen minutes, this assault—I was able to get around him and make my way out the door of the shower unit. When I came out to the hall, it was clear that the bell was continuing to ring, indicating that someone needed help in the shower room. No nursing staff were around. They could all hear the bell, but the bells go and go on these floors to the point where the nurses become numb hearing them. Had my co-workers realized that I was being so seriously assaulted, I don't doubt for a minute that they would have run to my rescue. They assumed, perhaps, that I needed assistance with a mechanical lift or maybe supplies.

The next part of Lara's story left us stunned. She went on:

After leaving the tub room, I get around the corner and I think to myself, "I have left this resident naked and alone in the shower room and he may hurt himself." So I went back. I assisted him in putting on his robe and then brought him out into the hallway with me. Then I locked the shower room and I went to the nursing station. I reported what had just happened to the RN who was at the nursing station at the time and she said, "Good thing you weren't hurt. You were lucky." I wasn't asked to sit down. I wasn't asked to give a detailed description of the assault. I was expected to go back and carry on working.

After about an hour and a half—I can only guess—I was walking around the floor unable to work. I was a zombie. I went back to the nurse again and I said, "I think I need to go home." She was shocked and asked, "Did something happen that I'm not aware of?" And I said, "No, I think I told you everything." She asked, "Well, are you hurt? Do you need to go to the hospital?" I said, "No. I'm not phys-ically hurt. I'm just not thinking right." So she said, "Well, I don't think I can send you home. I'm going to call the nurse manager." Hours passed. Then a manager finally came up and said, "Well, if you really feel you must go home, go ahead. But you're putting us in a difficult position because now we have to replace you."

So I did go home. All I could think about was that I was a feather stroke away from being raped in my place of work. So I phoned the police from my house. After the police questioned the managers and the resident at my work, they told me that [it was evident to them] the resident was fully aware of what he had done. The police told me that when they asked him why he assaulted me, the resident shrugged off the question by responding, "I didn't f— her." But the police said they couldn't lay charges because his chart said he had the beginning stages of dementia.

Lara wasn't provided with any counselling or other supports. She wasn't referred to a sexual assault centre. She said, "I think that it would have been less traumatic for me if I had felt supported." When Lara did return to work, she overheard the RN she had reported to discussing the incident with several colleagues. "She was laughing and said to her audience, 'She needs to grow up if she thinks that is getting hurt.'"

"She didn't care. I was in shock"

In talking to health care workers, we heard over and over again about the lack of support victims received following violent inci-dents. And we heard about the frustration they felt knowing the perpetrators of the assaults were suffering no consequences for their actions. Jessica had this to say after experiencing a sexual assault by a patient:

I was treating a patient, and another patient assaulted me from behind. He rammed me from the back and held my hips and

I could feel his penis pressing up against me. The [other staff] that was there went on about her business. She didn't care. I was in shock. Four hours later, I finished my shift. So, before I left, I said to one of the managers, "I need to talk to you about what happened." She said to me, "Oh, poor Mr. X. He must be sexually frustrated. You know his wife sold his house. Go on home. Don't worry. Everything is fine." I was numb, I couldn't sleep. I was feeling such anxiety.

Is violence really just part of the job?

How is such rampant violence going unchecked? How, in this era of #MeToo, is the silencing of victims being tolerated? Surely we can mitigate the emotional trauma so many victims experience. But what needs to be done about the problem and how do we get there?

We need to understand the immediate and underlying causes of violence and the roles played by race, gender, sexuality, and the inequitable medical hierarchy. We need to consider the limitations of the legal protections available to health care workers and whether some perpetrators of violence against workers should be charged under the law. We must identify the reasons for the lower rates of violence against health care staff in some other countries and whether they have protective conditions or policies that we can replicate or even improve upon.

2.

Under the Scope

"Hopefully doing this research will help"

As researchers, curiosity drives much of what we do, personally and professionally. We need to know what makes things tick. But, as *advocacy* researchers, our primary motivation is the pursuit of human rights and justice. We believe everyone has the legal and moral right to a safe work environment. Once we started to hear about health care workers being bruised, bloodied, broken, burnt out, and traumatized, we knew we had to get to the bottom of this public health nightmare and do whatever might be within our power to address it. We also feel an ethical obligation to share widely what we have learned.

In 2017 we set out to formally explore the problem of violence from the perspective of the health care workers themselves. We carried out two large, rigorously conducted, descriptive qualitative research studies.[1] Our first study focused primarily on violence against hospital staff and the second focused on workers in long-term care facilities. Articles we wrote drawing on the results of these studies were published in the peer-reviewed journal *New*

Solutions: A Journal of Environmental and Occupational Health Policy. The research participants told us they were hopeful that their contributions to this knowledge would make a difference. As one long-term care worker commented, "Hopefully doing this research will help. What's being allowed to happen is so shameful."

As we began our research, we were not particularly interested in gathering more statistics. The shocking prevalence of violence had been well established by other researchers. Instead, we designed our studies to explore health care workers' own stories and perspectives. We wanted to find out what exactly they were experiencing. What is it like to go to work knowing there is a strong likelihood that you might be abused or assaulted by your patients or their visitors? What do health care workers see as the immediate and underlying causes of violence? What do they believe needs to be done to prevent it, and what do they see as barriers to prevention?

After completing our formal research studies, we also conducted one-on-one interviews with dozens more health care workers. It turned out that their experiences closely mirrored those of the study participants and helped to confirm the validity of our findings, as did the heart-breaking stories published in OCHU-CUPE's *Voices* booklet.

We talked to nurses and PSWs, aides and porters, clerical workers, cleaners, and dietary staff in communities across Ontario. Many of the people we spoke with, especially those working in ERs, psychiatric units, forensic units, and long-term care facilities, told us that they regularly go into work fearing they will be physically assaulted by those they are providing care for.

We were assisted in each study by a member of CUPE, who acted as our research assistant. Linda Clayborne, an RPN with over forty years of experience, primarily in mental health, helped us with the first study, and Heather Neiser, a PSW with over twenty years of experience in long-term care, helped us with the second. Each was granted a research fellowship by the University of Stirling, our alma mater in Scotland, which hosted both studies. These two research assistants had years of experience and their help was invaluable. Not only did they have intimate knowledge of the problem of violence, but they were also very familiar with the union structure, which helped them to successfully recruit participants. They organized dates and locations for interviews and recorded the sessions. They also helped us to interpret what we were hearing.

Some study participants were specifically invited because they had experienced serious violence, but an open invitation was made to anyone who wanted to take part. Because health care workers providing direct patient care are statistically at a higher risk for violence than their co-workers who don't interact with patients, we pre-screened the participants to ensure that direct care staff were sufficiently represented.

To put individuals more at ease and encourage discussion, all of the interviews we did for the formal research studies took place in groups. Each session typically included four to five individuals representing various health care occupations, types of health care institutions, communities within the province of Ontario, ages, genders, ethnic and racial groups, and years of work experience.

"People get fired when they speak out"

Participants' anonymity was of primary importance. We had some difficulty recruiting health care workers because they were afraid of disciplinary action against them if they were found to have participated. At the outset of each group interview, participants expressed fear that their employer would become aware of their involvement or trace their comments back to them. Most knew about the case of Sue McIntyre, who was fired by her employer after publicly commenting at the 2016 conference on violence in health care. We were told, "People get fired when they speak out. Look at that nurse who got fired, who lost her job." One participant reported, "A family member warned me to shut my mouth while I was here. She said, 'You'd better be quiet, or they'll fire you.'" Linda Clayborne later explained to us, "I think it's because the hospital puts the fear of god into them. They're afraid of losing their jobs. We all signed confidentiality agreements. But you know what? I'm not going to break patients' confidentiality by telling the truth about what happened to me."

Before asking recruited health care workers to sign informed consent forms, we assured them that all reasonable measures would be taken to protect their confidentiality. Twice a potential participant chose to leave rather than face the risk of being identified and disciplined. All those who remained promised to protect the privacy of the other participants, and we, as researchers, agreed to follow the ethical guidelines laid out by the University of Stirling in the approved protocols. We recorded all of the interviews, which were then transcribed. In total, there were approximately 1,500 pages of transcripts, which we imported verbatim into a qualitative data analysis program.

The group interviews began with each participant describing an incident or incidents of violence that they had experienced or witnessed. In the second study, which focused on violence in long-term care, we added a technique that helped to break the ice and also spur discussion—an exercise called body mapping. Body mapping is a simple health survey instrument that uses large outlines of the human body posted on a wall or flip chart, marking pens, and/or stickers to elicit and record responses. We posted two separate images, labelled "Front" and "Back," on the meeting room wall.[2] We added a cloud over the head to represent mental or emotional injuries, such as stress symptoms or anxiety.

We asked participants to approach the body maps together and to apply colour-coded stickers to areas where they had personally been affected by physical, verbal, and/or sexual violence. We had them use different colours of stickers to indicate their occupational group and different sizes and shapes to denote how they rated the severity of the assaults against them and their effects. Large circles were used for serious injuries, such as sprains or sexual assault, rectangles for minor injuries such as bumps, bruises, or threats, and small circles for assaults that did not result in significant injury, such as slaps or name-calling. The health care

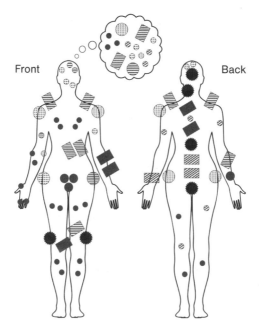

Front

Back

workers talked among themselves as they completed the exercise, and then we reassembled so they could describe what their stickers represented.

Together we saw that there were clusters of stickers in the groin, breast, and buttock areas, which we learned from the participants represented groping, touching, grabbing, or sexual assault. The arms and face were also shown to be common targets for slapping, grabbing, spitting, scratching, or wrenching. Stickers on the head represented blows resulting in everything from minor assaults to serious concussions. Participants told us about the bruises, strains, scrapes, scratches, bites, torn ligaments, fractured bones, shattered faces, lost teeth, and even brain injuries inflicted by frustrated, angry, confused, high, or intoxicated patients. Some said they are regularly slapped, pinched, punched, and assailed with objects. Here are some of their comments:

> On a daily basis I am hit, punched, spat at, sworn at, slapped, bitten. I've had hot coffee thrown at me. I've gone home with burns on my hands.

Oh yes, all the boob twists. And the pinches under the arm. It would be purple.

I'm still having issues with my eye.

I was hit so hard in the ear I couldn't even hear afterwards.

I had a fractured tailbone after being run over by an electric wheelchair.

I was just fixing his shoelace and he punched me in the back of the neck. I didn't see it coming.

I rolled him towards me, and he grabbed onto my breast so hard. I didn't know how to get him off but pulling made it worse. My breast was black and blue.

I put his pyjamas on, and I went to tie them. Then I saw his fist. Oh my god! Here it comes. Pow, right in the mouth. It cracked all my teeth and broke my nose.

Some had been so seriously injured they were off work or placed on modified duties for an extended period of time.

I ended up with a herniated disc from a resident pushing me, and I have just come back to full duties after five months.

He grabbed my arm and turned me around his chair and pulled me up and over. I had bruises on my ribs, and he sprained my wrist. I was in physiotherapy for weeks and I still have pain.

She pushed back as I lost my grip and I slipped. Something popped in my back. I had nobody to call for help. I felt like, "Oh my god, now I can't do my work. Now they're going to be short-staffed that day." I finished her care in excruciating pain and then sat down and just broke into tears. I was off work for months.

One of the nurses described the litany of assaults and injuries he had endured over the course of his career.

> I have a stab wound right here in my arm. A patient on a medical unit who wasn't getting a cup of tea when he asked for it stabbed me in the arm. At that time, we used to have real cutlery, including serrated knives. I had my ribs broken when I was working in the emergency room of a hospital and was put through the wall because a patient didn't like being told he would not be given drugs he asked for. I've had my leg severely broken. I've also had a chunk of flesh bitten from my body. I have had my head rung, my jaw twisted around. I've had my "family" parts assaulted on many occasions.

"I ended up with a split lip and concussion"

A young PSW arrived at one of the group sessions wearing a hat and sunglasses and, finding it still too bright, asked us to dim the lights. Her face was bruised, her lips swollen. When we asked what had happened, she told us:

> I was working a night shift. When I was on break, one of the patients went into someone else's room. The nurses asked me to get him. So I took the wheelchair and I walked to the room he was in. I found him in the bathroom. He didn't seem agitated. He was just really confused. I was talking to him and he mumbled something. And I just kind of went, "Pardon me?" He was leaning against the sink and suddenly he gave me an upper cut right in the mouth. I ended up with a split lip and concussion. I'm still off work.

A concussion can be serious, life-changing. It occurs when the brain, suspended inside the skull, is violently jostled. Victims may or may not lose consciousness. The U.S. Centers for Disease Control and Prevention describe concussion as a type of traumatic brain injury—or TBI—caused by a bump, blow, or jolt to the head or by a hit to the body that causes the head and brain to move rapidly back and forth. This sudden movement can cause the brain to bounce around or twist in the skull, creating chemical changes in the brain and sometimes stretching and damaging brain cells.[3]

According to the U.S. National Institutes of Health, symptoms can be mild to severe, depending on the extent of the damage to the brain.[4]

Multiple or repeated concussions can cause permanent brain damage. A condition known as chronic traumatic encephalopathy (CTE) has been identified among football players and other athletes. It can result in memory loss, depression, psychiatric conditions, Parkinson's disease, and even dementia. CTE is not just a concern for athletes. Victims of intimate partner violence have been found to suffer symptoms of CTE.[5] By extension, health care workers who are repeatedly exposed to head trauma may be at increased risk for CTE.

Headaches and pain pills

When we spoke with Amelia, the injured nurse who had been warned to take down her Facebook photo, she had just made the decision to leave her community-based nursing job, which she'd held since her partial recovery from the injuries she had sustained during the attack by an acute care patient. At the time of the interview, Amelia was still suffering disturbing after-effects. Confusion, memory loss, and difficulty in recalling words and details were making her feel she could not effectively do her job. She still suffered from headaches every day. Her vision continued to be affected. She was experiencing photophobia, double vision, and her balance was compromised. Her hearing was overly sensitive. She was having difficulty sleeping. Her future in nursing was uncertain.

Some victims are left with ongoing physical pain and disability following attacks. Scott, for example, whom you also met in the previous chapter, told us he was in constant, intractable pain after the vicious attack that left him with a severe spinal injury. He couldn't walk; he couldn't sleep. When we talked to him, he had undergone numerous procedures and surgeries. He described the most recent—the ninth!

> They had to shave my spine because they were going to mix DNA in with the cement that they injected into two rods, my eight screws, my four spacers. I was on fifty, sixty pills a day—opioids—which, as we all know as health care workers, is a huge, huge problem, and now I was part of that.

Dianne Paulin didn't readily recover from her injuries either. She has never been able to return to nursing. Seven years after she was attacked by her mental health patient, she told us, "I had severe daily headaches for almost a year. Every morning I still wake up with pain. I have a bulging disc in my neck from the assault. My ears still hurt every day from middle ear damage." And she said she suffers from ongoing depression.

"It's not over when the bruises heal"

Heather Neiser, our research assistant for the study on violence against long-term care staff, has herself been a victim of violence many times. And she has witnessed many brutal assaults against her co-workers. She told an assembly of health care workers, "The emotional damage this does to someone is sometimes irreparable. Cuts and bruises heal or fade. Memories, however, never leave. The way you felt when someone took your power and sense of safety lingers."

A nurse on a busy hospital unit described to us how she felt when a patient unexpectedly struck her.

I brought my supplies and just asked her, "Can I do your blood?"
She just looked at me. She put her hand out, I put the tourniquet on,
and I bent my head to get the needle and got slapped in the face. It
hurt me and it upset me so much. It was something about a slap in
the face. It's not only physically painful, but it's also demoralizing.

Looking at the completed body maps, it jumped out at
us—both researchers and participants—that many of the stickers
had been applied in the cloud above the head. They represented
emotional injuries, including the effects of racist, sexist, classist,
or anti-immigrant comments. Many participants said they suffer
from ongoing trauma. It spills over into their family lives. We heard
about the disturbed children and spouses of injured health care
workers begging them not to go back into the environment that
had caused them harm. It affects the health care workers' sleep,
their personal lives, their careers, and their sense of well-being.
Many live and work in a state of heightened anxiety.

One participant said, "I'm still not the same nurse that I used
to be. There are such lasting effects. It's not over when the bruises
heal." Another talked about being emotionally triggered returning
to work after an incident.

The next day when I went in, I knew I'd be going into the room with
the man that chased me down the hall. It all started coming back and
I was on guard. You can't give good care that way. You don't want to
get that swat in the head.

With few supports, some of the nurses said they end up taking
on the role of security, having to defend themselves or their co-
workers against aggressive patients. Some, especially those facing
violence on almost a daily basis, said that most days they feel so
defeated, they just want to quit because they believe it affects not
only their own well-being, but also their ability to properly care for
the patients.

The effects of stress related to risks at work that are beyond
one's control can have long-lasting and devastating effects. In the

book *Heartland: A Memoir of Working Hard and Being Broke in the Richest Country on Earth*, Sarah Smarsh warns:

> A life full of peril and lacking care leaves its mark not just on the body but on the brain. Under the surface, the amygdala—the brain's fight-or-flight center of primal fear—enlarges and remains that way, a physical reflection of the hypervigilance developed by necessity under chronic stress.[6]

Post-traumatic stress

Post-traumatic stress disorder (PTSD) is a far-too-common condition among health care workers. The Manitoba Nurses Union reports that 40 per cent of nurses experience PTSD symptoms related to trauma at work. The union lists five workplace triggers: violence, the death of a child (particularly due to abuse), treating patients resembling family or friends, the death of a patient following extraordinary measures to save a life, and a heavy patient load.[7] Violence, the union claims, "plays the largest role in the development of PTSD," also citing a "lack of employer and organizational supports, emotional labour and compassion fatigue" as core contributors. The U.S. National Institutes of Health estimates that one in five individuals who suffer from concussion or mild traumatic brain injury develop PTSD symptoms and/or depression in the months following the injury.[8]

Here's another important fact. The link between violence and mental health concerns is found to be much higher for women, who make up the majority of front-line staff. Studies have shown that women are twice as likely to develop PTSD.[9]

Timely and appropriate support and intervention have been shown to decrease the likelihood of ongoing psychological trauma.[10] The health care personnel in our studies described how traumatized they felt after an assault and how little compassion they felt they received. One of the health care workers we talked to said she experienced serious, ongoing symptoms of PTSD after being attacked by a patient. "I was numb. I couldn't sleep. I started to have anxiety." She received no immediate acknowledgement of her distress or treatment.

Although some participants praised their management team or immediate supervisors for their care and compassion, others felt that their own well-being took a back seat to the smooth, uninterrupted operation of their unit, which would often be short-staffed and plagued by time constraints. "There's no follow-up with management. They don't ask you if you're okay. They ask, 'Can you take Tylenol and stay here?'"

A nurse working in long-term care felt her safety was not being taken seriously by her manager.

> I had a patient who told me my mother should have aborted me, I should just kill myself, things like that. Tripped me, stuck her leg out the side of her wheelchair, then kicked me when I knelt down on the ground. This is not a behavioural unit, so I flagged that, charted on it, let the manager know. The manager said, "Oh, it's just her first week; she'll be okay." That same patient attacked another patient. They finally did transfer her to behavioural.

A nurse we spoke with personally described her own experience. She had come to the aid of a co-worker who was being assaulted by a strong, male, psychotic patient. She stepped between them and he then turned on her, pushing her, pulling her, dragging her down the hall, all the while screaming obscenities and insults. In her struggle to escape his grip, her arms were violently twisted. Several minutes passed before help arrived and she was finally rescued. She went home and returned to work the next day for about a week, but she felt her trauma wasn't being properly acknowledged. Furthermore, her attacker's behaviour wasn't being adequately controlled, putting the staff and other patients at risk. She was so upset that she decided she needed to take some time away from work to recover emotionally. She stayed home for about a week and a half.

I took the time off because I was really, really upset and mostly, because I wasn't getting any support. If they had just been compassionate and found me some modified work, and if they had gone ahead and dealt with the issue on the unit and done what they had to do to protect everybody there, I would have felt better. But they chose to turn their backs on me . . . I thought my managers were on the same team as me. I just always thought that if something like this ever happened, I would have support. I was so naive. I ended up having to really fight them to get what I needed. They said they didn't think the incident was bad enough to cause emotional harm. They said I didn't need time off, I didn't need to see a counsellor; maybe a little physiotherapy for my sore arm, but to get back to work.

Years after the incident, she stills feels burnt out, exhausted, and unsupported. Although it had always been her dream to be a nurse, she now feels she probably should have chosen a different career. She said, sadly, "Nursing isn't what I thought it would be."

The blame game

We heard considerable frustration from the health care workers we interviewed that not only were post-incident briefings not personally supportive, but workers often felt they were being personally blamed. Although it is not always the case, several participants said that when management is trying to determine the root cause of a violent incident, their first position seems to be that the staff person somehow triggered it by some misstep.

To me it's accusatory. They're blaming you . . . especially when they can target the lowest-ranked nurse.

I can tell you from looking at the responses from managers on incident reports, they feel they're mainly there to defend the patient. You're the one defending yourself.

If I report an incident and my manager brings me into the office, she's questioning me on what I did wrong. "Did you approach the patient the right way? You came in too fast. You didn't tell them what you were doing." . . . It's never the patient's fault. It's always our fault. What could you have done better? Well, maybe the question should be asked, "Well, you, as my employer, what could *you* have done to help not have this happen?"

Blaming appears to be an all-too-common practice. During a media conference about the issue of violence against long-term care staff, CUPE's Candace Rennick said:

I can speak from experience, being cornered in the private room of a resident who tried to force himself on me, grabbing my face to try to kiss me. I was able to remove myself from the situation without any further violation but when I went to my manager to report the incident I was told to and I quote, "stop being so nice."[11]

Another staff person working in long-term care was horrified by her treatment following a traumatic encounter.

There was a resident who kept following me around accusing me of taking his money. He followed me to the nurses' station. I tried locking the door, but he pushed it open, slammed me against the medication cart, put his hand around my neck, and was choking me. I tried screaming for help. I had my personal alarm and I tried pulling it, but it flew right to the medication cart. One staff came to my assistance, but she couldn't get him off of me. Finally, a family member came to my rescue and pulled him off me. The ambulance came. I had a big red mark on my neck. I'm sorry. [*crying*] I went into shock. I refused to go to the hospital because I had wet myself in the process of being choked . . . I returned to work after five days and my nurse manager called me into her office and said, "The other staff said you kept telling him to leave you alone, go away, I don't have your money. Why didn't you approach him in a gentle way?"

Being blamed can evolve into self-blame and self-doubt on the part of assaulted staff. Victim-blaming can cause serious psychological harm. Dr. Anju Hurria, a psychiatrist and professor of psychiatry at the University of California, Irvine, calls victim-blaming a "secondary trauma or a secondary assault." It can result in "greater distress, increased amounts of depression." It can also exacerbate symptoms of anxiety and shame.[12] As one worker put it:

> I'd be so traumatized that it would take days to fix it in my head. Did I do this right? How could I have done that? What did I do wrong to make it worse? What could I have done differently?

"She couldn't sleep for a week after seeing that beating"

Witnessing an assault, whether against a co-worker or another patient, can be traumatizing. A resident in an Ontario long-term care home brutally attacked another resident, who ultimately died from his injuries. It was devastating for the staff. A co-worker of a witness who was also pursued by the assailant told us:

> She couldn't sleep for a week after seeing that beating. All she could see was the residents coming down the hall. One man was covered in blood and the other man had black eyes and a bloody nose and had his ear half chewed off by the other resident. And then the resident that did the beating climbed over the desk and went after her!

A study in France examined the post-traumatic reactions of health care workers to experiencing or witnessing violence, such as "flashbacks, nightmares, avoidance, loss of interest in important or interesting activities, sleeping problems, hypervigilance, concentration problems, irritability and guilt." It found that, although direct victims experienced a greater level of distress, "witnesses of violent acts at work might experience similar psychological and behavioural outcomes as direct victims."[13]

Linda Clayborne, the nurse who assisted us in the first study, witnessed a vicious attack on a co-worker and says she is now wary of any footsteps behind her, even in her everyday life outside the hospital environment.

I have to be honest that I have it myself. It started when I was going to a code white, and as we were running up the hall, we could see a patient punching a nurse. He had her on the floor and he kept punching her and punching her. I remember I felt like I was running in slow motion. Do you ever feel that way? I just felt like I wasn't getting there, and there were other people running behind me. And all I could hear was the punches and just trying to get there. And even now today, if I'm in a grocery store and someone runs behind me, I feel that all over again. It brings me right back there. You're in protective mode. It's an awful, awful feeling.

A cleaner told us he had suffered a solid blow to the back of his neck by a patient while he was walking down a hallway. He was in pain for weeks. He was also left feeling very shaken and vulnerable by the unexpected attack. He told us, "After that, I found my anxiety level was really high. It took me about a year to feel comfortable again. I didn't like anyone coming up from behind me."

PTSD has continued to plague Dianne Paulin.

At first, I was crying all of the time. I was a total basket case. I was anxious, crying, depressed. I couldn't sleep. Even the medication sometimes didn't help. My mind raced all the time. I went to physio thirty-eight times in four months. Thirty-eight times! I was getting acupuncture. I was so sore, I couldn't function. I ended up losing my front teeth because they had been knocked loose. It was so hard on my son because of my moods, my emotional state. I'd be up and down like a yo-yo. It's hard to watch your mom cry all the time and to watch her in pain. It's just been a roller coaster. It still hasn't stopped.

The insidious nature of stress

It isn't only traumatic incidents that cause psychological harm. The day-to-day threats of violence, ongoing name-calling, racism, sexism, and other forms of discrimination and abuse take a heavy toll.

High levels of stress plague health care workers. According to Vittorio Di Martino, a consultant specializing in health and safety at work who wrote a report for the International Labour Office (ILO) and WHO on the relationship between violence and stress in health care: "Doctors, nurses and social workers are all high on the list of occupations with serious stress levels.... In practically all cases violence, including minor acts, generates distress in the victims with long-lasting, deleterious effects on their health."[14] Caring professions are inherently stressful. High demand, little control, and inadequate support are major contributors. So is violence or the threat of violence.

The symptoms associated with stress are many and varied. Both physical and mental health can be affected. Stress can cause such conditions as body pain, headaches, fatigue, digestive problems, weight gain or loss, autoimmune disorders, difficulty sleeping, feelings of irritability, hopelessness, anxiety, and depression, even high blood pressure and heart disease. It can lead to overuse of alcohol or dependency on drugs. It can affect relationships and family life.

The Oncology Nurse Advisor, a publication addressing the needs of nurses caring for cancer patients, explains:

> Cumulative stress is a common experience for people who work in chronically stressful situations. It results from accumulation of various stress factors such as heavy workload, poor communications, multiple frustrations, coping with situations in which you feel powerless, and the inability to rest or relax.[15]

This certainly describes the working conditions most health

care staff face. Several participants in one of the group interviews described the stress they were under at work.

> We're not only being harassed by families and the patients, but I also feel like I'm being harassed by my boss too. They are not on the floor. They don't know what's just gone on. It just becomes so overwhelming and I can see why so many of us are just so stressed.

Another participant jumped in with, "Yeah, the stress thing is just leaping off the page." Another concurred, "Yeah, stress, stress, stress." And another questioned "why we're not all banging our heads against the wall . . . my husband said I don't know how you haven't cracked yet."

A PSW working in long-term care told us:

> The longer you're in it, the harder it is on your body. It takes a toll. The majority of the people that retire from our facility, and this has just been in the last little while, their lives are very short afterwards.

Discrimination

A 2018 Statistics Canada report stated that people working in health care were more likely than those in other occupations to experience harassment.[16] Discrimination, sexual harassment, sexual assault, and violence go hand-in-hand. Frequent or unrelenting verbal abuse can be emotionally debilitating. Sexist, racist, anti-immigrant, and other discriminatory comments are dehumanizing and leave victims feeling demoralized.

Racism

Racism has been shown to cause PTSD, hypervigilance, depression, anxiety, hopelessness, and increased risk of addiction.[17] Racism can have a serious impact on one's physical health. A review of studies evaluating the physiological effects of racism found that victims experience increased output of cortisol—the stress hormone. Other studies found that experiences of racism may increase blood pressure, elevate heart rate, increase heart attack risk, reduce kidney function, and possibly even increase the risk of breast cancer.[18]

Recall that the OCHU-CUPE polling of long-term care staff found that the majority of those who self-identified as Indigenous, racialized, recent immigrant, or visible minority indicated that they experience related harassment, many on a daily basis. A Black nurse told us she had a resident who regularly snarled racist remarks at her. "She had a southern drawl and used to say, 'Oh, you. I had slaves like you.'" An Asian nurse said she often suffered such hateful comments as, "'Oh, an immigrant. Where did they find you? Downtown? Brought you here?'" Another was frequently sexually and racially harassed by a resident. "'Do *this* to me. That's what you're getting paid for.' He called me 'Ch—' [racist slur]."

A racialized health care worker in one of the group interviews said she believes that racism is not adequately acknowledged or addressed. She told us about a patient who was targeting Black staff.

> She was using her cane to whack people and calling them the N-word and calling them other degrading slurs—whatever she could say. And more than one nurse stated that this was happening to them, but it was never addressed in the [managerial] report. How would you feel if it wasn't addressed, each and every one of you? Would you feel human?

CBC News reported that a temporary staffing agency in Quebec regularly received requests for white women only from a hospital HR department seeking to recruit staff. A spokesperson for the temp agency said the HR representative rationalized the requests by saying, "If we send in somebody who is Black, or of a different background, [the client] will be mean, abusive, verbally, physically, to this worker, to one of my employees, and I don't want to put my employees in that position." To their credit, the agency refuses to abide by such requests, calling them discriminatory.[19]

Gender and sexual orientation

Sexism and gender discrimination are similarly destructive. For whatever reason, some patients feel free to unleash physical or verbal sexual abuse upon their caregivers. Gender-based violence is rampant in our culture. The Canadian Women's Foundation has shared some alarming numbers, such as the fact that half of all women in Canada have experienced physical or sexual violence, and women are ten times more likely than men to be victims of police-reported sexual assault.[20]

Some women are targeted more frequently than others. The McMaster University Sexual Violence Prevention and Response Office explores violence using the lens of intersectionality, which it explains "describes the experiences of those living at the intersection of two or more marginalized identities and is a useful framework for understanding the realities of sexual violence." The term, coined by Kimberlé Crenshaw,

> illuminates the reality that those who live at the intersections of multiple marginalized identities—like Indigenous women, women living disabilities or trans people of colour—experience sexual violence at higher rates.[21]

The targeting of marginalized individuals has implications for the health care industry workforce, which is primarily made up of women and is diverse in terms of sexuality and racial identity.

LBGTQ+ health care workers face their own discriminatory victimization. A nurse who is openly gay told us, "It's pretty scary." He says his sexuality was behind a violent attack that left him severely injured. "When he [psychiatric patient] came to us, as soon as he saw me, he was focused on me because of my sexual orientation. In his words, some 'f—' [sexist slur] gave his uncle AIDS and he died."

We heard that sexual harassment is so pervasive that victims seldom formally report it. But it leaves emotional scars. One of the long-term care study participants told us she faces sexual violence daily. "'You've got a nice set of tits on you.' I get that all the time, or they grab my butt. It's degrading. There are times that you just sit down in your car and cry." Another said, "He groped me when I was bathing him. It bothered me for a very long time, but I didn't dare say anything because I was worried about my job. I was a single mom and I had to work."

A young long-term care worker said she had a resident who would grab her and try to get her into his bed. Another regularly made sexual comments when she was bathing him or providing peri-care, such as, "I know you are enjoying this."

Heather Neiser believes that violence against health care staff is closely related to violence against women in society. She said, "Violence against women is too often normalized. If many women experience violence at home, why wouldn't it be acceptable at work? Then add what happens behind your door, stays behind your door. I learned that from a young age."

Burnout

The end result of much of the physical and psychological harm done by violence in a work environment with little support or control is burnout. We heard in both studies that the violence and related stress was so intolerable that many workers just wanted to quit their jobs. Some did. One of the nurses changed occupations, choosing to be a dietary aide to avoid the daily harassment and threat of violence. She said, "I quit my job because I was having nightmares." Some changed their occupations in order to avoid direct patient or resident contact. An experienced nurse told us, "I've been in nursing for over thirty years, but I decided to switch to housekeeping because I couldn't take it any longer." Some told us they are counting the months and years before they can retire. Some tell themselves that it could be worse or that they are tough and can take it.

A PSW told us, "You're drained. I've been doing this for thirteen years and probably in the last couple years I'm thinking, 'This is it. I got to do something different." One of the research participants told us:

> The staff are not happy because they're burnt out. It's not just about protection for yourself. They feel helpless and hopeless because they can't protect themselves and they can't protect the residents. I'm supposed to be caring for these elderly people, but there's not enough staff to. And you take that home with you.

Home care workers

Although our research involved hospital and long-term care staff, several had also worked in home care or were working part-time in both areas. The home care workers talked about many of the same risk factors for violence that we heard from hospital and long-term care staff, although some conditions were unique, such as the danger of working completely alone, and, of course, having no code white team to call in an emergency. They described experiencing physical and sexual abuse and verbal aggression, including racist and sexist remarks. They talked about the anxiety they felt entering the home of a new client, the fear they felt returning to the residence of a client who had been aggressive on a previous visit, and the disgust they experienced after being harassed or assaulted. Other household members can also pose a threat. A PSW told us she was sexually assaulted by the husband of the client she was caring for. "I was young, and it was awful to be violated like that. And he did it in front of his wife. I went home. I quit my job."

A recent U.S. study that surveyed over 1,200 home care workers found that the majority had experienced some form of aggression from their clients or others in the home in the previous year. Those who had experienced aggression suffered greater rates of stress, depression, sleep problems, and burnout.[22] Another study found that "risks like violent crime, verbal abuse or even an encounter with vicious animals are everyday occurrences, yet they often go unreported." As many as 80 per cent of home care workers did not report incidents for fear of losing their jobs.[23]

What now?

Just knowing how seriously violence affects its victims' physical and mental health is not enough. In order to devise strategies for change, we also need to understand what is putting health care workers at an increased risk. A deeper examination of the causes of violence is needed to provide illumination and direction.

3.

Finding an Abnormality

"How many people have to get hurt?"

Is violence against health care staff normal? Is it unavoidable? Does caring for people have to involve such a high risk of being physically or emotionally injured, sexually assaulted, traumatized, or killed? According to a report jointly released by a coalition that included the ILO and the WHO, working with people in distress is one of the principal risk factors for violence.

> Frustration and anger arising out of illness and pain, problems of old age, psychiatric disorders, alcohol and substance abuse can affect behaviour and make people verbally or physically violent. Violence is so common among workers in contact with people in distress that it is often considered an inevitable part of the job. Health-care workers are at the forefront of this situation.[1]

Heather Neiser disagrees with the notion that violence is inherent to the job. As she put it, "We are not boxers."

What do health care workers themselves see as risk factors for violence? As part of our information gathering, we posed open-ended questions to the research participant groups and let the discussions unfold. Together we explored immediate and underlying causes of violent incidents. From their own experience, workers identified dozens of factors that can lead to violence. Many of the factors are modifiable. In other words, there are mechanisms for minimizing or eliminating risks.

To help us analyze the dozens of factors the health care workers talked to us about, we organized them using U.S. Occupational Safety and Health Administration categories: clinical, environmental, organizational, social, and economic.[2]

Clinical risk factors

According to OSHA, clinical risk factors include "the influence of drugs or alcohol; severe pain; history of violence; cognitive impairment (e.g., dementia); and certain psychiatric diagnoses."[3] The study participants described conditions in their own workplaces that fit within this category, many of which took place in ERs, long-term care and geriatric care, psychiatric units, detox facilities, and forensic units (which treat mental health patients who are deemed NCR). The shortage of mental health beds, addiction services, dementia programs, and social supports leaves many people with no alternative other than to access the ERs, which are generally ill-equipped to handle the patients' particular needs.

An ER nurse recalled, "We had a situation where a patient's family member came through the emergency department with a club. He apparently didn't feel that the patient was getting the proper care."

A psychiatric nurse who had been seriously injured during a particularly vicious assault told us:

> I've pretty much dealt with violence since starting work in mental health. From having to do one-to-ones, five-point restraints, tackling violent people, restraining them. I was assaulted by a

patient and it was a severe assault. I was strangled. I was thrown. I was beaten. I had another patient that was withdrawing from heavy drugs and alcohol and he ended up cornering me in the hallway. He even picked up his mattress and he threw it at me. It's worse now than it was thirty years ago. We're not using the restraints as we did once as much. On the street component is the drugs. The drugs are different now. It's not like, you know, the sixties where it was just a couple of hallucinogens here and there and mostly people were kind of mellowed out. They're not mellow anymore. And these people are stoned for days, when they're doing crystal meth. Holy crap. That is scary, when someone's on crystal meth.

We heard about violent incidents that took place on general wards, in medical/surgical departments, day surgery, internal medicine, and stroke care departments.

I had a patient who had been trying to leave the unit. We couldn't allow him to just walk off the floor. As we were in front of the elevator trying to stop him, just calm him down and try to talk him down, he started to swing. We called a code white. It took over twenty staff members to hold him down, to try to get him to calm down and get him back to his room.

Several participants reported that patients are being improperly placed in acute beds rather than in specialized care. A nurse working in an acute care hospital told us:

We need appropriate funding for people to be placed where they should be . . . You have patients with drug problems. They need to have a place other than the hospital.

An ER nurse voiced a similar viewpoint. She explained:

And we need to get psychiatric patients off the units to the proper unit. They don't belong on a medical floor. We don't have enough psychiatric beds. There are even a lot of patients in the nursing homes who are young psych patients. They're taking up beds that we need for the elderly who are stuck in our hospital system because there's no place to send them.

The acuity of long-term care residents, which includes adults of all ages, is very high and is contributing to the risk of violence.

Residents are coming in sicker and with more dementia and they have more responsive behaviours like kicking, spitting, scratching.

When I was first hired, you had to be ambulatory to get into the building. Now they're on a stretcher. There are feeding tubes. There's oxygen.

One of my residents is this homeless guy that was a drug addict. He's a real handful to look after and he's younger than me. We had a lady in her twenties with brain damage from an accident and she shared a room with a woman who was over a hundred. They're all mixed in together.

Now people are coming in who are thirty, forty, fifty. The last several people that have been admitted are in their fifties and have mental health diagnoses. Long-term care is not equipped to deal with people who have mental health issues. We don't have outside support. We don't have a psychiatrist or a psychologist like they do in a hospital.

We have a resident who is an ex-fighter. He's hit a few people in the face. He was mumbling something, and I said, "Pardon me," and he went pop with his fist, right in the face.

One of my co-workers was in a room tending to a resident, and this man who had dementia got it into his head that it was his wife in the bed and that my co-worker was abusing her. He picked her up, threw her across the room, pounded her face, and there was blood everywhere.

Others identified wait times as a trigger for violent behaviour directed towards staff. Patient wait times are elevated in many health care facilities, a significant risk factor for violence that has been identified in the published literature. For example, a study of violence in ERs states, "A normally pleasant and well-adjusted patient can become irritated after a 3 or 4-hour wait, and a not so well adjusted patient may become dangerous after the same wait."[4]

Whether it's a psychiatric or medical patient or someone coming into an emergency room, if you don't have the staff to immediately address their issue—if they're kept waiting—they are more likely to escalate in their behaviour.

On our floor, if we're working short and a patient has rung for us maybe five times, they become frustrated. Technically we're not supposed to tell them that we're working short, so then they think that we're just ignoring them. And we're running around trying to get to all the bells and by the time somebody actually gets to them, they might have waited twenty minutes, and they had to go to the bathroom or they want a pain pill or whatever. And now they've gone from being a little bit mad to being really agitated. And if there's a family member in the room, they'll be really upset too. Then it escalates.

I think they're cutting back on everything. Patients are waiting for porters. They're waiting for nurses, because they have seven or eight patients each. And they're waiting to have rooms cleaned because there are not enough housekeepers.

Environmental risk factors

Environmental risk factors "relate to the physical layout, design, and contents of the workplace." These include such building features as "unsecured access/egress . . . ; insufficient heating or cooling; irritating noise levels; unsecured items . . . and lack of personal security alarms."[5]

One hospital worker described a situation in which she and two co-workers were trapped in a room by an aggressive patient and had been unable to call a code white.

> He had hold of both of my arms. The more I tried to get away, the stronger he got. He slammed me against some walls and pushed me down on the bed. Two of my co-workers came to help me and we ended up on the other side of the door holding it closed.

We were told that there are too few seclusion rooms, which are locked rooms in which a patient or resident can safely be held until they are sufficiently calm. Not having a secure room can compound the risk to staff when patients are out of control. A ward clerk, whose responsibilities include such administrative tasks as organizing and updating patient records and answering phones, told us about a frightening incident that took place when she was asked to enter a patient's room to fix a faulty soap dispenser.

> I went in to help, only because ward clerks tend to do a lot of everything. Just stepping in there, he came at me. He punched me in the head a couple times and in the shoulder, and I was trying to get out. So I yelled and then people came. But we had no place to put the patient, because we only have one seclusion room in the hospital on each floor and one of ours was being used by a patient with a serious neurological disease. That's his room. The violent patient had to be transported somewhere else.

Health care workers told us that there are areas within the

hospital that are not protected by alarm systems, or in some cases, the alarms were non-functioning. In one instance, the patient call bell, bathroom assist bell, code blue alarm for respiratory or cardiac arrest, and staff emergency alarms all made the same sound in the nursing station. Several alarms may be sounding at once, making it difficult to know which requires the most urgent attention. Coloured lights are the only indicators of the nature of the need.

> There is a bathroom emergency alarm and then up above the bed with our call system are the patient and staff emergency alarms. There's no different distinct sound between them.

Many of the participants said they do not have personal alarms that would allow them to signal for help.

> We have no alarms. It is funny, which people do have alarms—the doctors, the social worker, and the occupational therapist—but not the nursing staff.

> I had my cell phone out to try to call, but I couldn't. And when I went to press zero to call a code white, the patient kneed the phone out of my hand. So we just had to deal with it ourselves.

> I didn't know that there was anything wrong with us not having alarms until I was approached at a seminar. An employee from another hospital came up to me and said, "I work laundry and when I walk into the mental health floor, I have to pick up an alarm, and after taking care of the laundry, I come back and drop it off." And I said, "We scream. That's the best we can do is scream."

Some workers had been hurt when patients used loose furniture, commodes, dishes, building materials, or other objects as weapons. A psychiatric patient seriously injured one of the nurses we spoke with.

He grabbed me and hit me with the glass. I slumped to the ground and he was still pounding me. And next thing you know, all I can tell you I remember—I don't remember being on the floor—but I remember my tongue being tingly and then my memory was off. I tried to fight him off all the way down the hall. He put my head through the wall. There was blood on the walls from my elbows, my face . . . Many months later, I still suffer headaches and symptoms of depression.

Even long-term care residents can present a serious threat. Heather Neiser told delegates at a conference about a new resident whose fear and frustration turned violent. He used whatever he could get his hands on as a weapon. Before his tirade ended, he had struck her multiple times and had hit another resident. It took several staff to restrain him.

Social work came to admit him . . . he spat in her face and said a few profanities . . . the social worker left for the weekend with a simple "Good luck. He's all yours." By supper he was escalating from arguing with the residents to pushing and striking out. When finally redirected to his room he took the heavy lid off the back of the toilet, swinging it like a baseball bat, making contact with me before he threw it at the window in an attempt to escape.

Many nursing stations were considered unsafe because they do not have protective shatterproof barriers or adequate egress or escape options. We heard about patients grabbing items from the nursing station and throwing them at staff or jumping over the desk to attack an unprotected worker.

After a co-worker was sexually assaulted by a patient, the government inspector recommended that they put glass up. The hospital fought them on it. They said it stigmatizes the patients.

Environments within long-term care carry their own unique

risks. Study participants were critical of building design features that create barriers to communication.

> Those hallways are terrible. You work way over there, and you can't communicate.

> You can't even hear our overhead speakers when you're in a resident's room. Because you have to shut the door for privacy.

> There's a big section between the two hallways. I'm down in one. How is my co-worker going to hear me while she's giving a bath? And 90 per cent of the time, I'm working short. So who's going to come and help me?

Each long-term care facility has its own method whereby staff communicate that they need help. Some have walkie-talkies or whistles. Some have no mechanical means whatsoever to call for assistance.

> There are policies in some care homes against using your own cell phones. Which is fair enough. But they should have personal alarms on all the PSWs and registered staff because they're in rooms alone with people.

> He had me backed up in the corner, punching me, and I was blowing the whistle over and over, and it was in his face and it didn't even have any reaction. He was still pounding away; nobody heard the whistle. He just happened to back up a little bit and I was able to get out—but it was scary.

> A PSW was down in a room and she was very pregnant doing a one-on-one with this aggressive guy. It took a long time before somebody heard her and pulled him off. She was hurt.

> I've been in a situation where I've been at the end of the hall with a violent resident and he had me up against the wall and I was yelling.

And no one could hear me. I finally managed to get my own cell phone out of my pocket, and I called the RN.

If I can't breathe because I'm getting choked, a whistle's useless to me.

Resident agitation can be exacerbated by their immediate environment, which can then lead to outbursts directed against their caregivers. A review of the impact of building design and the physical environment on residents with dementia, who make up the majority of the long-term care population, found

> substantial evidence on the influence of unit size, spatial layout, homelike character, sensory stimulation, and environmental characteristics of social spaces on residents' behaviors and well-being in care facilities.[6]

These findings were similar to those of a study of female caregivers in Sweden in which residents reacted to the sense of confinement in cramped spaces, such as narrow hallways and small bathrooms. Feeling agitated and restricted, they can lash out at caregivers.[7]

The experience of hospital and long-term care personnel we consulted reflected the research findings.

> So they send these patients, who can't get into the specialized units they need, to these medical units—and they're loud. The environment is loud for them—people coming in, people coming out. So this is where we get a lot of our violence from, is from these patients. And the [staff] don't have time to help them. They've got ten, eleven other patients along with this violent one.

The long-term care staff we spoke with agree that much can be done to improve the residents' living environment, including giving careful consideration to how lighting can affect them at various times of the day or night.

The ministry tells you what kind of lights you have. We just got cited. The ministry came in and said the residents' rooms needed to be brighter. They spent millions of dollars rewiring the facilities because the lighting wasn't bright enough. I sort of get that, because I know one of things they talk about with people who have dementia is that bright light keeps them brighter, but it's not great if we're coming in at five in the morning. They need the option of a nice little dim light, a morning light and an afternoon light.

Organizational risk factors

Organizational risk factors include "policies, procedures, and prevailing culture of the organization related to safety and security."[8] The study participants identified many factors that could be considered organizational, including working alone, inappropriate staff placement, lack of trained security personnel, health care workers' responsibilities during code whites, inadequacy of de-escalation and other training, under-reporting, and limited use of restraints.

A long-term care worker told us she felt completely unprepared to handle the aggression she faced from the mentally or psychologically compromised residents—many of them quite young—on her particular unit.

> The levels of aggression on my unit have increased so severely in the last six months, it's phenomenal. And I have said repeatedly, "We are not psychiatric nurses. We are not trained to work in a psychiatric hospital!" To be a volunteer at a psychiatric hospital, the training you go through is much more intense than what I have ever received. Touching these people and caring for them on a daily basis, I have no training whatsoever how to protect myself against physical aggression. I have no training whatsoever how to de-escalate a situation.

In his report to the ILO and WHO, Vittorio Di Martino said

that the lack of adequate training was an important risk factor for violence—and one that is easily remedied.[9]

We also heard there is a lack of security personnel in many facilities. A nurse told us, "I was also trying to lobby for extra security, because it was just one security guard for the whole building."

Furthermore, security personnel are generally not available or trained to handle aggressive patients or residents, leaving the care staff to handle their own emergencies, such as code white calls.

> Security staff don't interfere in code whites. They just direct the police officer to the floor if they are called. I don't think they have any special training in any type of de-escalation. They wouldn't know how to help you.

Health care workers believe that when they have to function as security, their caregiver-patient relationships are adversely affected and they are made to feel professionally less effective. Some nurses even expressed fear of losing their licence because, without the support of security personnel, their interactions with violent patients take them beyond the traditional nursing care role.

There is a lack of communication between various occupational groups regarding potentially violent situations.

> The patient could have grabbed someone else and we wouldn't know. The violence isn't being charted. Even if it were charted, it might be so buried in the chart that you might not see it.

PSWs, dietary staff, and housekeepers are not included in nursing care meetings or discussions and don't have access to a patient's medical chart.

> They can walk right into a dangerous situation. They're not included in any huddle at the beginning of a shift.

There is inconsistent flagging of potentially violent patients, not only in their charts but in other visible locations. Some hospitals use coloured arm bands, some use symbols or signs on the door or over the patient's bed. A participant described the flagging policy in the facility where she worked. No sign signalling threatening behaviour was put in place until a violent incident had occurred.

Hospital policy is that, if they swing so many times, then you put up a sign . . . the sign goes up after incidents have happened.

Some patients, family members, and patient advocates feel flagging unfairly stigmatizes the patient. Health care workers told us there is no universal protocol for flagging nor any threshold for the evidence needed to trigger the practice.

The assault could well have been prevented with flagging—a white sheet of paper or arm band. But I've been told, "That's too much information, it's breaching confidentiality—stigmatizing them." And I think, "Come on! How many people have to get hurt?"

Language and cultural barriers can contribute to miscommunication and frustration between staff and their patients or residents. Participants made the following comments:

If someone's talking to you in a different language and they're not understanding you—if someone's asking you repetitive questions and they're not understanding what you're saying, it could be very frustrating; it can escalate things.

Or if you're touching them and you're doing care, they know they can't speak English so they know whatever they say isn't going to matter, so they bite you instead to get your hand off them.

Also, culturally—I've been backhanded by a patient for assisting him to bed too early. I haven't received a lot of education about how different cultures view this and that, even death when I worked in palliative care, which I thought was a little unusual, but you don't really know what's accepted. In some cultures, they don't like eye contact, others do. Well, if I look—I always look at my patient in their face—I'm looking for a lot of things, but they might perceive that as making intense eye contact and being rude.

Some participants said their last names were included on their name tags. They wanted them removed as a safety measure. A nurse recalled an uncomfortable episode in which a visitor said, "Very nice to meet you, [Jane Doe]. And you know, you shouldn't have your last name on your badge because I can just look you up and find out who you are and where you live."

As we heard previously, statistics regarding the actual incidence of violence are not available because most incidents are not reported.

I look at my co-workers who work on the locked unit. Their arms are literally covered in bruises. I was really upset and asked if they were reporting the incidents that caused the bruises. They said, "We didn't know we were supposed to."

We're spread so thin. And there's not even any time to complain. So if we're short and I get my arm twisted, and I haven't even had my break in the morning . . . or I'm running around, and I've got to get the charting done . . . or that person needs their shower . . . where do you fit in the time to do an incident report? Where do you fit in the time to take a step back and say, "I'm a person too. I got hurt!"

One of the deterrents to reporting incidents of violence is the fear of being blamed.

If you do report, the first thing they ask is, "How did you trigger the resident? Did you provoke it? What did you do to make this happen? What was your approach? Don't you think that they perceived you as aggressive, rushing in?" But I've only got two minutes to get the person up!

The supervisors don't really give you a lot of support. They may look like they're trying, but basically the blame still falls on you. "Why didn't you speak more softly? Why didn't you approach with more caution?" But in the moment, you don't see those things. All you're trying to do is get away from what's coming at you.

A lot of us don't report because we don't want a bull's eye on us. We feel if we keep reporting we're going to get written up.

Our findings matched those of many similar studies. For example, a 2016 study of violence against long-term medical care staff in North Carolina reported:

88% of sample participants failed to report workplace violence because of the fear of losing their job and the inappropriate way management will handle the situation.[10]

The organization of work and work practices in health care are determined by administrative decisions aimed at efficiency and productivity. Time management, budgetary interests, and management efficiency practices seem to supersede the principle of patient- or resident-centred care. In long-term care, work is clearly broken down into specific tasks: bathing, dressing, toileting, feeding. This tendency towards "industrialization"[11] means that practical tasks are the priority and less time is allocated to relational care, which involves a broader range of care services and meaningful two-way social interactions between residents and staff. Numerous studies have identified that strict hierarchical staff structures and the accompanying rigid assigned tasks allow for limited caregiver flexibility to address residents' needs.[12] This has a direct impact on residents' quality of life and may contribute to their agitation, fear, or confusion, which can then lead to aggression.

Of course, the residents are agitated because there's no time to spend with them anymore. If you spend five or six minutes with each one of them, even during suppertime, it's a bonus.

We would all love to do the kind of care that we would expect for ourselves—the calm, quiet, slow-moving care. A little chat in the morning. What you'd expect, especially if you are in your eighties and are really severely dependent on a care worker. But that is not the reality.

We used to be able to develop a relationship. We could talk. They took that out of our care. Now all we do is basically factory work. It's like putting hundred-pound bags of potatoes into bed. Good night. That's it. That's health care. Now it's an assembly line.

When staff are too busy to relate at more than a superficial level with residents, the opportunity to alleviate their psychological suffering is also lost, leading to the potential for more aggression.

We had a resident who was physically okay, but he had serious PTSD. In the middle of the night, he would have nightmares and he would need staff to sit with him.

You see them getting more depressed and not thriving. Sometimes they just need a hug or just holding their hand walking down the hall chatting away. Well, you try to do it in between your tasks. You're multi-tasking all the time. Even though you're trying to hurry down the hall to another one because they're ringing, you're holding hands and you're trying to make sure that this one is feeling comfortable because you know this one's going to act out if you don't.

I feel like I have to make these decisions almost every shift. Like, "Hmm, which one comes first?" And I don't really think that's fair. I always consider these three things: Are they safe? Are they happy? Are they comfortable? And I feel like I can manage one out of three at best.

Residents can sense their caregivers' stress and may mirror their state of mind. This can then lead to responsive behaviours, like lashing out.

Do our actions perhaps cause them to act aggressively towards us? I would say so.

Especially with our dementia patients. They need time to process. You can't rush them. You have to wait for them and, if you try to hurry them, they react.

They're mad. They're agitated because we're agitated. They want to go to bed yet they're sitting there for a whole hour waiting and then when I come into the room, they're mad at me. So, I'm the first one that's going to get kicked, punched, or spit at or called "You stupid b—" [sexist slur].

The hierarchy among long-term care personnel can lead to conditions that can increase the chances of violent behaviours. For example, physicians often do not communicate well with the PSWs and nurses who are closest to the residents. As a result, medications may be prescribed or withdrawn without consideration of the consequences. Indeed, there is ongoing controversy over the issue of medicating residents. In recent years the use of antipsychotic drugs has been reduced by more than a third.[13] Participants agree that chemical restraints should not be overly prescribed. However, there has been no corresponding increase in staffing and other resources to deal with the resulting exacerbation in resident agitation.

The doctor will come in and look at a resident. We're pulling our hair out saying, "Listen, something has to change here," and the doctor says, "I find her very endearing." So the problem remains.

The doctor takes away their medication. If I say, "This person is escalating. He's going to start striking," they say, "No, he's not that bad."

One of the strategies that was introduced in 2010 is Behavioural Supports Ontario (BSO). Their function is to assess behavioural issues among residents with cognitive or neurological deficits and establish care plans. However, not all facilities have in-house teams. Furthermore, as is the case with the reduction in use of medications, additional staffing is required to carry out the BSO plans.

> Behavioural supports are there weekly but don't add care staff. They're there to assist in advising on whether there's a change of medications to give, recommendations to the physicians, but they're not there to put time in with residents.

> You have fifteen care plans which you're supposed to know inside out and then the BSO gets involved and creates another ten strategies, which adds another five pages to the care plan. Where's the staff to implement those strategies?

Social risk factors

Social risk factors include the use of "weapons among patients and their visitors; the increasing use of healthcare facilities by authorities as criminal holds; and presence of gang members, drug or alcohol abusers, trauma patients, or distraught family members."[14]

Health care workers we spoke with reported that, in some locations, police have a practice of bringing violent patients into the health care setting without sufficient communications or controls.

> The police don't want to take them to the drunk unit. They don't want to be bothered with the ones that they know are going to act up. So they literally come to the emergency with them and leave. There's no security at this hospital.

A nurse told us about a situation in which a violent patient was brought into the ER and was left for the hospital staff to deal with.

> She came in with the police, wasn't searched or anything. They were trying to get her into restraints because she was throwing stuff at

them; she was threatening people. Nobody checked her, nobody patted her down. It turned out she had a six-inch blade.

Another nurse told us about an incident that left everyone on the unit rattled and fearful for days.

We had an incident in the convalescence unit. We had a patient there who had been pushed by his grandson down the stairs and got injured. He was sent to the hospital and, after that, for rehab. They sent him to us. There was a notation on his care plan that if his grandson were to come, we were not to let him go close to his grandfather. One night, that guy showed up and the PSWs were trying to intervene. He got mad. He pushed the PSW, but the PSW called the security and then the guy threatened all the workers. He left the unit because the security came, and then he came back with a knife. So they called a code white, but he left again. That night the PSW and the nurses were terrified. They were worried that the guy might still be on the unit or on the floor—just hiding—and might come out to stab them. And then the day staff were also terrified because every time we'd go into the room, we would have to check for him.

In the coding for our research data analysis, we also included lack of respect for health care staff and negative societal attitudes towards women, LGBTQ+ people, and racialized and immigrant workers as social risk factors.

Several health care workers said they had experienced a decrease in respect from patients and visitors in the past few years. They feel that when there is little respect, there is a greater likelihood of verbal and physical abuse.

You need to be respected and the supervisors and doctors need to demonstrate respect for you in front of patients and family members—otherwise they are going to pick on you.

In a growing number of facilities, signs have been posted

informing patients and visitors there is "zero tolerance" for abusive behaviours, including discrimination, harassment, and other forms of violence. Others have no such signage.

> I notice at the hospital coffee shop they have a sign that says they won't tolerate any type of verbal abuse. But there's no signs on our units that say that. We need signs like they have in emerg that say, "We will not tolerate verbal or physical violence." . . . There is a poster about if you're widowed and lonely, here's a singles website. But you won't put up a violence sign for us?

Discrimination was cited as a trigger for violence, ranging from verbal insults to sexual harassment and physical assault. One participant reported that he was frequently harassed because of his sexual orientation.

Many of the women described frequent incidents of sexually inappropriate comments or touching.

> They always grab my breast when I'm doing their care, or they grab my crotch. We don't report sexual violence because it happens so frequently . . . I have been grabbed many times.

> Sexual harassment is definitely a problem for women workers. If I go in with a male worker, the patient is not going to pinch his butt. They'll pinch mine or make a sexual comment.

> A patient referred to the nurses as whores and bitches.

> You feel disgusted with yourself after someone makes an inappropriate pass. It makes you feel violated.

Cultural and racial differences have become flash points for some patients. A hospital cleaner reported, "I've been called the N-word many times and I've been threatened." Another cleaner told us, "My Asian partner got beaten up. She got punched in the face. The patient thought she was a terrorist."

A participant recalled being warned by a patient's daughter that her father would likely react if a non-white health care worker tried to treat him. She was told, "My father has a problem with visually ethnic people. If the doctor is going to be Chinese or whatever, you're going to see a side of my father that's going to come out."

Distraught families and traumatized patients sometimes lash out at health care workers, verbally or physically, blaming them for the patients' discomfort, long waits, and lack of attention.

> This family member was chasing and barricading a co-worker. He was angry over a bruise on his parent's hand, which we had suspected was from basic blood work. I grabbed his attention and yelled, "You need to leave now. You can't do this; you need to leave." Then he starts chasing me, yelling. I finally get away and run to the nurses' station. I get in and start to close the door fast so I can call 911. He starts kicking the door and forcing it open.

> I go to give the patient an explanation and the family members rip my head off and want to talk to the doctor—rightfully so—it's the doctor who changed their orders. Things like that happen all the time and people get agitated with you.

Sometimes there is no apparent trigger. For example, a health care worker was assaulted by a family member while transporting a patient.

> The porter was taking the family down to the main entrance. The patient's husband was with her. And for some reason, he flipped out—pushed the porter and hit her. She continues to suffer symptoms of PTSD.

Economic risk factors

Economic risk factors are related to the funding levels of the institutions and decisions regarding allocation of funds, which "can contribute to risk factors on a personal level in the form of stress levels and on an organizational level in the form of short staffing."[15]

Inadequate resources, understaffing, and lack of appropriate services for patients with mental health needs have been identified in numerous studies as important risk factors for violence. Our study participants, without exception, identified limited resources as a contributing factor. They reported that understaffing contributes to patient frustration, boredom, fear, and anger, which can then lead to acting-out behaviours.

One of the staff was working nights and a patient bashed her head into a piece of equipment. She was by herself. She couldn't call for help. She didn't even have a phone. She suffered a concussion and never came back to work.

When there are not enough front-line workers, patients get neglected. Patients don't get the care they need, the immediate attention they need. That causes stress. Whether you're a psychiatric patient, a medical patient, a physiotherapy patient, or you are coming in to an emergency room, if you don't have the staff to immediately address your issue, then you're going to escalate in your behaviour, whether or not you're an educated person, a street person, or travelling through our community.

The staffing is there, but it hasn't changed over the years with the increased duties. It used to be nursing was responsible for transferring patients. Now you get one floor specifically with a half-dozen bed transfers, a couple isolations that you have to do start to finish, maybe a ward. And then you're supposed to do all the discharges on top and do your regular duties on top of that. And so they haven't taken into account the increase of responsibility. They should increase the staffing accordingly.

Breakfast time, we do the rounds. I haven't actually counted how many staff, but I know there's not enough. I can go in and take their breakfast and the person's saying, "I got to pee, I got to pee." I'll say, "Hang on." I push the buzzer because some of them don't know what to do with it and the desk will come on and I'll say, "So and so needs to pee." "Okay, we'll send someone down." And I could finish delivering the rest of my trays, and they still haven't had someone. Or else they'll complain and say, "I rang the bell an hour ago." And they wet the bed. And, you know, it's just not fair. And years ago, it was probably three patients to a nurse.

You don't really have extra staff to sit with them and calm them down or to help monitor them . . . Then that upsets the other patients and family members. And it comes back on you.

We have one resident who is a former football player. He's only middle-aged but has acquired dementia because of head injuries. He's six-two and he's big. It takes three to four people to handle him just to be able to do the peri-care, even put on his shirt, because he can strike. Nobody can handle him on their own. He gets just one care a day because in the evening they don't have enough staff.

We were working short that night. The float had gone home. We had an incident where we had a lady bleeding out and waiting for the RPN. I had a gentleman down at the end with the bed alarm going; by the time I got to him, he had already ripped the blinds off the wall, pulled the TV onto himself. And then he started grabbing at me.

They spoke of the problems associated with being short-staffed when workers who called in sick were not replaced. Some reported that violence, lack of support, and burnout were themselves contributors to the number of sick calls.

With everybody just burning out like they are, you've got no one to come in. There's a ridiculous number of staff that are not making their shifts because they can't cope anymore. I was just in a unit where they had three staff out of their seven call in sick. Supervisors were calling from five o'clock in the morning until seven and they couldn't find a single person who was willing to come in.

You're scrambling trying to find somebody to replace and nobody wants to take your call. On the weekend there were seven sick calls. And all these calls were to replace people at 6 a.m. for their shifts.

There was concern expressed that the increase in public-private partnerships (P3s) would further erode hospital staffing levels and, in turn, patient care and staff safety because the profit motive would drain money from patient care.

They talk about not having enough funding. But the health care system is becoming a profit-making system.

Some were critical of what they viewed as inappropriate prioritizing by management of the limited funds within the institution's budget.

We talked about the capital budget when my co-worker was assaulted, and the supervisor said he was going to do everything he could to fix the environment. But nothing's happened.

It's all about the budget . . . We have no security. When we've brought it to their attention, their answer is, "If we do bring in security, there will be staff layoffs."

The participants also said there has been a reduction in one-to-one care as well as therapeutic programs for mental health patients and long-term care residents, which were designed to calm and reassure them.

They need somebody in the evening. The patients just sit and do nothing. There's too much time on their hands. They get bored and they get angry and that's when the agitation gets worse.

Lack of institutional supports

There is another area of risk related to violence that concerns its aftermath. Staff who have been victimized by violence, or have been traumatized by witnessing it, are more likely to suffer long-term consequences if they do not receive immediate and appropriate supports. After speaking to dozens of health care staff across the province, we learned that violence is ruining health care workers' lives, leaving some of them disabled and in pain. It has driven many of them into states of chronic depression, fear, hopelessness, and anxiety. Victims of sexual harassment and assault are left feeling debased, traumatized, and unsupported. We heard that some management personnel are less than understanding and may not provide the needed emotional supports or time off to recover.

The functioning of the workers' compensation system can also contribute to the possibility of ongoing physical and emotional injury. PTSD, for example, is not uniformly recognized as a compensable injury for all health care staff. Long-term symptoms related to concussions and chronic pain from physical assaults are difficult to establish as compensable, often requiring stressful interactions with the compensation system staff and case managers. The convoluted system seems to be designed to make injured workers want to give up. And many do just that—especially if their claim has been initially rejected.

> He told me they [my employers] were appealing my claim, and he said, "Don't be upset. They appeal everybody's claim." I said to him, "Yes, I am going to take it personally, and I don't understand why you're appealing it."

A PSW sustained a serious wrist injury when a very heavy resident tried to fight off her attempts to roll her over in her bed. Her trust in the WSIB as a safety net was shattered by its bureaucratic barriers and seeming insensitivity.

She's resistive in the morning, so she will not help. We were just about to finish care, and I was just grabbing the soaker pads to roll her over so we can get her brief and the sling under. And she just was against me, so I pulled on her more, because she's heavy, to get her over. And I ended up crushing the cartilage in my wrist bone area and ended up getting tears and pulled my tendons. I had to have my bone cut—shortened—and a plate put in because it was not healing. Since returning to work, I've been on light duties. WSIB has been following me since. I don't have a lot to say nice about them right now either. I've been waiting a month to receive any money from all my lost time. I haven't received a penny from them. The way they treat me is not very nice, like it's my fault pretty much. And the caseworker is telling me I should have been back to work two weeks after my surgery. If I had an office job, answering phones, that would be fine. But my job is all physical. It's all with my hands and she can't seem to comprehend that. So she has neglected to put in any paperwork properly. She's had me have two return-to-work meetings with return-to-work specialists, trying to get me back to work. It's like they don't want to give me time to heal from the surgery.

Other staff spoke of similar experiences. Many said they were simply not granted enough time off to recover.

I took a couple of days off where I just couldn't manage because of the stress of the night before and . . . I was just kind of getting over my first injury, then another patient—because they could—grabbed my wrist, pulled my left arm down and pulled it out from my body. So now I'm going back through the same thing. I've been hurt twice in seven months, and now I'm feeling that they're trying to push me back to my regular job again.

Health care workers, of all people, should be able to expect prompt responses, courtesy, and co-operation from the compensation system. After all, they are working in one of the most dangerous sectors in the province. As one hospital worker said, after many frustrating encounters with the WSIB, "You would not believe what it's like, just having to deal with them." Another said:

> It's really hard to deal with every day. The WSIB sloughed it off. They said, "You should be back to work." But every day I deal with the post-traumatic stress from it. They don't get it—because they don't live it.

Dianne Paulin's life has been changed forever, not only by the injuries she sustained, but also by the mistreatment she feels she received from the WSIB.

> WSIB and the hospital have re-victimized me . . . It's been a battle—constantly, constantly . . . They tried to get me not to go to WSIB. They wanted me to go on long-term sickness instead of WSIB. And I went, "Why would I go on long-term sickness? I don't have a long-term sickness; I got beaten up; I got hurt. It's not because I got cancer or something." I said no . . . WSIB went three months without giving me a penny. Three whole months without a penny to live off of.
>
> My psychiatrist had told the hospital—had written them a letter—saying, "Dianne cannot return back to work." WSIB went against my psychiatrist, and the hospital went against my psychiatrist and they *made* me return to work.
>
> My caseworker phoned me and said, "You're going back to work on Monday." I said, "What?! I'm not ready to go back to work. Who said I was ready to go back to work?" And she said, "I did." . . . I wasn't physically or mentally ready to go back to work. So my case manager sent me back to work. My nurse at WSIB was not even aware that my case manager was sending me back to work.

Dianne was not able to handle the stresses of the job and was directed instead to a customer service job, making minimum wage. That didn't work out either.

Because I'm supposed to be working as customer service—even though my doctor says it's the worst place for me to be. He tells me that post-traumatic stress disorder doesn't go with customer services where people are complaining constantly. It would make my anxiety go right through the roof!

Another nurse, who asked to remain anonymous, described an incident that left her both physically injured and psychologically traumatized. She said that a resident in long-term care began screaming and threatening a PSW. Hearing the commotion, she ran to the aid of her colleague. She was immediately grabbed by the arms, while the resident whirled her around while shouting obscenities. The resident pushed her into a room and pinned her on the bed. Time elapsed but finally two other staff rushed into the room, and among the three of them they were able to free the injured nurse.

The physical injury was minor in comparison to the psychological damage that continues to haunt her years later. While she was granted access to a number of visits to speak with a psychologist, she never fully regained her confidence and sense of security. Her management was also unsupportive and remained insensitive to the trauma she experienced. "Work was also my safe place. I felt like I belonged there, I felt like people had my back. And then I found out they don't."

She also had numerous conflicts with the WSIB, who focused mainly on her return to work. The injured nurse finally demanded to see her compensation file and discovered a letter by her supervisor outlining reasons why the employer opposed her compensation claim.

I discovered a two-page letter on why I should not be approved for this injury. According to them, the injury was not as bad as some of the violent incidents that I had previously faced, and that violence was part of my job. That there were care plans in place and that I was trained to deal with them. And that I know that it was expected at my workplace.

This letter validated one of the important insights we heard over and over from the health care staff we interviewed. Management and even the compensation system recognize the risk of violence in these facilities but accept that it is just "part of the job."

The Ontario Network of Injured Workers Groups (ONIWG) is very critical of the barriers put up by the WSIB. The network claims the issue of pre-existing conditions is unjustly used to deny compensation to those who should be entitled to it.

> In and around 2010, the WSIB began a practice of aggressively reducing or eliminating benefits to injured workers who they claim have "pre-existing conditions." Essentially, rather than compensating somebody for a work injury, the WSIB searches through their medical records and tries to find something else that it can blame for their ongoing disability, essentially some other "condition" that it can claim is the "real" source of the disability.
>
> All too often, though, the "pre-existing conditions" that the WSIB points to never actually affected the person at all until they were injured at work. In many cases, they were never diagnosed by a doctor before the work injury, and never caused the person any symptoms.[16]

Dianne is convinced that that is what happened to her and why her claim was denied. She was forthright about her past, revealing to a WSIB counsellor that she had been abused as a child.

> When I was four years old something happened to me. So they say that's why I now suffer from post-traumatic stress disorder, that it has nothing to do with the assault whatsoever. So they blame whatever happens to you now on your childhood. Even though I was able to work for twenty-three years without a problem? That doesn't seem to matter—whatsoever . . . Of course, I'm depressed. I'm suicidal. I can't pay any of my bills! I phoned my caseworker at

WSIB . . . My caseworker laughs at me—in my face. My psychiatrist has forbidden me to talk to my caseworker now.

From risk factors to prevention strategies

We all know that an ounce of prevention is worth a pound of cure. We know what the risk factors for violence are, and we have a basis to prevent injury should violence occur and improve the outlook for those who have been assaulted and/or traumatized.

There seem to be, however, almost insurmountable barriers to implementing the many and varied prevention strategies that are identified. Understanding how the epidemic of violence against health care staff has been allowed to continue, relatively unabated in many workplaces, requires a deeper examination of the political, economic, and cultural environment in which health care functions. We will explore these underlying influences in part two. Perhaps we will then be in a better position to devise strategies for change.

Part Two
A Forensic Examination

Birth and Decline of the Health Care System

The roots of violence

As we heard over and over again in our research, much of the violence experienced by health care workers is related to under-funding and understaffing—a situation that seems to be getting worse. As one study participant told us, "The health care system has been so badly cut that there's not enough staff to provide the safety and security we need." It's difficult to imagine how violence against health care staff in Canada has become so serious and so widespread. Its roots may lie somewhere in the history of health care itself, the hopeful and public-spirited evolution of our modern system, and then its calamitous devolution and decline.

A brief history of government-supported public health care

The history of Canada's universal health care system is not straight-forward, nor has it evolved over the years into the system its creators first conceived of. The system's single-payer universality is still being contested, and there is ongoing pressure from some quarters to privatize.

Birth of universal health care

The first serious discussions about the need for publicly funded health care in Canada took place during the Spanish Flu pandemic.[1] The demand for access to medical care as a basic right for every Canadian was further fuelled by the devastation of the Depression of the 1930s, followed by the Second World War. Having experienced the hardships of such catastrophic upheavals, Canadians began to demand a different role from their governments. Activists advocated for such universal social programs as medical care and an old age pension system. But the idea that every person should have free access to medical care, as a human right, was not universally supported and was often vehemently opposed. In the mid twentieth century, the movers and shakers who controlled Canada's federal and provincial governments, as in other capitalist countries like the United States, still wanted the burdens of health care to be borne by each individual without the state's involvement.

Those who opposed any form of welfare, most of whom were financially comfortable, questioned the entitlement of the needy. Why should the government be involved in providing for such irresponsible parties? Why should taxpayers shoulder the expenses of the less well-to-do? Shouldn't each individual or their family be expected to bear responsibility for their own medical needs rather than taking handouts from the rest of society? And since society relied on the free enterprise market system to regulate and control the distribution of goods and services, why not let private companies offer health insurance for purchase? If parents were unable to pay to have a sick child seen by a doctor, or if a family had insufficient funds to adequately care for an elderly relative, they were seen by governments and the wealthy as having failed to properly prepare for such eventualities. Such burdened individuals would essentially be blamed for their own predicaments. The majority of

Conservative and Liberal politicians at the time held this perspective and opposed universal health care.

Saskatchewan leads the way

The first breakthrough to establishing a publicly funded health care system came in Saskatchewan in 1944 when the Co-operative Commonwealth Federation (CCF) won the provincial election. Its leader, Tommy Douglas, had promised to enact a comprehensive health care program, similar to the British National Health Service.

In 1947 the CCF introduced, for the first time in North America, a "universal and compulsory public hospital insurance program" in Saskatchewan.[2] It would take another ten years before Ottawa followed suit with legislation that launched a federal-provincial partnership providing for a public hospital insurance program for all Canadians.

With this national program in place, Douglas announced that Saskatchewan would proceed to create a universal, comprehensive public health care system that went beyond coverage for hospital treatment. Legislation proposing this broader coverage became the focal point of the 1960 provincial election. The CCF faced fierce resistance from a coalition of doctors, including the Saskatchewan College of Physicians and Surgeons. The Canadian Medical Association (CMA) and the American Medical Association supported the opposing coalition, as did many business groups and much of the provincial media.[3]

During the 1960 provincial election, the doctors and their allies sought to gain public support for their opposition to universal health care by putting out the message that this was forced socialized medicine and that it would take away patients' individual choices. Tens of thousands of dollars—a lot of money at that time—was spent on a propaganda campaign that included direct mailings to every household in Saskatchewan as well as media advertisements. The strategy failed, and the CCF won a majority government with a mandate to enact a universal, comprehensive health care system.

This clear electoral victory did not, however, end the strife. Physicians' groups continued to engage in a campaign to limit the scope of the public system. This effort culminated in a twenty-three-day doctors' strike in 1962. The government held firm to its plans, the doctors conceded defeat, and the strike ended. As political commentators Lorne Brown and Doug Taylor concluded in their article on "The Birth of Medicare," the outcome of the strike was that, in Saskatchewan, "medical insurance would remain government-controlled, compulsory, universal and reasonably comprehensive."[4]

A national health care plan

Prime Minister John Diefenbaker's government—faced with the Saskatchewan precedent—established a Royal Commission in 1961, chaired by Supreme Court Justice Emmett Hall, to explore health services across the country. Its purpose was to assess existing services and plan for future needs, in order to "ensure that the best possible health care is available to all Canadians."[5]

The hearings provided a public forum for farmer organizations, trade unions, community groups, and other social movements. The Hall Commission produced its report in 1964, recommending legislation that essentially mirrored the Saskatchewan government's model, thereby providing the impetus for what was to become our most treasured social program. Justice Hall commented:

> We, as a society, are aware that the pain of illness, the trauma of surgery, the slow decline to death, are burdens enough for the human being to bear without the added burden of medical or hospital bills penalizing the patient at the moment of vulnerability. The Canadian people determined that they should band together to pay medical bills when they were well and income earning. Health services [are] ... a fundamental need, like education, which Canadians could meet collectively and pay for through taxes.[6]

Hall famously quipped, "The only thing more expensive than good health care is no health care."

In December 1966, the federal House of Commons voted 177 to 2 to pass the *National Medical Care Insurance Act*, or what is referred to as medicare. It would pass responsibility for health care to individual provinces and territories. Costs were to be borne by the provinces, with subsidies from the federal government in the form of transfer payments. By 1971 all the provinces had met the conditions in the federal legislation that required that they provide "universal, publicly administered, portable and comprehensive" coverage.[7]

It was not an easy process. The establishment of the public health care system did not settle many of the contested issues, and some doctors fought back by extra-billing for services rendered. This went against the spirit and intent of the medicare legislation; in response, the *Canada Health Act* was passed in 1984, banning extra-billing. According to a group of professors of medicine, including Dr. Chris Simpson, past president of the CMA:

> The five core principles of the Canadian system were now established [under the *Canada Health Act*]: universality (all citizens are covered), comprehensiveness (all medically essential hospital and doctors' services), portability (among all provinces and territories), public administration (of publicly funded insurance) and accessibility.[8]

Decline of the universal health care system

There have been long-standing tensions between the federal government, which sets national standards and provides a portion of the funding to the provinces for health care, and the provinces themselves.

In the decades since the 1984 federal legislation that outlawed extra-billing, there has been constant political and social conflict over the administration, scope, and funding of Canada's health care system. Federal and provincial governments were facing the end of the post-war boom in the 1980s, which resulted in increasing budget deficits and spiralling debt. As researchers Drs. Pat and Hugh Armstrong have stated, "The federal government initiated bitter and complex negotiations with the provinces to restructure the cost-sharing arrangement."[9] The provinces in turn gained more control over how health care dollars were allocated. They also started to look to the private sector and its business practices as a way to control and shape how work was being done and by whom. A significant moment in this intra-governmental fight was the 1995 decision by federal finance minister Paul Martin to introduce legislation, named the Canada Health and Social Transfer, which significantly reduced federal transfer payments to the provinces for health care and other social programs.

Each of these fiscal crises resulted in significant increases in private, for-profit corporate involvement. This transformed the organization of work within the hospitals, as pressure mounted to reduce expenditures. Drs. Pat and Hugh Armstrong explain:

> Driven by corporate pressures, neoliberal ideology and rising costs, the provinces gradually introduced many business management strategies, from work reorganisation and time compression to the employment of lower-cost workers and the introduction of labour-saving technologies.[10]

In 2002 a Royal Commission on the Future of Health Care in Canada was established, named the Romanow Commission after its chair, former Saskatchewan premier Roy Romanow. Its purpose was to "improve the system and its long-term sustainability."[11] The commission's recommendations for short- and long-term investments and greater accountability were largely ignored, as provincial governments encouraged greater for-profit corporate involvement with the hope that it might reduce their expenditures.

Our shrinking hospital capacity

In 1976, Canada had almost 7 hospital beds per 1,000 people.[12] In

2017, that number had dropped to under 3.[13] Compare that to Japan, which had 13.4 beds per 1,000 in 2017, or France with 6.37. By 2019, the Canadian number had dropped to 2.5 beds; in Ontario, the hospital bed capacity is even more dire at 2.2.[14] The Ontario Health Coalition, a province-wide public health care advocacy group, has reported that Ontario has the fewest hospital beds per capita of any province in Canada, with a shortfall of over 14,000 beds in comparison to the rest of the provinces.[15]

Doug Allan is an impassioned researcher for CUPE. Having followed Canada's health care trends for many years, he is dismayed by how the system, especially in Ontario, appears to be unravelling due to increasing underfunding and understaffing. And he worries that the conditions, and the violence against staff that arises from them, are about to erode even further. We asked him what he sees coming in terms of violence against staff. He responded:

> I am very fearful that violence and other problems in the workplace are going to get significantly worse. There is a demographic change the likes of which we haven't seen forever—a very significant growth of the sixty-five-plus and especially the seventy-five-plus population over the next twenty years. The funding that the Ontario govern-ment proposes to have for hospitals and long-term care is totally out of whack with reality . . . that flies in the face of this demographic wave that is coming at us.

Hospital staffing is also lacking. Canadian Institute for Health Information (CIHI) statistics show that in 2015 there were 4.98 hospital RNs per 1,000 population in Canada and 1.34 RPNs. CUPE reported that there were almost 20 per cent fewer hospital nurses in Ontario compared to the rest of Canada.[16] The union also reported that in 2017 there were 21 per cent more hospital staff across Canada than in Ontario. In real numbers, that means that compared to the rest of Canada, Ontario is missing 45,000 hospital employees. A 2019 CIHI report found that Ontario had the lowest per capita ratio of RNs in the country and would require another 20,147 registered nurses to meet the ratio in Canada.[17]

The bed and staff shortages can be explained in part by poor funding levels. In a 2019 report entitled *Ontario Hospitals: Leaders in Efficiency,* the Ontario Hospital Association boasted that it was saving the taxpayers billions of dollars by reducing hospital admissions and shortening hospital stays.[18] It declared proudly that in 2019 Ontario spent only $1,494 per capita, compared to an average of $1,772 for all other provinces.

The funding for health care has not kept up with growing needs. Such "efficiencies" have real consequences for care. Natalie Mehra, director of the Ontario Health Coalition, warned Ontarians:

> Already the real-dollar funding cuts to Ontario's hospitals are biting into patient care. Hospitals are cancelling operating room days and surgeries to cut costs, closing clinics and, on last count, [cutting] about 500 full-time nurses, health professionals and vital support staff amounting to about 900,000 hours of patient care.[19]

Harris and the Common Sense Revolution (1995–2003)

What is behind Ontario's austerity and privatization in health care? In 1995, after a Liberal-led Ontario had been followed by an NDP term, the Ontario Progressive Conservatives returned to power. Mike Harris and his manifesto, paradoxically called the Common Sense Revolution, promised a return to a slash-and-burn fiscally and socially conservative government. The Common Sense manifesto provided a roadmap for a neoliberal agenda of austerity, conservative social policies, and deregulation. As Dr. Greg Albo, a professor of political economy at York University, suggests:

> The programmatic content was clear: cut taxes, spending, regulation, the partnership model, and the size of the Ontario public service; balance budgets; and reform administration in line with the new public management of marketization of the state. In other words, remake the form and policy regime of the Ontario state to restore its competitive position as a low-tax, low-cost regional economy within the NAFTA trade zone.[20]

During his first term Harris opened up avenues for corporate involvement and penetration into our public health care system by launching public-private partnerships to build and manage health care facilities. This measure was meant to take the cost of hospital construction and maintenance off the government's books, but the auditor general found that it actually cost Ontario taxpayers billions of dollars.[21]

Under the Harris government there were dramatic reductions to the health care system, with more than 11,400 hospital beds eliminated and dozens of hospitals closed or amalgamated.[22] Hospital and long-term care staff were reduced by nearly 25,000.[23] The twin problem of underfunding and understaffing that is so central to the problem of violence deepened.

Harris's severe retractions to Ontario's social programs generated a backlash. It was further fuelled by the Ontario Provincial Police shooting of First Nation activist Dudley George at Ipperwash and the poisoning of the Walkerton water system.[24] In the late 1990s, thousands joined a coalition of labour unions and community groups during multiple province-wide Days of Action. There were protests and occupations. The stage was set for a change in government.

McGuinty and Wynne Liberals (2003–2018)

In 2003 Harris lost the election to Dalton McGuinty's Liberals. Although McGuinty ran on a moderate platform, including a promise to protect the health care system, he did not repudiate or reverse the Harris strategy of austerity. The new Liberal government accepted the general tenor of the Harris regime's neoliberal perspective and continued to employ budgetary constraints with corporate-friendly programs.[25] In the area of health care, the government budgets and policies continued to promote the corporate-sponsored P3 hospitals, the privatization of health services, and general underfunding of the health care system.[26] For example, the Liberals privatized services that had previously been covered under the Ontario Health Insurance Plan (OHIP), including eye exams and physical rehab services.[27] It was also under the Liberal government that hospital spending in Ontario started to fall below that of other provinces.

Kathleen Wynne, who served as premier from 2013 to 2018, continued the cuts, with serious reductions in front-line staff. The Ontario Health Coalition commented, "Wynne and her Liberal government are hacking and slashing hospital budgets in a way that's more chaotic than Mike Harris ever was."[28]

Ford's Conservatives (2018–)

The 2018 Ontario election of a majority Progressive Conservative government, led by Doug Ford, brought a significant turn to the right. Ford's win represented a return to the Harris era of dramatic reductions in government spending. In the new government's first budget, health care expenditures were cut and many more reductions were promised. Funding for such social programs as women's shelters and Ministry of Labour workplace injury prevention programs was reduced.[29]

In 2019 the Tories passed the *Hospital Restructuring Act* to create a Super Agency that enhances the minister of health's powers to privatize and close services. According to a Linda Haslam-Stroud, former president of the Ontario Nurses Association, the act gives them "super powers far above and beyond anything other governments have had." The association's campaign material calls it "a wrecking ball."[30]

The consequences of the Ford government's austerity-driven agenda of slashing public protections and services was uncovered as the pandemic began to devastate our hospitals and long-term care facilities.

Canada's bad report card

Even before the Ford government started downsizing health care in Ontario, Canada's reputation was already suffering. A 2017 report by the U.S.-based Commonwealth Fund, an independent organization that ranks the health care systems of eleven countries each year, places Canada near the bottom of the list.[31] It uses many indicators in its evaluation, such as access to medical care, wait times, infant mortality, and number of medical errors. In its 2017 report, Canada ranked as one of the more affordable countries for health care. The country loses points, however, because there is no universal pharmacare and prescription drug costs can be exorbitant for those without private coverage. Not surprisingly, U.S. health care was ranked as the least affordable.

Wait times

The Commonwealth Fund found that Canada's patient wait times are elevated. Fifty per cent of patients report waiting two hours or more in the ER before being seen by a doctor, a higher percentage than in any other country examined.[32]

It didn't surprise us to hear, through the course of our research and examination of published literature, that wait times have been shown over and over again to be triggers for aggressive behaviour. As William Watson, writing for the *Financial Post* about the Commonwealth Fund report, commented, "Most Canadians I know get more than agitated when trading emergency-room stories."[33] Many Canadians have tales of long waits in the ER, sitting for hours holding a feverish child, pressing an increasingly bloody towel over a wound sustained while trimming the hedges, comforting an aging parent whose belly is inexplicably and painfully enlarged. As anxiety, fear, and frustration increase, so does the urge to lash out at the administrative or health care staff who seem to be ignoring patients and their very immediate needs.

We, ourselves, have had the agonizing experience of waiting for several hours before being seen by a doctor. In one particularly nasty case, after one of us was brought to the hospital by ambulance with a crushed and partially severed big toe, we sat for five long hours in the waiting room as pale, moaning patients were called in. Throughout the wait, blood continued to drip onto the floor from the offending toe and the pain and anxiety seemed too great to bear. Needless to say, being human, we were irate, both the injured party and the supporting partner. Somehow, we held it together and remained civil, and thankfully, there was ultimately a good outcome for the savaged toe.

Dr. Alan Drummond is an emergency and family doctor who has practised in various communities in Canada. In an opinion piece for the *Ottawa Citizen*, he wrote, "The ER has morphed into a chaotic melting pot for all society's ills and the glaring deficiencies of a health care system gone horribly wrong through a systemic lack of understanding and poor stewardship."[34] According to Drummond, this process has been going on for some time now; he says overcrowding and long wait times began to erode the health care system in the mid-1990s.

Clearly long ER wait times are a violation of our trust in the public health care system. But instead of governments ensuring that more resources are directed towards ERs, hospital beds, health care staff, and alternative services, the public is blamed for the clogged system. We are told that we are showing up at the ER with problems that should be treated elsewhere—in community or walk-in clinics, our family doctors' offices, or urgent care centres. The problem with such attempts by health care administrations to deflect culpability is that alternative services, including family doctors, are often unavailable or in short supply.[35] Statistics Canada reports that, in 2016, almost 16 per cent of Canadians were without a "regular health care provider."[36] Walk-in clinics and urgent care centres operate within very limited hours. The ER may be these patients' only access point for care.

Dr. Drummond echoes the experiences of the ER staff we spoke to who feel targeted by angry patients and family members:

> Crowded ERs breed patient frustration, anger, aggression and occasional horrific violence. On every shift, in every emergency department in Canada, a staff member is subjected to harassment, abuse and assault. Recently, a nurse at the Montreal General

Hospital was strangled; in Smiths Falls, a clerk was repeatedly stabbed.

He explains:

> Contrary to the widely held view, crowding in the ER has absolutely nothing to do with inappropriate overuse by patients presenting with non-urgent problems. Rather, it is a function of hospital overcrowding and the inability to transfer admitted patients from the ER to the wards.[37]

Hallway medicine

The nightmare of so-called hallway medicine is haunting Canadians now in many provinces. In 2019, the Ontario Premier's Council spoke with 340 patients about their experiences. The council reported:

> A recurring theme from their stories is what it feels like to wait for health care services in environments that don't support rest or healing. Many patients described uncomfortably low levels of privacy in emergency departments, and feeling a complete lack of dignity when telling their personal stories and sharing their medical history with a health care provider in a hallway, where everyone could hear. For some people, even something that should be simple—like helping patients to get to the washroom on time—was challenging under the current conditions.[38]

When hospitals are operating at or beyond capacity, they are unable to handle crisis situations. Even predictable cyclic demands, such as flu season, put overwhelming pressure on overstretched staff and facilities. Ambulances are turned away, ERs overflow, and even more sick people end up on gurneys in the hallways during these surges.[39] Patients who have been admitted but are left waiting in the ER for an available bed face longer and longer waits. Drummond blames the shortages of available beds for the stacking of patients in the ER who have been admitted but are waiting for a room. He laments the loss of dignity and suffering of elderly patients languishing in brightly lit hallways.

Patients find such treatment dehumanizing, neglectful, and uncaring. Neil Macdonald, a journalist with the CBC, wrote of his own traumatic ER experience in June 2019. His account illustrates how waiting can raise one's ire to uncharacteristic levels. Macdonald was suddenly beset with intense, disabling hip pain and was transported by ambulance to the hospital. The attendant injected him with morphine for the pain, warning him it could be morning before a doctor would see him. The paramedic was right. Macdonald waited. And waited. And groaned. After trying unsuccessfully to get information about how much longer he might be left to suffer, he lost patience. "Finally, I just yelled, and I hate yelling. You've completely lost control when you yell." His yelling, however, was rewarded with a dose of Fentanyl. It took until the next morning for him to be admitted to the hospital. And then he was subjected to more waiting to have tests completed. The experience has left him bitter. He suggests that "we should stop bragging about our health care system, and start yelling about it instead."[40]

Are we Canadians doomed to spend long hours in the ER? Medical researchers who have studied wait times believe that there are better ways of servicing patients. Dr. Howard Ovens, the chief medical strategy officer for the Sinai Health system in Toronto and Ontario's provincial lead for emergency medicine wrote:

> I think there are some examples in Canada, but more so in other countries, where they have been much more thoughtful about medical coverage, access to imaging, access to administrative oversight for flow, and have taken out some of these wrinkles and tried to improve care and flow around the clock.[41]

Doug Allan sees long ER wait times as symptomatic of a system that is strained beyond capacity. "They are like the 'canary in the mine' because everything backs up there. If there are not enough long-term care beds, patients can't get out of the hospital;

they can't get out of the emergency rooms so the wait lists increase right there."

An unmanageable pace

Overcrowded ERs and hospital wards translate into rushed, fatigued, overburdened staff. The older, more experienced nurses and other health care staff we spoke with recalled that the pace of work during the early years of their careers was more manageable. Their recollection is that they had fewer patients and responsibilities, and more support. A nurse who was nearing retirement remembered:

> It was great to come to work. I used to come to work on this floor and, at the end of the day, a twelve-hour shift, you never would feel like this . . . I'd want to go out for dinner after. I had energy. I was happy. I loved my co-workers. It was great. My love for my co-workers never changed, but the work did.

One of the more experienced nurses interviewed for the OCHU-CUPE *Voices* booklet said:

> I've noticed a change in the past few years—mainly the past five years. We don't have as much time to care for them. So it's a little more mentally stressful. . . . We had a lot more time when I first was a nurse—to care and spend time with them. And you see their behaviours change due to the fact that we don't get to spend time with them at all anymore. I'd say at least fifty percent of the time has been decreased, and it's frustrating for us.

Another nurse, who said she is run off her feet on every shift, told us:

> All the cutbacks. Everything's been cut back. People's positions have been eliminated. And we pick up part of that slack. For some reason, everything always seems to fall on the nurses. I don't know why, but

just part of my job now is discharge planning. We lost our specific staff person, so we're doing all kinds of stuff that the discharge planner would have done. And so it just takes more and more time away from the beds.

An ER staff person said:

I think [violence] has been escalating because of the cutbacks in other areas. Like the police don't want to sit with a violent patient so they get dumped. And the health care system has been so badly cut that there's not enough staff to provide the security and the safety for the people that are there.

The inability to satisfy patients' needs and wants is demoralizing for health care workers, and lack of support adds insult to injury.

The workload increased; the sick calls increased because my co-workers were too stressed. They took stress leave because they could not cope. The patients have changed—the complexity of the patients . . . they're so sick. You're juggling IVs. You're getting thrown up on. Your patient is spiking a fever . . . Meanwhile the patient in the next bed is yelling and cussing you out because you won't go get them a spoonful of peanut butter, or go get them hot tea, or drop what you're doing and go get a cold water. You can only do so much, and I try to do my best. In the last six months that I was on [the complex care] floor, I don't think my manager ever told me I did a good job once and I don't think I ever had a patient say thank you.

Waiting for specialists

Then there are the waits to see the specialists—the urologist for your recurrent bladder infections or the neurologist for your crippling sciatic pain. The Commonwealth Fund found that 30 per cent of Canadians wait two months or more to see a specialist, again a higher proportion than in any other country. (We, ourselves, waited eleven months for an initial consult with an orthopaedic surgeon for a rotator cuff tear.) The Commonwealth Fund report tells us that 18 per cent of Canadians have to wait four months or longer for elective surgery—again the greatest percentage of any of the eleven countries examined. The CIHI states, "Approximately 30% of patients who required a hip or knee replacement or cataract surgery did not have their procedure done within the recommended wait times."[42]

Waiting isn't just frustrating or inconvenient. It can deeply affect quality of life. Delayed treatment can make it impossible to go to work, putting economic pressure on the affected individuals, their families, co-workers, and friends, and even our social safety net. And it can lead to the overuse of addictive painkillers.

Mental health

One of the reasons for overcrowding in ERs and related violence against staff is the shortage of accessible mental health services in Canada. There is also a scarcity of mental health beds.[43] According to a report by Health Quality Ontario, "Emergency department mental health visits can be an indication that people did not receive timely and appropriate care for mental illness or addiction in the community."[44] The report states that, in 2016, only four in ten young people who visited the ER with a mental health issue or addiction problem had been provided with any mental health care in the previous two years through another health practitioner or service.

The Canadian Mental Health Association (CMHA) commissioned a survey to find out what Canadians think about mental health services. It found that "over half of Canadians (53%) consider anxiety and depression to be 'epidemic' in Canada. . . . Eighty-five per cent of Canadians say mental health services are among the most underfunded services in our health-care system."[45] The report stated that there are many people with mental health problems who are not adequately treated and end up in the acute care system.

The 2016 *Annual Report of the Office of the Auditor General of Ontario* found:

> For the past five years, specialty psychiatric hospital funding did not keep up with inflation or the increased demand for mental health services. To deal with this, these hospitals have had to close beds, which has resulted in patients now waiting longer to access specialty psychiatric hospital services.
>
> These hospitals have also changed their employee mix to include more part-time staff. It is not clear that current resources, including staffing, allow enough activities like group therapy, or therapy involving the use of facilities available at the hospitals (such as swimming pools) to occur. These are important to a patient's treatment and patients feel there are not enough of them.
>
> Specialty psychiatric hospitals have not been able to deal with safety concerns to the degree that staff have requested. We also found that important patient file documentation, such as inclusion of patient risks in patient care plans or updates on the status of a patient's treatment, was missing from patient files.[46]

One of our study respondents talked about how mental health services and bed shortages can clog up ERs and can also contribute to the potential for violence against staff.

> We had a code white not long ago. The patient was waiting to be transferred to our psychiatric unit. The doctor had ordered "transfer when bed available." The patient was completely agitated. She was young. She was having a psychotic moment and she wanted to leave, but she couldn't leave because she needed to be transferred. I think it took about three days before she was able to get that bed. I worked in the ER last year for a month. And in this one area where they have admitted patients who are waiting for beds, out of ten patients, five of them were psych patients waiting for beds. And on the weekend, waiting for psych beds, they're not going anywhere. The psychiatrists don't discharge people on the weekends . . . It never used to be

like that. Everything's changed and I'm praying just to finish off my last seven months and get out of there, after thirty years.

A psychiatric nurse described the problem:

What's happening now? Say you're having a manic episode and you are bipolar. You go to the ER and maybe you've been off your medications for a while, because maybe you didn't have any money or access to a doctor to renew a prescription. Common problem. And you're going to ask that person to wait four or five hours before they're even assessed by a nurse? Please! And you ask, "Why is there violence?"

Aggression among patients in forensic units is particularly difficult to predict or control, as we learned from the life-altering assault on Dianne Paulin. She didn't see the attack coming. But the system is well aware that many forensic patients are capable of violence. It is often the very reason they have been placed in the criminal justice system. There should never be too few staff to exercise the buddy system when entering a patient's room, transporting a patient, or providing treatment.

Safety features can be engineered into the building of the facility, and effective, accessible communication is a necessity. If such protections had been in place when Dianne was attacked, she might still be working in her chosen career as a nurse. Instead, she is facing poverty and depression.

Today my life is really unpredictable. I look at myself as damaged—I'm damaged goods. I can't go back to work, ever. So I am left doing whatever I can around the house and trying to make some kind of money to survive. I borrow money. I'm always trying to do something . . . I put my house up for sale . . . I've gone to four different places to see if I can consolidate all my bills, because I'm still financially unstable . . . Every day's a new day, and it's a challenge, and I don't know what I'm doing from one day to another.

The rates of violence

Can we confidently claim that violence against health care staff in Canada has increased over the past decades? We are, unfortunately, lacking the data we need to say for certain. There are very few sources of statistics on violence prior to the year 2000. We did, however, find a few. For example, a survey of Ontario nurses published in 1992 found that 35 per cent had been assaulted in the previous year.[47] By comparison, the 2017 survey of hospital staff done by OCHU-CUPE reported that 68 per cent of nurses and PSWs had been physically assaulted—that's almost twice the rate.

Ontario workers' compensation numbers also provide evidence of an increase in violence. In 1989, 111 nurses were allowed lost-time claims for violence-related injuries; in 1990, 100 were allowed; and in 1991, 96 were allowed.[48] By contrast, in 2017, there were 860 allowed violence-related lost-time injury claims among health care workers—about eight times as many.[49] While the earlier statistics were related to violence against *nurses* and the 2017 numbers were for *all* health care workers, we can safely extrapolate that the claims for nurses did significantly increase, as they make up the majority of the occupational group. The compensation lost-time injury rate increased by 25 per cent in the short period from 2013 to 2017.

Linda Clayborne, who has seen dramatic changes during her forty-one-year nursing career, is distressed by the increased threats to staff.

> I worked on a variety of units. I worked in geriatrics for a time and I finished my career in schizophrenia services. Of course, there's violence in nursing. I'll go on record as saying that when I started out as a nurse, it wasn't anything near what it's like now. And it's getting worse. The whole health care system has changed.

The architects of our public health care system likely never imagined it would be facing such challenges today. The levels and severity of violence staff in our contemporary system encounter were probably never anticipated. We have had many discussions with Dr. Craig Slatin, professor emeritus, University of Massachusetts Lowell, about health care in North America. He believes that violence can be traced directly to the trend towards defunding of the system that began in the 1980s when hospitals were made to "function more like a business than a critical health service." He said after the model had changed,

> the staff were no longer able to balance their workload. They were understaffed, overworked, and fraying at the edges. Patients were not getting the care they needed . . . Patients were getting harmed and angry. Patients' families were getting angry. Health care workers were getting angry. Health care administrators grew crueller—some intentionally and some due to the frustration of not knowing how to resolve the conflicting management goals and purposes. And violence in the health care workplace became malignant. Harassment and assault had become part of the job.

CBC's *Fifth Estate* surveyed about 4,500 nurses in 257 hospitals in Canada in 2018. Forty per cent said they are experiencing such high levels of stress and burnout they fear making mistakes that could put their patients at risk.[50]

In 1984, Dr. Andrew Jameton wrote a book on ethics in nursing practice.[51] He recognized the problem of stress among nurses and its resulting "moral distress." Moral distress, a concept that is still widely recognized today, is caused by "being in a situation in which one is constrained from acting . . . on what one knows to be right"; it can arise from "constraints stemming from proximate and background challenges of health care organizations."[52]

Dianne Martin, CEO of the Registered Practical Nurses' Association of Ontario, wrote an article for the *Ottawa Citizen* about the alarming level of burnout among nurses.[53] Martin said that Jameton's concerns were never more relevant than they are now, claiming that "nurses in Ontario today are facing an unprecedented degree of stress over the challenge of providing the level of care patients need and that we have spent years training to deliver." She acknowledges that the stress nurses are feeling is apparent to their patients: "When we're distressed, patients feel it." The Canadian Nurses Association (CNA) has declared:

> Factors in today's health system environment contribute to nurse fatigue, including increased worker stress, increased workload, understaffing, increasing expectations from patients and families, high levels of patient acuity, unexpected emergencies with staffing or patients, sensory overload, functionally disorganized workplaces, and relentless change within the workplace.[54]

Among other demands, the CNA called on governments to increase staffing and enrolment in nursing faculties.

As we have seen, the crisis in health care has been decades in the making. The public and health care staff are paying the price for government austerity measures and the prioritizing of efficiencies over quality and timeliness of care.

5.

Birth and Decline of the Long-Term Care System

Unimaginable conditions

Aggression against staff in long-term care homes exceeds even the appalling levels found in many acute care settings, such as hospitals and clinics. Inadequately cared-for residents in understaffed, underfunded, impersonal, institutional settings understandably lash out against their rushed, overworked immediate caregivers.

Anyone who has spent time either working in or visiting someone in long-term care can attest to the dehumanizing conditions that seem to have become normalized. We visited numerous facilities in 2020 searching for one that would be suitable for an aging and increasingly dependent family member. Having been given a list by our Local Health Integration Network (LHIN), we arrived at the first facility with anticipation and optimism. We were impressed with the fancy entrance lobby, the cute little tuck shop, and the carpeted and nicely decorated reception area. But when the tour of the floors and resident rooms began, our initial impressions were completely reversed.

We started on the second floor. The stench of urine and feces hit us as we stepped off the elevator. We saw dozens of people lined up in wheelchairs in the hallway beside the nursing station—heads bowed, some moaning or calling out, some reaching out to us with their eyes pleading for help. The resident rooms, most of which were shared, were stark and impersonal. The lighting was harsh and the surfaces were hard and scrubbable, in other words, practical. There was nothing cozy or comforting or homelike about it. Staff were few and far between, and residents were clearly being left unattended and untended to.

We shook our heads and moved on to the next facility, hoping that the first one was an anomaly. It was not. After multiple tours we agreed that, if it were to come down to it, we would move heaven and earth to scrape together enough money from everyone in our rather large family to keep our loved one where she was with extra caregivers to supplement our own labour. We ended up spending many hours each day devoting ourselves to bathing, dressing, feeding, and caring for her. As it turned out, she died in February 2020, just as the COVID-19 pandemic was beginning to unfold in Canada. We are grateful that she was spared the horrors that emerged in facilities throughout the country, especially in Quebec and Ontario, where thousands of residents were infected and died, exposing unimaginable conditions.

A brief history of long-term care in Canada

Perhaps the disregard with which we currently treat our elderly was foreshadowed in the shameful history of long-term care. The federal government did not include care of the elderly and those with complex needs when the public health care system was established in the 1960s. Long-term care arose from a very different history.

In Ontario, from the late nineteenth century to the 1940s, the facilities that were established to handle vulnerable, elderly, impoverished citizens were essentially "poor houses." These callous institutions became known as Houses of Refuge. They were often located outside of urban centres, away from public scrutiny. Elderly people who were too frail to work were segregated into a particular section of the building, living in large dormitory-style rooms shared by ten to eighteen others.[1] Residents would lose their right to vote or to leave the institution without permission. If they were still able to physically work, they were forced to do so without pay to cover their costs.

The government believed it had only minimal responsibility for such unproductive people. Provincial politicians argued that care for the poor elderly was a responsibility that families had to bear rather than taxpayers and the state.

Throughout the early part of the twentieth century, as life expectancy increased and more people lived beyond the age of sixty-five, the political pressure to address elder care increased. Dr. James Struthers, a professor emeritus at Trent University, published a critique of the historical elder care system. He stated:

> The responsibility, according to provincial officials, lay with families, not the state. Old people, they argued, were being foisted upon the government in order to shift the burden of their care "from the home to the state." Building more institutional care would simply take away . . . the filial obligations for the support of the aged parents which is the main bond of family solidarity.[2]

Dr. Struthers wrote that government poorhouse inspectors—as late as 1946—reported horrendous conditions in which vulnerable elderly residents were "crammed into 'temporary' beds in the attics, basements, and hallways of the province's houses of refuge."[3] These inhumane conditions, exposed by health inspectors and media reports, as well as a growing public realization that the government needed to play a more significant role in the care of our senior citizens, resulted in new legislation.

In 1949 the Ontario government passed the *Homes for the Aged Act*. This legislation began a significant influx of money for residential care. Local municipalities and various charitable and religious groups joined in the construction of Homes for the Aged that were somewhat more homelike, rather than institutional. However, rooms were often shared with other residents, and married couples were separated.

In the 1950s, further pressure to provide elder care was generated by Ontario's participation in the federal government's hospital insurance initiative. There was now growing demand for hospital spaces. Elderly patients were being viewed as "bed-blockers," as their stays in hospitals were extended because there was no suitable alternative for their ongoing care.

The solution to the 1950s long-term care bed shortage was to turn to private, for-profit nursing home enterprises. In 1959 the owners of the private facilities organized into a lobbying group—Associated Nursing Homes Incorporated of Ontario. After the association had received provincial government funding for a decade or so, Ontario's health minister told the premier:

> I have learned to my bitter sorrow that they are concerned about one thing only, making as much money as possible and giving as little as possible in return to the patients. . . . The sooner this is gotten into on a public basis, the sooner we will be able to provide good quality health care for this segment of our population.[4]

Dr. Tamara Daly examined the history of long-term care and found that it was largely allowed to evolve without much direction or support from government. There were clear periods of time in which commercialization proliferated. Several federal and provincial regulatory acts were passed between 1965 and 1990, and public funding was expanded. A shift towards neoliberalism had already begun; it grew in earnest from 1990 to the present, during which time numerous pieces of legislation have been enacted but resources for long-term care have been circumscribed by increasing "austerity," "regulatory rigidity," and "consolidation" of smaller facilities into large, corporate for-profit care homes.

> When viewed in historical context, it is clear that a commercial logic governed the development of the sector almost from the beginning

of the post-war period. Past and current actions by provincial and municipal governments have resulted in few commitments to promote non-profit or public organizations compared with for-profit organizations.[5]

The private sector is now heavily involved. In 2020, over half of Ontario's long-term care facilities were privately owned and operated.[6] All long-term care facilities receive some government funding, but residents are expected to contribute financially.[7]

Long-term care bed shortages keep those needing daily support in hospital beds, which are also in very short supply. CUPE researcher Doug Allan told us, "The long-term wait lists have increased from about 19,000 in 2011 to 36,000 in 2019." He said the provincial government had been following "a policy of no new long-term care, just ignoring the emerging wave of the elderly population that's becoming even greater."

Dr. Chris Simpson, past president of the Canadian Medical Association, and his colleagues are critical of the shortage of long-term care beds that leaves "seniors who are not acutely ill also wait[ing] in hospitals for assignment to a long-term care facility, for months and, on occasion, years."[8] In Ontario, this observation is supported by the auditor general: "As of March 2016, about 4,110 patients were occupying hospital beds even though they no longer needed them. Half of these people were awaiting placement in long-term care homes."[9]

Residents are sicker now

One of the contributors to the unmanageable staff workload and the resulting resident frustration and related aggression, or so-called responsive behaviour, is the significant change in the character of long-term care that has taken place over the past two decades. Many residents now require much higher levels of care.

Until recently, elderly residents made up the majority of the population of long-term care homes. Now residents include physically and mentally challenged adults of all ages, and 18 per cent of residents are now younger than seventy-five.[10]

A report by the Ontario Health Coalition stated that part of the long-term care bed shortage can be attributed to the cutting of chronic care and psychogeriatric care beds in hospitals.

> Ontario's long-term care homes have not been resourced to increase care levels commensurate with the offloading of significantly more complex patients. Our research shows that long-term care beds are funded at approximately one-third the rate of chronic/complex care hospital beds.[11]

In 2010, when home care became a greater focus for the Ontario government, the criteria for admission to long-term care was changed. Residents were required to suffer higher levels of physical or cognitive impairment to be admitted.[12]

Statistics from 2019 show that 90 per cent of residents in long-term care have some level of cognitive impairment, while 32 per cent have severe impairment, an increase of about 3 per cent over the previous five years. "This represents almost 5,000 more people who need more support with daily activities," reports the OLTCA. And nearly half of residents exhibit some degree of aggressive behaviour.[13]

A research participant who worked as a dietary staff person in long-term care throughout his long career said:

> I've been there for over thirty years, and I remember when I started there, the residents used to walk in with their suitcase . . . Now, thirty years later, most residents are pushed in from the hospital, especially in this area where we have the mental hospital that closed beds; those residents have got to go somewhere, so they land in our long-term care.

A PSW who participated in one of the focus groups told us about the changes she has seen over the years:

I would say probably in the last ten years it's gotten worse. And mostly because of cutbacks in staff. So that you don't have a partner there to help you deal with the residents. And there's been a change in the type of residents we see coming into long-term care too, and that has a lot to do with the cutback in hospital beds. At one time in our community, there used to be a whole floor at the hospital for people [with higher needs]. Then that hospital closed and they all came to us. All of a sudden, we're getting these extremely heavy-care residents coming in with multiple diagnoses . . . They're as young as in their thirties with brain injuries right up to people that are a hundred . . . It has created an entirely different work environment than what it used to be years ago.

Understaffing

While the acuity of residents has increased, staffing levels have not kept up.[14] Improved funding for long-term care is key to enhancing staffing levels to better perform both basic and relational care, to providing safe and resident-friendly facilities, to increasing programs such as music, recreation, and outdoor time—all of which can improve residents' quality of life and in turn reduce agitation. A long-term care worker described her frustration to us. "We ask management for better education and something to help us deal with residents who are being aggressive. Their response is, 'Where are we going to get the money for that?'"

As one long-term care nurse we spoke with said, "Short-staffing is kind of like drunk driving. You know, most times you will get away with it. But every day people's lives are at risk."

There are government-mandated staff-to-resident ratios, but the guidelines are difficult to interpret and easy to manipulate. An independent report on staffing levels in long-term care in Ontario published a decade ago revealed that understaffing seriously affects quality of care. It recommended that levels of all direct care staff be increased according to the particular character and needs of the resident population. The report also called for at least four hours of hands-on care per day per resident.[15] This need remains unmet today, although an Ontario private member's bill, Bill 13, dubbed the Time to Care Act, was introduced mandating the four-hour minimum standard. It has passed second reading but, at the time of writing, had not yet become law.[16]

In a 2019 report, *Situation Critical,* which lays out the deficiencies in Ontario's long-term care system, the Ontario Health Coalition points out that in 2016, the most recent data available at the time, residents received only 2.71 hours of care per day; as a result, "residents are fed too quickly, cannot get enough food down, and lose weight, becoming frail and risking dehydration or starvation."[17] Dr. Struthers told us emphatically:

> I'll say this again and again and again. The conditions of work are the conditions of care. You cannot have good quality care delivered to long-term care homes without adequate staffing, without a staff-to-resident ratio at least double what we currently have.[18]

Staff-to-resident ratios differ from one facility to another— often depending on whether they are private or not-for-profit. All of the long-term care staff we spoke with estimate that they are able to spend only a few minutes per resident during the stressful morning routine, regardless of the home's funding source.

> Do the math. On Sunday I had ten residents to care for; three of them were showers. I start at 6:30 a.m. and breakfast is at 8 a.m. So I have ninety minutes.

Dr. Struthers calls this "an industrial model of care," adding, "It doesn't provide for safe and sufficient resident-friendly or person-centred care." He told us:

> Certainly I was able to observe incidents of violence and, more importantly, constantly observe the extent to which staff members were rushed. PSWs in particular and nurses doing medications were

constantly being rushed or harassed or frustrated in the inability of time they had to sit down and have conversations with the residents to try to deliver relational care, to try to provide their own approaches to dealing with anxiety and agitation and anger on the part of the residents they tried to care for.

Our research participants would agree that their workload leaves little time to relate to the residents as human beings with emotional needs. A PSW who said she is run off her feet, especially during the early morning routine, explained:

You just say, "Good morning" and "I'm here to get you up for breakfast. I'll be right back." And then you run back, and you wash their face, their hands, their underarms, under their breasts while they're in the bed. And then you roll them, as you're putting on their incontinence product, pull their pants up, and then they'll either get up on their own or you put the bed up, turn them, get them sitting. Then you have to take care of all the dirty linens, put all their washing material back in the closet, and wipe it all down.

Another PSW described the impossible workload demands being made on her:

I think it has to be the worst thing when you're in there and the call bells are ringing and this one over here is screaming and that one is yelling, and you're always thinking, "Oh my god. No break today." I've still got three cares to do, breakfast is in twenty minutes, and I've got to have them all in the dining room.

And to top it off, overworked staff who cannot keep up with resident care can be verbally abused by family members who are not satisfied with the care being provided.

When we're short, we're getting blamed if Dad hasn't had a bath or is soiled. We're the first ones they target. And we're not allowed to say, "I'm sorry, we're short-staffed today."

According to the older long-term care staff we spoke with, there was a period when they were able to provide personal care, attention, and comfort to individual residents in an unrushed manner. A PSW recalled what conditions were like when she first began her career in long-term care years ago.

> When we first started working there, the patient-worker ratio was totally different. It was, like, one staff to five residents. Now it's one to seventeen. You had time to paint their nails. Your carts had cream to massage their feet and backs.

Another PSW told us:

> When I started there thirty years ago, the PSWs were able to sit down on the bed beside the resident and read a letter that they got from somebody out of town, or whatever . . . It was more one-on-one, even though they had eight residents to take care of; now they take care of fifteen to sixteen residents—with dementia and everything.

An older nurse who worked with dementia patients said, "I can remember a time when I was never afraid. I was never expecting to get hit . . . you wouldn't be getting them out of bed at 6:30 in the morning. And we had more staff."

During one of the group interviews, several participants explained to us how the nature of the work had changed over the years—especially the workload.

> The issue is that twenty-five years ago, the residents walked in and stayed . . . Of the twelve residents in your care, only four or five of them actually were total care. Now you have twelve residents and all twelve are total.

> So it's more fast-paced—we call it almost, like, a warehouse. It is really stressful for the resident, because you're rushing them; you're waking them up and it's like, [*claps hands*] let's go, and I have five

minutes to get this done and then I've got to move on to the next one and the next one.

Dr. Struthers and his colleague, Dr. Ruth Lowndes, have extensively researched the intricacies of long-term care. They found that, like our hospitals, understaffing negatively affects care as well as staff well-being, resulting in "heavy workloads, routinized care, and unsafe work conditions."[19]

In 2018, the Registered Practical Nurses' Association of Ontario published a survey of its members working in long-term care.

The majority surveyed reported experiencing high moral distress because of such issues as:
- Having to rush the daily care of residents due to lack of time
- Seeing resident and specialized nursing care suffer due to lack of funding to hire more nurses
- Poor communication between staff members leading to challenges in patient care[20]

We saw similar results in the OCHU-CUPE long-term care staff poll. Nurses and PSWs are experiencing such high levels of stress, burnout, hopelessness, depression, and exhaustion that the majority feel like quitting their jobs. Our own research shows that they attribute most of their stress to understaffing, overwork, and the threat of violence.

In their examination of the state of long-term care in Canada, Dr. Lowndes and Dr. Struthers wrote:

Overall . . . we found that relational care is devalued, and medical, task-oriented, and quantitative approaches to work and life are prioritized within LTRC [long-term residential care]. Shifting toward a greater emphasis on relational, social care, however, is imperative to improving the quality of resident life, as well as workers' job satisfaction, in these highly gendered settings.[21]

Dr. Hugh Armstrong, researcher and board member of the Ontario Health Coalition, is like-minded. He told a roundtable gathering in Sudbury:

> I think the biggest issue is insufficient resources . . . there are other issues too, we have a disproportionate focus on the clinical or medical side of care and an insufficient focus on the social or emotional side of care.[22]

The hiring of more PSWs, Dr. Armstrong said, is essential. Unfortunately there is a shortage of available PSWs. The community colleges have experienced declining enrolment in recent years. And many PSWs leave their careers because of burnout and lack of recognition.

The resident experience

A homelike environment has been shown in study after study to reduce resident agitation. Stressors in the immediate environment can lead to outbursts directed against caregivers.

Residents in many long-term care homes are housed in double rooms, contributing to a lack of privacy as well as increasing their exposure to irritating disturbances, lights, and noise that can contribute to aggression.

> Listening to all the sounds, noise, smells, having staff in and out of your room non-stop throughout the day. That commotion contributes to agitation.

> Sometimes there are people that holler all night. So, you can imagine if your roommate is hollering twenty-four hours a day. It can really irritate you. You can't sleep and you're not well. The problem is that there's no place else to put that hollering person.

Perhaps one of the most troubling practices is that of separating couples when facilities can't readily accommodate them together.

> I see an increase in behaviours—especially from married couples that want to see each other. They were married for sixty-eight years and always had the same bed, and then they move in and are not allowed to be in the same room anymore. Some of them have been living in the home for three or four years and they're not able to live together. We classify certain rooms by gender, so if a room is classified as a male-only room, no females are to be in that room. Or they'll throw one on the third floor and keep one down on the main floor, and if we have time as caregivers, we'll try to bring them together to see each other once a week.

Some facilities are seriously lacking basic cleanliness, presenting a dehumanizing and unhealthy environment for residents and staff. Some of the buildings are quite old, but even newer facilities can lack proper maintenance. A PSW working in a relatively modern long-term care home talked to us about her disgust regarding ongoing insect infestations.

> The building has lots of leaks. And the cockroaches! . . . I can't deal with that. We have a huge cockroach problem right now. I went to help my other staff member, who was busy, do snack cart. And I see cockroaches running up the snack cart! I was ready to walk out of the building right there.

Another was subjected to a bedbug infestation at work. "The bedbugs, when I came to my floor, I took them home. I had to take the time off. I had to take 130 garbage bags to the laundromat and wash and rewash everything."

Enjoyment of life

Studies have found that residents with dementia benefit from taking part in simple outdoor activities, which, according to Canadian researchers Dr. Habib Chaudhury and colleagues, convey "a positive impact on mental health, quality of life and mood, as well as reduced agitation, aggression and reduced use of behavioral medications."[23]

According to the long-term care staff we spoke with, most residents are never able to go outside unless they have a family member or private caregiver who will take them. Dr. Struthers talked to us about how negatively residents are affected when facilities are understaffed and "residents didn't have a chance to get outside and move around . . . That, in and of itself, would produce overmedication and agitation and anger and violence, both against other residents and against staff particularly." Imagine spending the final months or years of your life never breathing fresh air, seeing the clouds, feeling the sun on your face, or enjoying the cool shade of a maple tree.

Music, singing, and other activities have also been shown to reduce aggression in some residents with dementia.[24] The staff we spoke with witnessed this themselves. We were told, however, that recreational or entertainment programs are often unavailable—either because of time pressures, scheduling problems, or illness outbreaks.

> There's usually nothing scheduled on the weekends. And usually every night around seven o'clock all programming comes to a halt. They need something in the evening. There's too much time on their hands. They get bored and they get angry and that's when [the violence] gets worse. That's also when the staff levels go down.

> When we're on outbreak [usually due to colds or flu], all activities get cancelled for the duration of the outbreak, so that could be for three weeks, it could be for three months. And that makes them

go stark crazy. And they can't leave their units either. And we're on outbreak a lot. In a bad year we can be on outbreak a total of six months.

A PSW we spoke to during the early months of the pandemic told us that abuse against staff, already a serious problem, has been exacerbated by the lockdowns, cancelled programs, and restrictions on visitors. One of the residents whose routine was changed because he was prohibited from going out angrily lashed out at her.

He punched me. There has always been a lot of violence with residents, especially when they have dementia; they can get very agitated or aggressive. His anger kept building up and after a few weeks he was at his max. We had been saying that he's really getting frustrated, he's really getting angry and someone needs to come in and figure out something for him. It didn't happen until I got punched in the face.

Limited choices

One of the discussions we had with a group of long-term care staff still haunts us. A cook, nearing retirement age, talked to us about the kinds of meals they used to be able to prepare for residents—freshly made entrees and desserts. He said that was before the provincial government cut the meal allowance in half about twenty years ago—from eight dollars per person to approximately four. The current allowance is not much more than the dollar amount it was before the cuts. Taking inflation into account, the allocation for food is shamefully low. In 2019, Ontario long-term care facilities received $9.54 per day per resident from the government for meals.[25]

Efficiencies have also cut the quality and palatability of residents' food. The cook told us the breakfast toast, for example, is made hours before it is served—"It's soggy, not toast." Meat is cooked the night before and then left in a steamer, rendering it grey and stringy. And residents have limited choices. Those with food preferences based on their cultural backgrounds may not be pleased with the selections they are offered. The cook gave the example of someone used to a Mediterranean diet requesting a pasta dish and being told, "No, sorry, it's pork chops tonight."

The mealtime experience is further negatively affected by lack of personal interaction. Although family members or paid companions will sometimes be present to help out, the staff are often rushed and frazzled trying to attend to everyone's needs. The long-term care workers we spoke with found that such unpleasant or stressful mealtimes often triggered violence. A PSW told us about a chronically unhappy and angry resident who often reacted to the limited food choices and took out his frustrations on staff and even the other residents.

> Breakfast, lunch, and dinner, same routine every single day. We have two meal choices. You go around and you show him, and he'll slap the plate out of your hand. The other residents are forced to listen to that every single day. You can just see the mood change in the dining room when he's in there and he starts.

And the frantic mealtime pace, coupled with limited staffing, clearly contributes to responsive behaviours. A group of long-term care staff explained:

> They throw food at us, throw their cups. Spit.

> They fight amongst their tablemates.

> We have to remove them so people can have a nice dining experience because it's all about the dining experience when you're in residential care.

Dr. Pat Armstrong contends that we can evaluate the level of care residents are receiving, in part, by the cleanliness and selection of clothing they are wearing. She and her colleagues found that there is little opportunity for residents to pick what they are going to wear on a given day. Dr. Armstrong's research team witnessed "residents in mismatched clothing, in sagging urine-stained pants and with blouses undone."[26] This disregard for residents' appearance and personal choices not only affects their dignity, but it also takes away from their sense of themselves. Clothes are important because they are "about gender, class, culture and care. Indeed, clothes are central to our personal identity." Being denied such basic dignities as choices of clothing and being kept clean can result in anxiety and anger.

Resident-on-resident violence

The same conditions that lead to violence against staff can result in residents behaving violently towards each other. More often than the public realizes, angry, confused, frustrated, and fearful residents may assault their neighbours in the adjoining room, in the hallway, or next to them in the dining room.

A few high-profile cases of resident-on-resident violence have made the headlines. In 2017, James Acker, an eighty-six-year-old resident with dementia in a Dundas, Ontario, long-term care facility, was attacked in his sleep by another resident with dementia. He died several weeks later from his injuries. On National Seniors Day, six months after her father's death, Tammy Carbino addressed an audience at a meeting of the Canadian Association of Retired Persons.

> We've been told, at 2 am a resident left his room and walked down the hall toward my father's room, which was approximately 4 rooms away. A personal support worker (PSW) saw the resident leave his room and called out to him as he walked down the hall, however he was unresponsive to her calls. The resident entered my father's room and began to viciously punch, bite and beat him repeatedly in the face, head and hands. The PSW followed the resident into my father's room and yelled at the resident to stop but could not persuade him off my father. She then yelled for assistance, at which time another PSW entered my father's room and together, they

screamed and yelled at the attacker. Essentially, the two PSW's who witnessed my father being beaten to death had neither the means or training to stop the attack.[27]

As usual, there were minimal staff on duty that night. They did what they could to rescue Mr. Acker, but quickly found themselves at risk as well.

Mr. Acker's family is outraged by the conditions that led to his attack and continues to lobby the government for changes. As his daughter said:

The cause of his death has been confirmed as a non-culpable homicide. This means the attacker is not criminally responsible for my father's death (as he too, is a person living with Alzheimer's disease), but the system sure as hell is!

A shocking picture of Mr. Acker's bloodied and bruised face appeared in newspapers and on the evening news. But many such attacks—even homicides—occur with little public awareness.

In the six-year period from 2014 to 2019, there were twenty-nine reported homicides in Ontario's long-term care homes.[28] Natalie Mehra, executive director of the Ontario Health Coalition, told the Canadian Press, "The level of homicide in Ontario's long-term care facilities is higher than virtually anywhere else in our society."

There may be many more homicides that are not reported as such. CBC recently reported these examples:

One woman died of an unwitnessed fall and the report indicated she may have been pushed by another resident.

In the second death, a woman was found on the floor of her room. A fellow resident's shoes were found in her room and her blood was on his pyjamas. A document after the incident stated the long-term care home believed the other resident may have wandered into the woman's room and pulled her out of bed.[29]

Besides the homicides, there are hundreds of assaults by residents against other residents each year—and the incidence is rising. In 2016, there were 3,228 reported incidents of resident-on-resident violence in Ontario—up from 1,580 in 2011.[30]

Quality time and mitigating violence

Extensive research shows that calm, personal, relational inter-actions between staff and residents are important for keeping residents from becoming agitated and possibly aggressive. Having adequate time for meaningful personal interactions also enables the staff to observe potential problems as they are developing. Dr. Albert Banerjee and Dr. Pat Armstrong recognize that time pressures and understaffing make responsive behaviours against staff more likely. Lack of relational care, rushing to complete tasks, and lack of quality time and attention to residents' signs of agita-tion can result in a bloody nose or worse. However, they report, "given sufficient time, workers can 'tune in to' residents, even those with dementia, so that they understand their preferences, provide appropriate care and mitigate violence."[31]

The Alzheimer Society of Canada asserts that residents' responsive behaviours "are meaningful responses to the environ-mental and reveal underlying concerns, such as pain, loneliness or not wanting personal care."[32] However, as one of the nurses we spoke with said, "Although it's responsive behaviour, it doesn't minimize the fact that you're being assaulted; nobody wants to use that word."

Time-consuming data collection

As too few staff are dealing with heavier and heavier levels of care, and less and less relational care is being done, staff are also being increasingly drawn off on documentation. Systems have been put in place to gather comprehensive data—purportedly as a means to determine how well each resident is doing and what care they are receiving. It is also about providing evidence of the need for the full allotment of government subsidy. Significant staff time is now being spent by the requirements for completing the Resident Assessment Instrument—Minimum Data Set (RAI-MDS). Dr. Struthers talked to us about the problems associated with the electronic capturing of care data.

> We have created datasets like RAI-MDS to try to quantify what constitutes good quality care that can result in funding. And the new public management approach is the only thing that counts is what you can count, and that is things that you can measure: bed sores, number of falls, nutrition, diet, medication, illness.

A long-term care worker explained the implications of the increased demand for data.

> They haven't given us any more staff, but they've implemented all this documentation that they have to do. Where in the past, that time they're spending now documenting, they used to spend with the residents. The residents aren't getting that time anymore.

Several people we talked to said, given the enormous time constraints they are under, they can't possibly accurately document all the required details—so they end up fudging the data in order to personally be in compliance and avoid disciplinary action. They estimate, for the record, how much water a given resident has had at a meal or how many changes of briefs they had. "If you don't get that done, you get reported," we heard. "You get disciplined."

The effect on staff

It is difficult for staff to provide adequate, compassionate care when they are being run ragged. The long-term care staff talked to us about how the combination of violence, fear, stress, workload, disrespect, lack of compassionate support, as well as feeling professionally inadequate due to time constraints, leads to physical and emotional exhaustion.

> When I go home and I'm trying to sleep at night, I can still hear the poor man screaming. I'm not able to let that go. Or that poor woman lying in her bed that I didn't have time to tend to. That bothers me even more.

> They're not machinery. We're not dealing with car parts. We're dealing with actual human beings that you can't rush and that deserve better than what we're giving them. At the end of my shift I feel exhausted, mentally and physically.

> Not only are we subject to abuse, we are working short because people are exhausted, people are tired so they're calling in sick. I'm so exhausted, sometimes I cry on the way home.

> If a resident has died overnight, I don't want to think that yesterday he was cold, and I didn't have time to get the sweater he asked for on the last day of his life.

> It just sucks the life out of you. You think, "I'll go in and I try to do the best I can." And you come out and you feel so defeated. We have the most thankless job there is.

Surely the staff who are caring for the most vulnerable in our society deserve respect and all the protections possible. And surely our elderly and vulnerable citizens, during the final months or weeks of their lives, deserve better than they are getting in many long-term care facilities. For younger, dependent residents, this tattered and often neglectful system may represent their entire living environment for many years. The staff who care for these high-needs individuals have expressed anguish about how they and their residents are being treated. But because staff cannot openly reveal to the public the reality of their working conditions or the residents' living conditions, their concerns are not heard.

Doing this research has unfortunately left us jaded and upset about the lack of quality residential care available to those who need it. Underfunding and understaffing reveal a shameful disregard for the well-being of our elderly and dependent citizens. Our granddaughter, who was eight years old at the time, had been privy to many discussions about our research. She informed our daughter, her mother, that she plans to move in with us someday. She explained, "They'll be almost ninety then and they'll need me to look after them. We don't want them to have to go into a home."

Part Three

Prescription for Healing

6.

Treatment Strategies

Can anything really be done?

In 2018, an ER nurse in the Winnipeg Health Sciences Centre (HSC) was brutally assaulted by a patient. The attack left her with long-lasting psychological injuries, such as frightening flashbacks, panic attacks, and depression. She told CBC News:

> It's absolutely awful. I tried to go to counselling. I'm on antidepressants now. I feel totally defeated. Just defeated. Because nobody's really doing anything about it. Every single day there's a violent incident in HSC emerg. Every day. And no one seems to acknowledge it. . . .
>
> People are lashing out, hitting us, attacking us. Guns have been pulled out, weapons have been pulled out, we've been threatened, punched, kicked, spat on, everything. Everything. I feel like I'm going into a knife fight without a knife.[1]

So the question emerges: Can anything really be done to protect health care staff from violence? The answer, according to the health care workers we talked to in our research, is emphatically *yes*. The voluminous research that has been published concurs. For over two decades studies have provided myriad potential remedies.[2] Some would require significant financial investment, such as hospital redesign and increased staffing. Others require only small changes, such as removing last names from staff name tags or facility names from staff parking passes. Interestingly, many of the health care workers' ideas for violence prevention coincide with ideas for improving the quality of care for patients and residents.

One recommendation made by academic researchers is that *all* violent or abusive incidents be treated seriously, including derogatory verbal comments and threats. The importance of recognizing verbal assault as a form of violence cannot be overlooked, since it has been shown in domestic relationships to be a risk factor or precursor for battery.[3] When verbal and low-level abuse are tolerated, more serious forms of violence may follow.[4]

Prevention is sometimes categorized as primary, secondary, and tertiary.[5] Primary prevention aims to stop violence from occurring in the first place. Secondary prevention is meant to help potential victims from being hurt should violence occur. Tertiary prevention includes strategies for protecting victims of violence from further harm or ongoing harm. Let's look at what is required at each of those levels.

Primary prevention is key

In 2013, a newly minted nurse who was working alone in a mental health facility in Kamloops, British Columbia, was seriously injured when a patient punched her in the face and knocked her to the ground. Seven co-workers and the police finally rescued her from her attacker, but not before she had been so deeply psychologically traumatized that she would never be able to return to her job in the facility. Tracy Quewezance, a union official with the B.C. Nurses' Union, said, "Nurses are working short, caring for patients that even the jail can't handle."[6] The brutal attack and its ongoing effects likely could have been prevented if proper conditions and safeguards had been in place. This is true of most violent incidents. The majority of the solutions proposed by the health care workers we interviewed fall within the realm of primary prevention. Here are their ideas.

Staffing levels

It should be no surprise that, in interview after interview, adequate staffing levels topped the list of violence prevention strategies. We know that when in-patients have been waiting for long periods of time to be attended to by health care staff, they can feel neglected. They might be in pain and awaiting medication, thirsty or hungry, or need to use the bathroom. They might be lonely or fearful and need some comfort. They are often trapped in their beds or chairs, and the wait can seem endless. Some will take out their mounting frustration on the first person who approaches. Their anger can present as aggressive behaviour ranging anywhere from rudeness to verbal abuse to physical assault—in extreme cases, even homicide.

As a nurse in a large urban centre explained, increasing the staffing levels during the evening and night shifts might prevent frustration-related violence. A long-term care worker explained, "That's when the incidents are happening. We have lots of code whites on the night shift or right at change of shift when all the staff is busy doing charting."

Having sufficient staff to meet patients' or residents' particular needs would go a long way towards reducing their agitation. When dealing with potentially aggressive individuals, it is also imperative that enough staff be available to work in teams of two or three—or more if necessary. As one of the health care workers we spoke with said, "You need to be regularly working in pairs. There is safety in numbers." Another said:

> If you could call three staff to come into the room [of an aggressive resident], you'd be protected. If you had one that could hold their

hands, you could talk to them and distract them while the other two are doing care.

Depending on the department or the facilities, a certain number of sick calls from staff seems to be expected and accepted. It can be difficult to find replacements at short notice. Some of the staff we spoke with said they and their co-workers are reticent to accept calls to come in to work because they so desperately need time to recover, mentally and physically.

Ontario is operating at abysmally low staffing levels—far below other provinces or countries in the OECD. The fix for short-staffing seems simple enough. Facilities need to have enough personnel on hand on a regular basis. They also need to have more stand-by staff on the roster to fill in for those who have called in sick. Looking even more critically at what needs to be done, conditions for staff need to be such that they don't require so much sick time to recover from stress and exhaustion.

The health care workers we interviewed also felt that it would be helpful to be able to let patients, residents, or family members know when they are working short. It might make them feel a little more sympathetic towards the harried staff and less likely to lash out.

Dr. James Phillips, from the Beth Israel Deaconess Medical Center in Boston, has taken a long, hard look at the problem of violence. He pored over many studies looking for modifiable risk factors for Type II violence, or assault of a health care worker by a patient or family member. After completing his review of potential solutions, he concluded, "Perhaps most important are recommendations that health care organizations revise their policies in order to improve staffing levels during busy periods to reduce crowding and wait times."[7]

In long-term care facilities, higher staffing levels are crucial in order to reduce resident aggression against staff and each other. As a long-term care nurse said, "The biggest thing, I think, is that we need to start to help develop therapeutic professional relationships with the residents . . . but we don't have the time to do that."

Dr. James Struthers told us:

You cannot have good quality care delivered to long-term care homes without adequate staffing, without a staff-to-resident ratio at least double what we currently have . . . Because again and again we hear, and we can see it from what workers tell us, and what family members tell us, what staff and what residents tell us, that the most important part of getting good quality care is getting to know the residents, having continuity of care, having time to care, having time to sit down to talk, to touch, to hear, to listen and to communicate and to understand the person that you're delivering care to, and to understand the symptoms that that person might be acting out . . . Because they can't deliver a caring environment, they can't deliver good quality relational care, they can't take the time to reduce agitation and anxiety and aggression on the part of the people that they have to deal with on a daily basis . . . If you create staffing levels that are twice as high per resident in Canada, which is the case in Sweden and Norway, then you're going to get less violence occurring in the home and better working conditions and living conditions for residents.

Design of the work environment

With some careful planning, health care facilities can be engineered to eliminate many risk factors. Some of the fixes are as simple as securing loose furniture and eliminating other potential weapons, such as hard, heavy, or sharp objects.

Units, especially those requiring constant monitoring of patients or residents, should be designed to improve the sight lines. Some of the long-term care staff we spoke with said a circular design with the nursing station in the centre would be ideal. Barriers can also be installed at nursing stations for added protection.

Seclusion rooms need to be made available for out-of-control patients or residents. In some facilities, there are none at all. In others, the rooms may be all occupied or be in use for other purposes due to overcrowding or lack of beds. That creates a real problem when an aggressive patient needs to be isolated.

Staff should also have secure areas—safe rooms with safe exit options—that they can easily access. One health care worker told us, "We created a safe room where nurses could run to, lock the door, and we have a phone."

Protective technology

Security cameras and easily accessible emergency alarms should be installed where needed. Personal alarms should also be made available to all staff coming into contact with patients, residents, family members, or the public.

The injured ER nurse from the Winnipeg Health Sciences Centre believes further measures are needed, given the increase of meth-fuelled violence and the ready availability of weapons. She told the reporter:

> I want to come into work feeling safe. I want to come into work like not worried that I'm going to get a black eye. Or worse. Or get stabbed. What I want to see done is I want metal detectors. That would help me feel a lot safer. And probably the patients too.[8]

Flagging

In October 2019, a sixty-two-year-old patient in a Sudbury, Ontario, hospital stabbed a nurse with a screwdriver after she entered his room. She was seriously injured. It came out that the patient had threatened a staff person the previous day with a wrench, but no formal report had been filed and he hadn't been flagged as being potentially violent.[9] It should be obvious that the patient should not have had access to tools that could be used as weapons—particularly after he had brandished one the day before the more serious attack.

Our interviewees and the published studies agree that patients who have displayed aggressive behaviour or escalating agitation need to be clearly identified in their charts as well as in a manner that is visible to all staff, such as with wrist bands, colour coding, or signs. While this isn't a guarantee of protection, it does at least provide some warning that the patient may strike out.

Several of the health care staff we spoke with said it would also be useful to have province-wide access to chart information—including flagging—to inform them of previous behaviours in patients who have been transferred. The issue of flagging, however, is fraught with controversy because it can stigmatize patients or residents who are situationally desperate or confused and may be also be subject to discrimination. Long-term care staff, for example, mentioned that the practice, which they felt would be helpful to warn them and other staff of potentially aggressive residents, isn't done in their facilities. A PSW told us, "We need a flagging system to warn us about residents who have a history of violence. We used to flag the door, but they stopped it for privacy reasons."

Flagging may not, on its own, provide much actual protection. The question remains regarding what concrete actions are to be taken when a potentially violent patient or resident is identified. Will more staff be assigned to care for the flagged individual or other special measures be instituted? Andria Bianchi, a bioethicist at the University Health Network in Toronto, told the *London Free Press*, "There's no use in flagging or identifying something without a plan to manage it."[10]

Zero tolerance

We were travelling home on a VIA train from Toronto to Windsor after attending an OCHU-CUPE conference on violence against staff. We had heard one health care worker after another describe the lack of concern they felt their employer was displaying about the issue. The subject of zero tolerance signage came up, and it seemed most of those present didn't have such signs in place in their workplaces. As our train was pulling out of Union Station, the conductor began his announcements. We were struck by the fact that he included a statement saying that VIA would not tolerate any "verbal or physical abuse, threats, harassment, or intimidating behaviours." We have since seen signs displaying similar messages in our own doctor's and dentist's offices, at medical labs, and even in coffee shops or on local public transit. Signage in itself, however, is not enough. Dr. Katherine Lippel, who wrote an article entitled "Conceptualising Violence at Work through a Gender Lens," explains:

> A key factor in reducing exposure to psychological violence, including bullying and harassment, as well as sexual harassment is to find ways to make these behaviours unacceptable in the workplace. This is achieved not just by posting policies declaring them to be unacceptable but by changing the workplace culture so that there is a shared perception that such behaviour, that may have been prevalent and accepted years ago, is no longer tolerated either by management or by workers and their unions. The active participation of unions in educating the workforce with regard to sexual harassment or bullying can be far more successful in reducing these behaviours than top down orders from management or zero tolerance policies that raise the stakes for perpetrators, possibly exacerbating ill-feeling in the workplace.[11]

In 2019, the Ontario Ministry of Health and Long-Term Care and the Ministry of Labour provided administrators with a few tools to help protect their staff from violence. While they fall far short of addressing underlying causes, they do recommend that signs be posted saying, "Violence in the workplace cannot be tolerated." It's a baby step in the right direction. The enforcement of zero tolerance policies remains a stumbling block.

Management, doctor, and co-worker respect

Several of the health care workers we talked to said they had experienced a decrease in respect from patients and visitors over the past few years. They feel that when there is little respect displayed, there is a greater likelihood of verbal and physical abuse. We were told, "You need to be respected and the supervisors and doctors need to demonstrate respect for you in front of patients and family members—otherwise they are going to pick on you."

In an article about workplace incivility, occupational health nurses Natasha Collins and Bonnie Rogers wrote that negative and hurtful interpersonal interactions are growing in workplaces—both in the public and private sector—and that they not only cause personal harm, but also carry a heavy financial cost as co-operation and teamwork break down and burnout increases.[12]

The American Nurses Association produced a position statement on "Incivility, Bullying, and Workplace Violence." It condemns all forms of violence against staff—including violence that is perpetrated by co-workers, management, and other professionals. It also draws a link between general incivility and violence.

> [Incivility] may . . . include name-calling, using a condescending tone, and expressing public criticism. The negative impact of incivility can be significant and far-reaching and can affect not only the targets themselves, but also bystanders, peers, stakeholders, and organizations. If left unaddressed, it may progress in some cases to threatening situations or violence.
>
> Oftentimes incivility is not directed at any specific person or persons. However, it may perpetuate or become a precursor to bullying and workplace violence; therefore, it cannot be characterized as innocuous or inconsequential.[13]

The statement makes a number of recommendations for employers to follow. They are intended to prevent violence, acknowledge and support those who have suffered a violent incident, and mitigate ongoing harm, including conducting "a root cause analysis to understand all factors contributing to workplace violence."

Violence protection training

Staff who are working in high-risk areas or with high-risk patients need to be properly trained in de-escalation techniques. Yet the health care staff we spoke with were very dissatisfied with the training they received. Often it consisted simply of a brief online course. Many felt they would benefit from comprehensive in-person training—regularly updated—to better equip them to recognize signs of potential violence or conditions that might lead to violence. A nurse working in long-term care told us:

> We need better training, [such as] Crisis Intervention Training, which is more in-depth. It's more hands-on. It teaches you valuable skills and it would be an ideal thing for a long-term care facility. The key word is intervention—it actually teaches you how to stop it.

Appropriate staff placement

Staff must be appropriately assigned. Where there is a likelihood of violence, only those staff with specialized training and experience should be put in place. We heard many stories about younger nurses—new graduates—being thrown into situations where aggressive patients seemed to be aware of the staff person's inexperience and fear and took advantage of it. In his report for the ILO and WHO, Vittorio Di Martino wrote:

> The age and experience of workers is another factor that can either increase or diminish the possibility of aggression. Previous experience of handling similar difficult situations, which is obviously associated with age, should enable workers to react more wisely than inexperienced staff. This explains the higher risk of violence towards young nurses' aides compared with the risk for more experienced older nurses.[14]

A German study of aggression against health care workers found that being under thirty years of age almost doubled one's risk of being verbally or physically assaulted.[15]

Reduce agitation

Many strategies could be employed to reduce the agitation, frustration, fear, humiliation, disrespect, and anger that patients, residents, and their advocates or family members experience within what sometimes seems to be a heartless, rushed, deficient system. Besides providing an adequate number of appropriately assigned staff in order to reduce wait times and allow for relational care, many practical measures can be put into practice.

Provide translators and cultural sensitivity training

A study of patients in two large Toronto hospitals found that about a quarter were not fluent in English.[16] Although interpreters are provided, they have to be pre-booked and are often unavailable when needed. Several of our study participants expressed their own frustration regarding their inability to explain to their patients or residents what they were doing for them.

> They might not speak English and they can't tell me what they want. My employer says they have translation services but there are no translators available. I've worked with all sorts of people where I've been expected to speak Portuguese, Italian, Spanish. It's a contributor to violence because, if I could talk to them, maybe we could figure out why they're so upset.

Provide recreational programs

Having too much time on their hands between care activities can lead to boredom, stress, fear, and related agitation and anger among patients and residents. Research has found that the biomedical model of health care, which sees patients primarily as biological entities or sets of symptoms to be medically treated, ignores the importance of addressing patients' psychosocial needs.[17] The British Medical Association recommends that patients be able to engage in creative and recreational activities. Music programs, arts, crafts, and games have been shown to improve mood and reduce anxiety. Gardens, sunny patient rooms and common areas, and nature scenes can help. Boredom, monotony, and inactivity have also been shown to increase confusion and agitation in long-term care residents with dementia. As one worker observed:

> When a music group comes to the unit, there's less stress; it's more calm. Or if they have activities, there are only a few people walking around. There's less commotion. And we can do more important things for the resident. And you have more time to spend with them.

Communicate about wait times in the ER
Research has established that violence occurs frequently in crowded ERs. International investigators Cheshin Arik and colleagues have found, "The atmosphere in ED [the emergency department] is usually stressful, especially among patients and escorts who always consider their medical problem as urgent, requiring immediate attention."[18] Their fear and anger can escalate as their wait increases; this escalation can result in verbal or physical violence against staff.

When we were presenting the preliminary results of our first study to health care staff at their annual occupational health conference, several attendees raised the idea of posting ER wait times. Studies have shown that when patients and their family members are forewarned about long waits, they are less likely to became agitated and angry.

When we, ourselves, needed to visit an ER after an accident during a family vacation in New Hampshire, we noticed that wait times were posted on lighted signs outside the various local hospitals and urgent care centres. It helped us to decide which facility to choose.

Of course, in many communities, there is only one hospital, so shopping for shorter wait times isn't an option. Many Canadian hospitals do post expected wait times online, but not everyone is in a position to access the internet when they are suffering from an illness or injury that requires an ER visit. And patients have to take into account sudden unexpected demand and the triaging process, which might put those needing more urgent care ahead of them.

But even the simple courtesy of checking in with waiting patients would help. Have you ever wondered if you have been forgotten or overlooked as the clock ticks endlessly? It's unnerving. Effectively and frequently communicating with ER patients about their status and likely remaining wait time could go a long way towards reassuring them and reducing their anger.

Virtual visits with doctors or urgent care centres might also cut down on the number of patients using the ER. During the COVID-19 pandemic, there was a significant increase in telephone and virtual consults. Provincial and territorial governments established temporary billing codes specifically for telemedicine and virtual care.[19] Perhaps we should cautiously consider maintaining some aspects of this model, where applicable, when the pandemic is under control. We say *cautiously* because many critics, including the Canadian Medical Association, have expressed concern that virtual visits might exclude those who do not have access to or an adequate comfort level with technology. The CMA also warns:

> Its disadvantages include the inability to perform most physical examinations or procedures, difficulty establishing new therapeutic relationships, dealing with some complex mental health issues, missing body language and nonverbal cues and lacking the full degree of comfort and support that can be provided in person.[20]

Create a positive environment
Improvements can be made to the overall atmosphere in a hospital or other care facility, making it more calming and conducive to relaxation, rest, and healing.

> It's loud at the hospital. You've got call bells. You've got overhead announcements. And it's not a quiet environment for the patients . . . It agitates them.

Simple trips out into the sunshine have been shown to elevate residents' mood and improve their behaviour towards each other and the staff. A growing body of research demonstrates the value of providing access to the outdoors for those living with dementia. For example, a report produced in Australia found:

> Gardens designed specifically to support people with dementia provide therapeutic activities designed to maximise retained cognitive and physical abilities and lessen the confusion and agitation often associated with the condition.[21]

Develop alternative long-term care models

Long-term care staff offered several ideas for improving conditions for residents, and by extension, reducing the risk of violence against staff.

> We can't be putting the old and frail with the young and mentally disturbed.

> We need more family involvement. And when residents are admitted, families should sign a code of conduct acknowledging how and how not to treat staff.

> They have to hire more BSO [Behavioural Supports Ontario] nurses. Can you imagine four hundred beds and only one BSO?

> We don't have enough male PSWs. I think that male PSWs should be looking after male residents as opposed to women doing it. And they might not be whacking at them as often as they whack at women.

Interestingly, many of the prevention ideas put forward by the participants mirror those suggested by the Ontario Long Term Care Association,[22] namely, increased funding, increased staffing, more one-to-one care, redesigned buildings, and in-house BSO teams.

There are many innovative models of care that consider the overall well-being of long-term care residents, including the importance of outdoor activities and access to nature. Some go well beyond the typical institutional model in their designs, in some cases creating secured villages that include shops, theatres, gardens, and other spaces that bring a sense of normalcy to those requiring dementia care. One example of such a facility can be found in Holland. Hogewey dementia village is designed to provide residents a homelike setting and activities that increase their quality of life and sense of belonging and fulfillment, while providing care and safety. Yvonne van Amerongen, an employee at Hogewey, who also helped develop the concept, explained it to CBC News, which reported:

> Each household has at least one health-care worker present who helps with housework and other tasks.
>
> Residents are free to stroll all through town.
>
> "You will see [residents] sitting in a restaurant with a glass of wine or buying a box of chocolates from the supermarket," says van Amerongen of those who still understand the concept of money. A worker and a resident from each house walk to the market daily to buy groceries.[23]

Hogewey has been criticized for its deception of those in care, but defenders of the model observe that the mock village life has had many positive effects on the unsuspecting residents.

> "There's no trick here," says van Amerongen.
>
> She says that while some Hogewey residents recognize the caregivers as nurses, others simply think of them as "a nice friend."[24]

In the 1990s Dr. Bill Thomas decided he was going to make the atmosphere in a New York nursing home more like, well, *home.* As the medical director, he initiated a broad range of activities for the residents in order to combat boredom and feelings of worthlessness. One of the most daring innovations was the introduction of "plants, cats, dogs and birds."[25] He called his model the Eden Alternative. The resulting improvement in the residents' overall satisfaction, health, and well-being was remarkable. A few years later he developed another model that he called the Green House model; it is "based on small, homey communal living spaces, where residents share meals around a single large table and caregivers focus on just a few residents each."

The long-term care staff we spoke with agree that the atmosphere within most Canadian facilities is too stark and institutional.

> I would like to see a more homelike setting. I think we need to make it more resident focused. We're just taking them and saying this is your home and you're expecting them to adapt.

Several innovative long-term care models are, in fact, being developed in Canada. One of them, while perhaps somewhat less visionary than those created by Dr. Thomas, is the Butterfly model. The *Mississauga News* reported:

> While dementia care has traditionally been task-oriented, the Butterfly care model emphasizes a transformation in the way patients are cared for, with a focus on their emotions and the creation of home-like environments and daily activities they enjoyed earlier in life.[26]

Staffing is key to the success of the model. CUPE, the union representing one such facility in Peel, Ontario, says that it whole-heartedly supports the concept. It is concerned, however, that the staffing levels remain too low to deliver enough relational care without staff suffering burnout from the additional demands the model makes upon them.[27]

Both the Green House model and the Butterfly model have resulted in "happier residents, fewer falls, diminished violence, lessened antipsychotic medication and lower staff turnover."[28] A resident who was chronically aggressive—using his cane and fists to try to fight off his caregivers—was ousted from several long-term care facilities before being moved to the Peel Butterfly home. When he first arrived, the staff suffered "six weeks of bruising before suggesting the life-long farmer collect hardboiled eggs in the courtyard before tea. It tapped into his past, and the job clicked." That did the trick. He remained for another two and a half years, until his death, as a happy, co-operative, content resident. The staff attribute his transformation to the innovative program.

Dr. Pat Armstrong and colleagues compared various models and approaches in a report for the City of Toronto. They found that the Wellspring, Butterfly, Green House, and Eden Alternative models share common perspectives. They determined that there were advantages to each and that the Butterfly model and another approach, called Gentle Persuasion, reduced resident responsive behaviours. They concluded that "the mixed evidence does not lead to a recommendation for a single model but rather to a strategy to learn from all the models, adapting promising practices to specific homes and their populations."[29] The *Toronto Star* summarized:

> All [of the models] have significant benefits, Armstrong's report concludes, and all emphasize the "importance of care relationships" that embrace the interests of each individual living in the home. Key to success, the report said, are extra staff and flexibility for them to develop those relationships with residents.[30]

Workplace violence prevention programs

Under Ontario's previous government, a task force recommended that health care facilities develop policies and programs to prevent violence and that they be developed with the full engagement of members of the public, the health care staff, and their unions.[31] Dr. Craig Slatin agrees.

> Violence prevention experts are not accustomed to workplace dynamics, and they fall back onto their training about individual perpetrators. This orientation will usually result in failed prevention approaches in the workplace. We need workplace violence pre-

vention professionals who understand that workplace conditions and systems must be designed to mitigate and prevent health care workers' exposures to workplace violence. This requires a commitment to engagement of workers and their unions in developing workplace violence prevention and response strategies, ensuring adequate staffing to prevent workplace violence and harm from potential uncontrollable acts of violence, participatory violence mitigation and prevention training developed with and delivered by worker-trainers, appropriate security systems, commitments to fully report incidents of violence and near miss incidents and to report occupational injuries and illnesses that result from exposures to acts of violence as such—without contestation, and implementation of necessary engineering and administrative controls. These programs and protocols have to be based on comprehensive audits grounded in root-cause analysis conducted with engagement of workers and their unions.

Interestingly, the management team for Toronto East General Hospital put forward a similar view regarding the importance of involving workers in the development of programs.

> Despite these legislated requirements, violence against healthcare workers continues as recently reported in the media. . . .
>
> Ultimately, healthcare workers have the right to work in an environment that is free from all forms of abuse and to not fear coming to work at risk of being injured physically or verbally by patients, visitors or their peers. As leaders we must have zero tolerance to all forms of violence in our workplaces. We must take personal responsibility for building the partnerships between staff, labour unions and other stakeholders to make violence reduction interventions a real success. After all, our healthcare professionals and patients are counting on it.[32]

Needless to say, the development of policies is not enough. The agreed-upon measures need to be fully enforced, and the needed resources must be made available in order to enable the enactment of the policies.

Identifying and reporting hazards

Comprehensive hazard identification and hazard reporting must be encouraged, and procedures streamlined to facilitate such reporting. Inspections and documentation should include all existing risk factors for violence, such as flaws in engineering design and gaps in security measures, along with such systemic factors as understaffing. All hazard and inspection reports need to be shared with joint worker-management health and safety committees in order that improvements can be collaboratively planned.

Mental health and addiction facilities

Patients with psychiatric disorders, addiction, and criminal backgrounds related to mental health conditions need to be placed in appropriate facilities, not on general wards in unequipped hospitals.

> In our hospital a lot of our violence is because of our patients who are waiting to be put in nursing homes. And the other part of it is not having enough psychiatric facilities so they are on the nursing units until they get a psychiatric bed.

We are in no way suggesting that patients with mental health needs necessarily pose a threat of violence, but appropriately staffed and dedicated mental health facilities are better equipped to deal with any possible aggression. Appropriate placement would improve the safety of the staff, as well as the health and well-being of patients requiring such specialized care.

Consistent regulations

As it stands now, each province and territory has its own government ministry of health and long-term care. Regulations, funding decisions, staffing levels, and so on, are established at a provincial/territorial level. Policies regarding violence against staff are determined at an even more local level—within the hospitals or care facilities themselves. There should be consistent province- or nationwide protections against violence in all health care facilities, as well as additional tailored protections where required.

We, along with other witnesses, had the privilege of presenting to the federal parliamentary Standing Committee on Health in June 2019. The resulting government report included several important recommendations.[33] It was recommended that the federal government support the establishment of best practices for staff protection from violence by

- developing national standards for violence prevention training for health care workers;
- providing targeted funding for violence prevention programs;
- creating avenues to share best practices across jurisdictions; and
- funding research evaluating best practices.

Because so much of violence against staff is structural in nature, it was also recommended that

the federal government work with the provinces and territories to address staffing shortages in health care settings by updating the *Pan Canadian Health Human Resources Strategy* to reflect the health care needs of seniors, the well-being of health care providers and the shift towards community-based care.

The committee also recommended targeted funding to "support upgrades to Canada's aging long-term care facilities and other health care infrastructure to better meet the needs of patients."

Secondary prevention

There are many strategies available to protect workers from violence within the category of secondary prevention, which aims to detect problems early and stop them from escalating or recurring.

Avoid victim-blaming

In order to protect the mental well-being of staff who have been assaulted, management must communicate a clear mandate of support. Blaming an assaulted worker compounds their trauma and creates an atmosphere of fear and distrust. Before digging into the details of an incident, the process of debriefing needs first to consider the state of mind of the assaulted individual and provide needed sympathy and understanding.

We can learn from the experience of battered spouses, who historically have hesitated to report abuse because they feared they would be blamed, at least to some degree. The counsellors in today's shelters and the police who deal with domestic violence are trained to treat victims with respect and compassion—and to take them at their word. The same compassion should be provided to traumatized workers.

Incident reporting

Many incidents are never discussed, much less formally reported. The paucity of data regarding the prevalence of violence against staff keeps the problem hidden. One of the health care workers we interviewed, while sympathetic to those who do not formally report incidents of violence, is nevertheless exasperated by the resulting lack of documentation. She said, "We have to report incidents—report, report, report—because it is not right to be getting spit at or hit in your job."

We were told that the fear of blame and reprisal is a significant obstacle to incident reporting. Workers also said that the procedure is not encouraged and is quite onerous. A nurse explained,

"When you're short-staffed, there's no time to do incident reports. It seems like they make the incident reports so difficult for you to weave through, it just becomes too much to do." Another said, "I'd have to stay fifteen, twenty minutes after my shift to report if somebody got seriously injured. But people make threats all the time. So to do that all the time would be very time-consuming." The computer programs themselves can be difficult to use.

> When there is a code white called, there is to be an electronic inci-
> dent report filed so it's documented through our computer system.
> Now a lot of it doesn't get put in. It's not easy. They've revised the
> program many times and they just haven't gotten it user-friendly
> yet. The staff say, "I'm too busy. I can't fill that out."

Published studies recommend that all incidents, no matter how seemingly minor, be reported. Simplified reporting procedures would help. Computer systems must be made more accessible. Time needs to be set aside for filing reports. In his comprehensive review of the literature on violence, Dr. James Phillips concluded:

> When threatening language and signs of agitation are identified,
> interventions should be initiated quickly. The cautious application
> of a so-called zero tolerance reporting policy, in which all episodes
> of workplace violence are immediately reported to supervisors and
> security personnel and are addressed with the perpetrator, may
> prevent escalation.[34]

To ensure that the reports are at least reviewed, they, along with all hazard and inspection reports, should all be discussed by the joint worker-management health and safety committee in each workplace. The committees should be mandated to investigate all violent incidents resulting in injury, near injury, distress, or trauma, and all situations that indicate there is a risk of violence. The filing of formal reports is essential. As a health and safety committee member explained, "The only way that violence against staff gets to the health and safety committee is if the staff fill out one of the incident reports." Solutions, if any, should be agreed upon and implemented and responses should be provided to the staff who filed the reports.

Management and employees both have a role to play in gathering incident data. The government, in fact, now requires that this information be gathered and submitted annually. A 2017 amendment to O. Reg. 187/15 under the *Excellent Care for All Act, 2010*, requires hospitals to include mandatory indicators in their Quality Improvement Plans (QIPs), to be specified annually by the minister of health and long-term care upon the advice of Health Quality Ontario. In 2019 Health Quality Ontario produced a document, "Quality Improvement Plan Guidance: Workplace Violence Prevention," mandating that all hospitals collect data on violence against staff. Hospitals are advised as follows:

> The goal of addressing workplace violence is to reduce the number of violent incidents that occur and foster a culture of reporting. However, by necessity, the QIP indicator measures the number of violent incidents that are *reported by workers*—and workplace violence is known to be underreported.
>
> As your organization improves reporting and develops a culture of safety, the number of reported incidents of workplace violence may rise. This effect is expected and should be encouraged. It will be necessary to look beyond the number of incidents reported to truly understand the types of incidents being reported and the broader issue of workplace violence within your organization.[35]

The report presents strategies to overcome the problem of under-reporting. It advises that hospitals should embrace the following recommendations:

- The Ministry of Health and Long-Term Care and the Ministry of Labour should make health care staff aware of what should be reported as workplace violence under the *Occupational Health and Safety Act* (namely, not just actual physical force, but also attempts to exercise physical force; and statements or behaviours that are reasonable for a worker to interpret as a threat to exercise physical force).

- Hospitals should ensure that reporting systems capture workplace violence incidents that result in psychological injuries, as well as those that result in physical injuries. This will require changes to local system tracking and related processes, as psychological injuries are not always as immediately apparent as physical ones.
- Lack of action has been identified in the research literature as a common reason for staff not reporting workplace violence in hospitals in the United States. While the situation in Ontario is not known, Health Quality Ontario suggest there should be clear messaging from hospitals' leadership, the Ministry of Health and Long-Term Care and the Ministry of Labour about what action will be taken based on workplace violence reports. In addition, these groups should be clear how staff should report workplace violence incidents and what they should do if they feel action is not being taken.

In order to comply, employers need to overcome their reticence to fully document violence and to ensure that staff who file incident reports do not face any negative consequences for doing so.

Part of the job?

If managers regularly dismiss acts of violence as insignificant, they may also view protective changes as unwarranted.

> Violent occurrences are made light of by our management. I've seen the comments . . . It's accepted. It is part of your duties. If you don't like it, maybe you should look at a different type of job in a different type of field.

But not everyone we talked to was willing to see abuse as inevitable or accept it as intrinsic to the job.

I think there's a culture that accepts aggression from residents. Since they don't mean it, it's not the same. They don't know what they're doing when they spit on you. Well, I believe I still have the right to be at work and not get spit on, even though that person has dementia. Those things shouldn't become a normal part of your job.

In order to move forward towards a violence-free work environment, it is important that the idea that violence is just part of the job be eradicated.

In the past few years, it seems to be getting a lot worse. We still have a lot of non-reporting. I'm not sure if staff are afraid to report it or they're thinking it's part of the job. I have heard staff say, "Well, it's part of the job." And I've also heard new staff, that have just graduated out of the college, say, "They told us in school that it's just part of the job—it's to be accepted." And I think that's such a shame, that we've got these young RPNs coming out of the college and they are still teaching them, putting this disgusting thought in their heads, that this is expected to be part of your job—to be hit, assaulted, bit, sworn at, threatened.

Security

Many of the staff we talked to said that security is lacking or insufficient in the facilities they work in. They believe they would be better protected if there were an increase in the number of security personnel with higher levels of training. In some cases, they should be equipped to intervene with violent individuals. Another suggestion was to increase the number of health care staff with specialized training to deal with violence. A nurse who was interviewed for the OCHU-CUPE *Voices* booklet said:

On this particular day the patient was off the unit. Security called us about some questionable behavior he saw . . . so when the patient returned, and we spoke with him about it, he became extremely agitated. He just rushed at us and started swinging punches. He punched me three times before I kind of just did my best to wrangle . . . tackle him to the ground with some other staff. The first few punches I was just kind of holding him back, telling him not to punch me. Obviously, that didn't work. I ended up with a swollen eye. Nurses got concussed in the melee. Several people got cuts, scratches, things that really never should have occurred in the first place had the risk been managed properly.

The Winnipeg ER nurse we heard about earlier told CBC News that security personnel are also at risk of violence: "Our security guards are getting hit probably on the daily. Every day. They don't have enough power to deal with what we're facing in the ER right now."[36] According to the Manitoba Government and General Employees Union, which represents the security personnel, its members are not adequately trained. They need both mental health training and the designation as officers of the peace to protect them legally if they have to use force.

Increasing the availability of trained, higher level security staff would help with another of the suggestions that was put forward—the reconstituting of the code white teams to require the inclusion of trained security personnel.

We had our own security at the time. So if they were on the forensic unit, they would go to the codes and we would do the one-to-ones, which was great, because those guys really knew how to work the patients. These guys—the new contract security—only make minimum wage, so they send us in first. They're security! That's what they're there for, to help us, you know? But they don't. They just stand in the corner. I don't know what to say about them. They're people; they need a job I guess . . . but I think in psychiatry, they shouldn't skimp on security.

Tertiary prevention

Several after-the-fact tertiary prevention strategies can help to mitigate psychological trauma staff experience after being abused or assaulted. Published research and the health care staff we talked to stressed the importance of post-incident supports such as specialized trauma counselling, and financial supports such as compensation, adequate time off work, and coverage for physical therapy.

Dr. Donna Gates, a professor of nursing in Cincinnati, Ohio, along with two colleagues, carried out a study of violence-related stress and productivity among ER nurses. They wrote:

> Immediate interventions, during the first hours or days after a trauma, can provide the victim with the support system currently lacking in most health care facilities. . . . By providing a support system composed of peers and administrative representatives, employees have an opportunity to process the event and put it into perspective, thus minimizing the short and long-term symptoms related to stress and anxiety.[37]

Support

Many of the health care workers talked about the hurt and disrespect they felt because of their management's apparent lack of sympathy or concern after a violent incident. One participant emphasized the need for those in positions of authority to be trained in "compassion." Interestingly, Dr. Phillips's research uncovered evidence that management support is important, not only for tertiary prevention, but for primary prevention as well. He found that, "at the facility level, supervisor support was found to be protective against harassment and all types of violence."[38]

Assaulted workers suffer beyond the violent incidents that occur. One simple measure would be to ensure that all supervisors conduct the debriefing process with a focus on the well-being of the assaulted staff, rather than quizzing the victim about their own behaviour, leaving them feeling blamed, insecure, and at risk of being disciplined. Post-incident supports must be enhanced. PTSD, a serious and common result of violence, is not always recognized or adequately treated. Dr. Gates and colleagues found:

> Ninety-four percent of [emergency department] nurses experienced at least one post-traumatic stress disorder symptom after a violent event, with 17% having scores high enough to be considered probable for PTSD. . . . Interventions are needed to prevent the violence and to provide care to the ED nurse after an event.[39]

Physical and psychological effects need to be mitigated through adequate treatment, recovery time, and specialized counselling. According to the U.S. Occupational Safety and Health Administration:

> Victims of workplace violence could suffer a variety of consequences in addition to their actual physical injuries. These may include:
> - Short- and long-term psychological trauma;
> - Fear of returning to work;
> - Changes in relationships with coworkers and family;
> - Feelings of incompetence, guilt, powerlessness; and
> - Fear of criticism by supervisors or managers.[40]

Although verbal and sexual harassment may not result in serious physical injury, the harms from these forms of violence must be recognized and addressed. Ongoing support, such as one-on-one or group counselling, should be offered to anyone who feels they might benefit from it. In addition, supervisors and management personnel should be provided with sensitivity training in order to understand the needs of staff who are, or have been, subjected to violence, as well as to appreciate the importance of showing them respect and empathy.

Workers who have been sexually harassed or assaulted need specialized counselling by practitioners who have been specially trained, like those providing support in sexual assault centres. Employee assistance programs (EAPs) may not offer enough support for an individual who requires long-term specialized care. We also heard from health care personnel that EAPs are not always trusted by workers, who fear their confidentiality will not be completely protected.

A study by a group of researchers in China examining the role of various types of supports in preventing violence and/or its ongoing effects concluded:

> Vulnerable groups, such as healthcare workers and patients, need organisational and social support. Thus, it is not difficult to understand healthcare workers' need for more assistance from the organisation and society. If they cannot obtain sufficient support after exposure to violence, a decline in their quality of work and other adverse consequences can be expected. Previous studies have shown that higher levels of organisational support for those who have experienced violence are effective in reducing their tension and stress. A trusted and just work environment may reduce violence against nurses. Therefore, we should increase organisational support to healthcare workers who have been exposed to violence by providing psychological care, supporting their efforts to claim compensation, establishing and improving violence-reporting systems, and training them to improve their competence in responding to violence.[41]

Workers' compensation

Staff who have been injured by an aggressive patient or resident often find themselves in an uphill battle with the workers' compensation system. The health care workers also talked to us about the need for the compensation system to recognize PTSD, cumulative stress, anxiety, and other mental health issues related to violence. According to Fred Hahn, president of the Ontario Division of CUPE, currently "94% of Chronic Mental Stress [WSIB] claims have been denied, a denial rate higher than any other claims and one that's discriminatory towards workers suffering from mental stress."[42]

The compensation system uses a concept called "presumption." A law was passed in Ontario in 2018 that granted the presumption of work-relatedness for PTSD for nurses and other frontline health care workers. The law guiding compensation states:

> If the accident [injury or health problem] arises out of the worker's employment, it is presumed to have occurred in the course of the employment unless the contrary is shown.[43]

Presumption is somewhat vague in its definition. Furthermore, the presumption is "rebuttable." That means the employer or the WSIB can argue that the worker's PTSD arose from some situation or event outside of the work environment. You might recall that this is what happened to Dianne Paulin when the fact that she had been abused as a child was used to challenge her eligibility for benefits. As she said, shaking her head sadly, "They blame it on your childhood."

The duration of the effects of an "accident" can also be contested. In a 2016 letter to Premier Kathleen Wynne, the Ontario Network of Injured Workers Groups expressed dismay that the previous return-to-work policy, which provided "time to heal," had been replaced under the Wynne government by a new policy, "Better at Work," which requires an almost immediate return.

> There was a day when the WSIB recognized time to heal for injured workers. . . . The WSIB had a "Best Approaches Document", dated November 2005, and called "Recognizing Time to Heal—Assessing Timely and Safe Return to Work." . . . Here are some useful quotes:
> - "It is recognized that there are cases where 'rest' is an appropriate form of treatment and required in order to speed recovery and facilitate a successful return to work."
> - "We cannot ignore the impact of pain on an individual and on their functional abilities, especially in the early stages of recovery."

- "The patient should use common sense and listen to what his/ her body is trying to tell him. The patient should not ignore the warning signs of overdoing it, or allow a mild increase in discomfort to put him/her off work . . ."
- "The patient may be advised to see a medical practitioner for specific advice to facilitate timely recovery, either because of the severity of the initial injury, or if recovery appears to be slower than expected."
- "As outlined earlier, there are cases where 'rest' is an appropriate form of treatment, and required in order to speed recovery and facilitate a successful return to work."
- "Neither the WSIB nor the employer should insist on a return to work too early in these situations. Too early a return to work could cause damage, result in further injury for the worker, and more time away from work."[44]

ONIWG argues that this was "a very useful document to guide WSIB decision makers" and should be reinstated, as there is no good evidence to support the new policy of requiring early return.

The entire compensation system needs a revamp. It needs to be made more streamlined, less fraught with pitfalls and frustrating red tape. And it must be worker-friendly. Scott Sharp, who has suffered endless frustration, financial loss, and demoralizing treatment at the hands of the WSIB after his 2015 attack at the Guelph General Hospital, agrees it needs to change. He told us:

> They want you to throw up your arms and give up. I just had an individual [caseworker], who has been with WSIB for [many] years, and he said, "For the last seven I've been so disgusted with my job, but, because of my pension, I stick to it." He says their agenda is to mess with you. He says it is to make you frustrated, get you depressed, everything in the book in order to put pressure on your family, financial, so that you'll throw up your arms and quit and walk away.

ONIWG agrees that the compensation system's bureaucratic

and obstructive policies reduce the chances a worker will be compensated. It produced a report about the unreasonable practice of "deeming." An injured worker, who can no longer work in the job that led to the illness or injury, can be denied compensation because they are deemed to be capable of carrying out a different job—often a "phantom" one. This also happened to Dianne, when she was sent to work as a customer service representative after being unable to successfully return to her career as a nurse. The injured workers network report argues:

> Ontario was once a forerunner in this country when it came to treating injured workers with dignity and respect. Rather than trying to win a race to the bottom, it is high time we return to a position of leadership, and once again show Canada that when someone gets injured while contributing to our economy, they should not become a burden on their families, their communities, or taxpayers.[45]

Speaking out

The silencing of victims is psychologically damaging. In order to prevent ongoing harm, workers need some mechanism for sharing their experiences, fears, and trauma with others. We heard from study participants that staff who were assaulted, abused, or harassed are told they are not to share their experiences even with a family member or close friend. Staff are especially concerned that if they speak publicly about incidents of violence or the conditions at work that put them at risk for violence, they might be disciplined or terminated. When we asked a long-term care worker what would happen if she were to tell a reporter about what she is dealing with at work she answered, "I would be fired. Because [it would be considered] a breach of confidentiality. I signed a paper saying that I would never discuss *anything* to do with my job outside of the facility."

While not everyone is comfortable sharing their personal experiences and feelings, legal protection from reprisal must be in place to safeguard those who want to speak out.

Making prevention a priority

In a statement in response to the 2018 attack on the Health Sciences Centre ER nurse, the Winnipeg Regional Health Authority said

> it has made "significant efforts" to make changes to the security at HSC, including restrictions to visiting hours, panic alarms for staff and increased security mobile patrols and implementing card-access for staff.
>
> Alterations to the visiting hours led to a "significant drop" in incidents taking place which required security intervention after hours—down 39 per cent in December and 66 per cent in January compared to the year prior.[46]

A committee focusing on violence prevention policy at the Toronto East General Hospital stated in 2015 that a number of steps had been taken to protect staff from violence. It claimed that code white response times were reduced with the provision of personal alarms for staff. "After introducing these at our hospital, we saw Code White response time fall by more than 53%, to an average of 57 seconds." It reported that de-escalation training, alarms, and patient flagging have also "helped reduce use of force incidents at our hospital."[47]

The efforts of the management teams at Winnipeg Health Sciences and Toronto East General are laudable. The health care unions, however, say much more needs to be done as violence continues to plague workers in facilities across Canada and beyond.

A rally to stop violence against health care workers was held by CUPE in Kingston in March 2018. The union declared:

> A small investment in a Plexiglass barrier would have prevented a patient from stabbing a Perth/Smiths Falls hospital admitting clerk in the neck. Better alarms would have enabled nurses at Hamilton's St. Joseph's Health Centre to summon help when a patient, asked to take his medication, became violent. A nurse at a Royal Ottawa site was stabbed repeatedly by a previously violent patient and the

hospital fined earlier this summer for failing to "reassess the risk of workplace violence" as required by the Occupational Health and Safety Act.[48]

Many of the other solutions and prevention strategies put forward by the participants of our research and recommended in previous studies were also endorsed by the 2019 federal Standing Committee on Health, including collecting statistics on a nation-wide basis, increasing de-escalation training, public awareness campaigns, increasing health care staffing, and improving long-term care facilities.

Our recommendations

Based on our research, we offer the following observations and recommendations:

- Health care workers care about their patients. They need to be equipped to do their jobs well, to practise their chosen professions with compassion and care.
- Health care funding needs to be substantially increased. Staffing levels must meet the increasing demands. We need more beds, reduced wait times, and programs to minimize patient frustration, fear, and anger.
- The protections currently in place in the various health care facilities represented by our research study participants appear to be piecemeal and inconsistent. Universal province-wide protections need to be legislated.
- Assaulted workers must be provided with appropriate comfort, support, and empathy. It should not be automatically suggested they are to blame. Ongoing support and counselling should be available to those who would benefit from it. Consideration should be given to the needs of those who face verbal and/or physical aggression on a regular basis, such as those working with dementia patients.

- Management personnel should be required to undergo sensitivity training in order to understand the needs of staff who are, or have been, subjected to violence as well as to appreciate the importance of showing them respect and empathy.
- Health care workers must be provided with protections, such as personal alarms and additional staff when dealing with potentially aggressive patients or residents.
- The handling of code whites should be revamped, and specially trained security should be available.
- Violence training needs to include health care worker input and regular refresher courses. In order for system-wide changes to come about, the well-being of health care workers has to become a priority. The public must be informed of the real situation facing health care workers, from violence to understaffing and burnout. Community members have a right to know.

These are all immediate, practical recommendations that could be implemented to reduce the threat and impact of violence in the health care workplace. We know how to prevent violence, how to prevent injury when violence does occur, and how to improve the outlook for those who are affected by it. What, then, are the barriers to implementing prevention strategies that have proven to be effective? For insights into that question, we'll examine the lingering effects of the political history of health care and long-term care in Canada and the cultural impediments to social change.

7.

Rocky Road to Recovery

Hurdles to achieving the cure

Although in many ways it's clear what needs to be done, a number of obvious, and not so obvious, factors can be identified that hinder the elimination of violence in the health care system. The political history of health care in Canada—its rise and fall—not only set the stage for the epidemic of violence against staff, but also created barriers to change. For a start, perhaps we should begin to consider these obstacles to be hurdles, rather than barriers, because with sufficient will, financial resources, thoughtful planning, and implementation of strategies, they can be overcome.

What is stopping health care workers and the public from overcoming these obstacles? That's a big question with a complex answer. Over the years, we have learned—from personal experience and from our work as environmental and workplace health and safety advocates—that when you try to change conditions that contribute to poor health, premature death, and environmental harm, you are up against powerful vested interests. The architects and beneficiaries of our political economy are determined to maintain their control.

An ecological framework

The hurdles operate at many levels, from personal to bureaucratic. Understanding what they are and how they function can provide a starting point for developing strategies for change. One way to tackle the complexity is by breaking it down into layers using what's called an ecological framework, an approach that "conceptualizes violence as a multifaceted phenomenon grounded in an interplay among personal, situational, and sociocultural factors."[1] The World Health Organization, for example, used this approach to explore interpersonal violence at various levels, recognizing that the layers overlap and influence each other.

> The ecological framework is based on evidence that no single factor can explain why some people or groups are at higher risk of interpersonal violence, while others are more protected from it. This framework views interpersonal violence as the outcome of interaction among many factors.[2]

For the purpose of exploring factors involved in violence against health care workers, we have adapted the framework, identifying five different nested layers. Picture the model as rings in a slice of a tree trunk: individual factors are at the centre, surrounded by interpersonal relationship factors, then by organizational factors, encircled by societal and cultural factors, and lastly by policy and governance factors. By recognizing hurdles at each level, we can begin to consider ways in which to overcome them at that particular level and at multiple levels.

Individual

At the heart of the tree rings is the individual. This central layer is affected by each surrounding layer. Not everyone is subject to the same degree of violence, abuse, and exploitation, nor is everyone affected equally. Some health care workers have the protection of unions, while many do not. Registered occupational groups may be somewhat protected by their college. Other workers do not have such bodies to guide and assist them.

For example, PSWs in Ontario, even though they perform direct patient and resident care, do not have a regulatory college to provide them with protection, direction, and professional recognition. Allied health care workers are likewise unaffiliated. Individual staff do not believe they are in a strong enough position to advocate for change. Then there is the matter of one's paycheque. Writer and activist Upton Sinclair famously quipped how difficult it is to get a person to understand something when their salary depends on not understanding it.

And members of the public, on their own, who wish to support health care workers or are experiencing frustrations with the devolved system may feel similarly powerless.

Psychological hurdles

We have come to understand that the most insidious impediments to fighting for change may actually be our own fear, frustration, insecurity, powerlessness, and even self-blame. We say that without judgment. As citizens of a capitalist society controlled by economic interests, we are behaving just as those in the driver's seat have programmed us to behave. So let's dig deep and think about ways to reframe the problem of violence against health care staff.

Health care workers' energy and will to fight for change may be eroded by the trouncing their confidence and mental health have taken due to the normalization of violence, paired with the seeming lack of regard they experience from their employers and government. Rather than challenging the system to provide better protections, many health care workers said they turn to their own personal coping strategies—yoga classes, a glass of wine after work. Some choose to try to ignore the risks. Some become fatalistic. Some claimed to be able to compartmentalize and leave work at work. Most, however, said they arrive home stressed and exhausted. Research shows that, left unaddressed over time, the practice of merely coping with such emotions can cause sleep problems, anxiety, and depression. Such effects can be wide-ranging, varied, and completely individual.

Many people learn to blame themselves for the abuse they are subjected to or for being unable to cope with it. Rather than addressing the real issues, employers and the compensation system will sometimes accuse workers of not being resilient enough. Much has been written about the importance of resilience—and there is some truth in it. It is important to try to nurture oneself and to learn how to maintain a sense of optimism. But is it true, as philosopher Friedrich Nietzsche famously stated, that what does not kill us makes us stronger? Psychologists Dr. Tomas Chamorro-Premuzic and Dr. Derek Lusk suggest there is a "dark side" to the expectation of resilience. They write, "Too much resilience could make people overly tolerant of adversity. At work, this can translate into putting up with boring or demoralizing jobs—and particularly bad bosses—for longer than needed."[3]

In an article about burnout, family physician Dr. Talia Sierra likewise warns that using terms like "resilience" and "grit" tends to lay the blame on those who are experiencing difficulty coping, rather than addressing the causes of burnout.

> The problem is that we *can't* withstand everything. Burnout is a *normal* human response under excessive stress. *Anything* that is exposed to undue amounts of stress will break. People are no different. Clinicians are no different. We are *not* unbreakable.[4]

It is not far-fetched to assume that some health care staff who are regularly subjected to violence are suffering from symptoms of battered person syndrome, a term that is generally used to describe the emotional damage caused by intimate partner violence. The U.S. Centers for Disease Control and Prevention includes the following as forms of intimate partner violence: sexual abuse, stalking and threatening behaviour, physical abuse, and psychological aggression, such as "name-calling, humiliation, or coercive control, which means behaving in a way that aims to control a person."[5] Even after extracting themselves from an abusive relationship, survivors can experience ongoing symptoms of PTSD. They can experience sleeplessness, panic attacks, and flashbacks. The stories we heard from health care workers echoed many of these characteristics.

Gaslighting is also a form of violence. It is a hostile tactic used by abusers to destroy a victim's sense of themselves and erode their confidence in order to control them. Gaslighting is "a form of psychological abuse where a person or group makes someone question their sanity, perception of reality, or memories. People experiencing gaslighting often feel confused, anxious, and unable to trust themselves."[6] That definition reflects the treatment some health care workers described experiencing when they reported incidents to their supervisors. A psychiatric nurse who was seriously injured by a patient was interviewed for *Voices*. She said she was disturbed by the lack of care and concern she received from her employer. "No one even sent me a card saying hope you're feeling better soon . . . I was told, 'It's your fault.'"

A nurse who participated in our research was approached by her supervisor about how she had handled an aggressive patient who had assaulted her. She said that the way her actions were challenged made her begin to doubt herself.

> Then I start questioning myself. "Okay. Did I do this right? How could I have done that? What did I do wrong to make it worse? What could I have done differently to make it better?" And you do that as a worker.

Such lack of respect, concern, and support can contribute to feelings of poor self-worth. It can also contribute to individual feelings of isolation and alienation, which can be further compounded when one's co-workers have been conditioned to avoid rocking the boat or challenging management. In fact, co-workers may see one's attempts to challenge the status quo, even through the process of formally filing incident reports, as somehow a threat to their own security.

Under-reporting as a hurdle

A 2019 federal House of Commons parliamentary report entitled *Violence Facing Health Care Workers in Canada* noted that under-reporting of violent incidents and a resulting lack of statistical data are impediments to addressing this crisis.[7] Despite the danger to themselves, staff tend not to blame patients or residents who, because of mental illness or impairment, are not in control of their actions. They often view aggression from those with dementia with a degree of sympathy or detachment.

> At first it broke my heart. Now I'm used to it. I know that because they're sick or they have dementia, they probably don't even mean it; they don't realize they're angry. They don't know what's going on anymore.

As a result, verbal abuse, sexual harassment, and physical violence that do not result in significant injury are seldom formally reported. Caroline Criado Perez, author of the book *Invisible Women,* states that women in general tend not to report such workplace incidents. She attributes this data gap to "organisations not putting in place adequate procedures for dealing with the issue. Women don't report because they fear reprisals and because they fear nothing will be done—both of which are reasonable expectations in many industries."[8] As Dr. Karen Messing suggests in her book about women workers and solidarity, *Bent Out of Shape*, women have also been socialized to keep quiet about the way they are treated simply to keep the peace.[9]

Many of the staff we spoke with expressed doubt that the reporting of incidents would be of any benefit. They felt the reports are just a waste of time, and that they would not result in improvements or protections.

Sense of defeat

Working people and the general citizenry can feel like very small cogs in a very large wheel. Our sense of insignificance in the broader scheme of society, our own experiences and frustrations in trying to deal with bureaucracies, our financial insecurities in the face of a rapidly changing and impersonal economy, the inaccessibility of accurate information and a growing sense of distrust of the professionals—all serve to stultify resistance.

In a colourful collection of workers' stories collected by sociologists Dorothy Nelkin and Michael Brown in the early 1980s, it emerged that workers' sense of powerlessness may be the single most important impediment to improving occupational health and safety.

> We heard complaints that managers poorly understood the realities of the shop floor, yet ignored the judgments of workers who were in a position to offer solid contributions. [The workers were] resentful of a hierarchical system that discounted the validity of their experience.[10]

Workers' concerns may be dismissed as hysteria or ignorance or they may be placated by paternalistic authorities claiming to have the problem under control. Outspoken political analyst and commentator Noam Chomsky has grappled with the problem of workers feeling defeated before they even begin to demand justice.

> There was still a high level of [working-class culture] when I was growing up in the late 1930s. It took a long time to beat it out of workers' heads and turn them into passive tools; it took a long time to make people accept that this type of exploitation is the only alternative, so they better just forget about their rights and say, "Okay, I'm degraded."
>
> So the first thing that has to happen, I think, is we have to recover some of that old understanding. I mean, it all starts with

cultural changes. We have to dismantle all of this stuff culturally; we've got to change people's minds, their spirits, and help them recover what was common understanding.[11]

Some of the health care workers we spoke with expressed a sense of hopelessness and voiced concern that it may be impossible to eliminate the threat of violence. A nurse working in mental health told us adamantly, "You're never going to be able to prevent it." Another said, "I have to numb myself to it all. If I thought about it all the time, I'd probably have constant migraines—because there's nothing I can do." And yet another said, "My kids were upset, my youngest one especially didn't want me to go to work. My appetite diminished. I had a lack of confidence. I just got really deflated, really feeling like, why did I become a nurse?"

This sense of defeat presents a formidable obstacle to individual or collective advocacy.

Another hurdle is "learned helplessness."[12] The phenomenon was first described in relation to human behaviour in the 1970s by psychologist Dr. Martin Seligman, who theorized that it could lead to depression and inertia. He suggested that "people repeatedly exposed to stressful situations beyond their control develop an inability to make decisions or engage effectively in purposeful behavior."[13] Learned helplessness is one of the more significant blockers. What's the point of sticking your neck out if there is seemingly no chance that you can win?

And then there is the issue of the power needed to effectively fight for change. Michael Lerner, a therapist and researcher, has studied how many of us end up living lives that are much less fulfilling than we wish them to be and how our sense that there is nothing we can do to improve our situation leads to a cycle of further hopelessness.[14] He explains that our sense of powerlessness corrupts the way we see our own potential and leads to us accepting a less than satisfying existence.

One's socio-economic class position can strongly influence one's sense of power—or lack thereof. There are certainly well-developed power structures in place to control us. There are individuals and organizations that have very real power, usually because they have the wealth to impose their will and to influence government decisions that serve their interests. Individuals in positions of authority, such as managers or supervisors, can impose tyranny on those who fail to yield to them and their demands. They can control them by using fear and intimidation, such as blaming workers for being assaulted. According to Lerner, we tend make ourselves even more powerless by yielding to the system's power structures and by accepting failure without really trying—creating a self-defeating dynamic he calls "surplus powerlessness."[15]

In order for individuals to engage in efforts to improve their circumstances, whether in their personal lives or work lives, they need to feel deserving of safety, compassion, respect, and fair treatment. Exploited individuals have to reject outright the messaging that is being constantly directed at them. They need to reject the gaslighting and the disempowering messages they are hit with on so many levels. Members of the public have to reject the notion that you can't fight city hall.

Overcoming individual hurdles

The way out of the problem is collective resistance, individuals working together to demand change. For this to happen, though, we need to learn to rely on each other, to trust each other. This can be difficult when we have been so skilfully divided by the oppressive nature of our work, the broader culture, and the hierarchy that shapes us.

One of the first steps towards justice for health care workers is to repudiate the assertion that violence is part of the job or that boys will be boys. These are manipulative lies intended to disempower workers—to make them feel like giving up. There is safety and power in numbers. While collective resistance is key to making systemic and structural changes, we can all exercise some agency at an individual level. We can choose not to quietly endure the grabbing, sexual comments, and racist insults and threats.

Health care workers *can* tell—within bounds. A nurse who was interviewed for the OCHU-CUPE *Voices* booklet said she felt a moral obligation to tell the public what is really going on behind the health care institutions' doors.

> I'm speaking out now, because people are going to get hurt. People are already getting hurt. And it's just going to get worse. It's not going to get any better because they're not listening to anybody about any safety issues that we have. Staff should not be getting barricaded in the rooms. Staff should not be getting hit with chairs. Getting hit with remotes. . . . Getting hit with whatever they can find. I had a patient make a weapon out of a toilet seat!

While health care staff work to support the efforts of their union or association or their elected representatives to gain legislated whistle-blower protection, they can internally file incident reports and talk to their co-workers. They can report, within the confines of confidentiality agreements, to their union or association, their health and safety representatives, elected government representatives, or perhaps the office of their provincial ombudsman. For their own sake, for the sake of their co-workers, and for the well-being of the public, who need a safe system, health care workers need to be much freer to talk about their experiences.

> I think it's unfortunate that I can't talk publicly about having urinals thrown at me, having patients grab you and twist your arm, threaten you, having patients tell you that you're worthless and mean nothing. I don't think it's right that my identity has to be hidden. But I fear I'll be reprimanded. I don't want to lose my job, something that I love. And that's what the thoughts are surrounding this job. It's not fair. And I'm sure there are many other people who would love to speak out about their experiences . . . but they are too scared. Or too burnt out, and saying, "What's the point?" And it's heart-breaking.

Because the system does not provide the safeguards or supports health care workers say they need, some have resorted to calling the police for help. There are many reasons why police involvement might not be ideal, including systemic racism and lack of understanding of the needs of patients who are suffering from mental health problems, dementia, or addiction. Serious attempts by governments and management to control violence and a bolstering of specific support services and the social safety net would reduce or eliminate the need to involve law enforcement. However, without such measures in place, individual workers may feel they are left without much recourse.

Addressing the personal needs of health care workers is important for their safety and overall well-being. Besides protection, they must be given respect, recognition for their concerns, and mental health supports, such as trauma debriefing after a particularly harrowing incident or ongoing counselling to help them cope and recover from day-to-day traumas.

There seems to be general mistrust in employee assistance programs. Some who did take advantage of their EAP found it too limited and largely ineffectual. For example, after a particularly traumatic incident in a long-term care facility, staff were offered the option of minimal trauma debriefing—on their own time. "They did bring somebody in. You could go talk to them on your lunchtime if you wanted. They only did it for a couple of weeks."

Interpersonal relationships

Interpersonal relationships with one's family, friends, social networks, peer groups, co-workers, and by extension, unions or associations, can provide powerful supports and incentives. There are many ways in which our relationships can affect us—both negatively and positively. Some health care workers have understanding family members to support them when they return home exhausted or upset. Others live alone or are hesitant to let their partners or children know what they are going through, for fear they will worry or even demand the workers quit their professions. As a nurse explained, "It's actually affected my life, my relationship. It's affected my husband. I can't even talk to him about this hospital. He just says, you need to leave. We were talking about it this week, and he said, 'I told you a year ago to leave.'"

Let's talk about it

We all need to be able to talk openly about such issues as violence, fear, discrimination, and burnout with people who are confronting similar challenges. Unfortunately, the silencing of health care workers about violence on the job makes it difficult for them to reach out to anyone, other than perhaps co-workers or union representatives, about what they are experiencing. Rebecca Solnit, who wrote a book about the silencing of women as a form of control, says:

> Being unable to tell your story is a living death. . . . Violence against women is often against our voices and our stories. . . . Silence is what allowed predators to rampage through the decades unchecked. . . . Having a voice is crucial. It's not all there is to human rights, but it's central to them, and so you can consider the history of women's rights and lack of rights as a history of silence and breaking silence.[16]

A racialized hospital employee who has experienced related harassment and insults in the course of her work said:

> I don't think it matters what the violence is, whether it's a racial thing, a sexual thing, a physical thing, an emotional thing—what has to happen is, the person who has been violated needs to be validated that, "Yes, this occurred, and yes, we're hearing that you have these feelings and that this has hurt you, and that there is an incident." I think so often it is just swept under the rug and hidden away. And that's the worst thing that can happen for all of us. We need to be validated; we need respect.

Getting the issue out in the open within one's own close circle of influence can build support and solidarity. Health care staff might be surprised to hear about how co-workers themselves are feeling and about their experiences and ideas. Sharing with co-workers can be an important mental health strategy. A nurse who was seriously injured by an out-of-control patient said no to the EAP program, instead relying on co-worker support.

> My colleagues have just been so wonderful. They're so tired and so burnt out, some of them, but we all still try and just hold each other so tight and be supportive and see what we can do for each other because we can't depend on our corporation supporting us. As I heard somebody just saying, since we work in the health care field, that they have never seen such a corporation that does not care.

Another said, "I'm so privileged to have great co-workers. Thank god. We have to look after ourselves because there's nobody out there that's going to look after us."

Peer support is important. Allies are important. They are also key to getting a successful campaign against violence off the ground. We'll explore further the importance of building alliances in the next chapter.

Organizational

The next tree ring out is the organizational level—institutions and workplaces. The structure of an organization can cultivate an environment in which violence is allowed to proliferate. We asked Dr. Craig Slatin about the issue of employer responsibility for protecting workers from perpetrators of violence. He provided this thoughtful response, even going so far as to suggest that a lax employer can also be considered a perpetrator.

> The analysis and interventions for domestic violence and also community violence tend to focus on the perpetrator—holding the individual perpetrator accountable . . . Of course, individuals [patients or visitors] are the immediate source of an incident of

violence against a health care worker, but the employer has the responsibility to ensure that the workplace is free of hazardous exposures. Individual acts of violence in the workplace result from the lack of violence prevention programs or their failure.

Decisions that affect the safety of health care workers are being made by public servants and administrators who are following directives from government or, in the case of private care, their CEOs. Some of the health care staff we interviewed were somewhat sympathetic to their immediate supervisors, whom they understood to be acting within the confines of their institution's budgets, protocols, and rules. It puts the supervisors, who are often themselves medical professionals, into an uncomfortable position where they themselves potentially face moral injury when having to supervise care they know to be inferior due to a lack of resources. Some may come down hard on staff, ordering them to keep going when they know they are exhausted and suffering.

Administrative evil

That raises the question of the culpability of those in positions of power or authority who are simply carrying out their mandate despite its potentially harmful impacts. This ethical concept has been dubbed "administrative evil" by academics Guy Adams and Danny Balfour. That may seem like an extreme term, but it can be rather fitting when mandates carried out as part of one's job may cause others to suffer. Adams and Balfour write, "The common characteristic of administrative evil is that ordinary people within their normal professional and administrative roles can engage in acts of evil without being aware that they are doing anything wrong."[17]

The pair describe administrative evil as a continuum stretching between two extremes—horrendous acts such as the Holocaust at one end, down to "little white lies" at the other. Such disasters as the poisoning of the drinking water in Flint, Michigan, or the mercury poisoning of the First Nations communities in Grassy

Narrows and Whitedog fit the definition. The individual, agency, or committee making decisions, providing directions, or issuing orders may not be fully aware of the implications of their actions. So can they really be blamed? According to Adams and Balfour:

> If administrative evil means that people inflict pain and suffering and death on others, but do so *not* knowingly or deliberately, can they be held responsible for their actions? We believe the answer is yes, but when ordinary people inflict pain and suffering and even death on others in the course of performing their "normal" organizational or policy role, they usually justify their actions by saying that they were just following orders and doing their job. This reflects the difficulty of identifying administrative evil, and the possibility of missing it altogether, or perhaps worse, calling mistakes or misjudgments evil. We maintain that identifying administrative evil is most difficult within one's own culture and historical time period.[18]

The decision to curtail staffing in Ontario's hospitals, the lack of regulatory protections for health care workers subjected to violence, or the failure to adequately support those who have been injured might well fit the criteria of inflicting pain and suffering and death in the course of carrying out one's regular duties. While governments are in the driver's seat around funding and regulations—and should not be let off the hook for their decisions—those carrying out the government's mandate have clear responsibility as well.

Structural violence

The position of health care workers within the structure of their workplaces puts them at a distinct disadvantage. Presenting an overview of literature on occupational violence, Dr. Katherine Lippel explains, quoting from Dr. Albert Banerjee and colleagues:

> The term "structural violence" has been used "to identify the heavy workloads, low levels of decision-making autonomy, low status,

rigid work routines and insufficient relational care as forms of violence. Not only are these poor working conditions experienced as sources of suffering, but they prevent care workers from providing the kind of care they know they are capable of."[19]

Dr. Lippel writes that when organizations are focused on the bottom line, workplace safety can suffer.

> Exposure to a broad range of psychosocial risk factors, including organisational factors, has been found to be associated with bullying and harassment. Job strain (high work demands with low decision latitude), job insecurity and a poor psychosocial safety climate are known determinants of workplace bullying, findings confirmed in reviews of the international scientific literature and in studies from Australia, Belgium, and Québec.

Underfunding

Underfunding is frequently cited as a significant obstacle to preventing violence. Management's attitude towards staff's concerns is reflective of the budgetary constraints they are working under. The prioritizing of efficiency and task completion leaves little room for addressing patients' or residents' frame of mind or staff's ability to provide the degree of compassionate care that patients and residents need for their human dignity and to keep them from lashing out in frustration, anger, fear, or confusion.

Task orientation

Health care work is becoming increasingly task oriented and produces measurable outcomes that are documented and used to shape budgets and justify funding requests. In an article criticizing the assembly line nature of care, Dr. Pamela Hartzband and Dr. Jerome Groopman use the term "medical Taylorism" to describe the disturbing trend in which efficiencies are prioritized. Patient or resident needs are reduced to their particular medical or personal care problem, rather than the individual being treated as a whole person with complex needs.[20] They also view the increasing use of technology as part of the medical Taylorism trend.

While technology has brought with it speed of access to digital records, and during the COVID-19 crisis, it became the only means by which some patients or residents were able to communicate with their families, aspects of technology may be interfering with patient care. Those making decisions about the allocation of staffing resources and time management need to take into account that, in part because of the learning curve, digital data entry can sometimes be more time-consuming than hard-copy charting. This in turn affects patient care, and by extension, worker safety when frustrated patients become exasperated with what they experience as neglect. It may go even further than just a time issue. According to Dr. Arthur Kleinman, a professor of psychiatry and medical anthropology at Harvard University, "Clinicians have become so tied up with technologies, and so tied up with delivering the technologies effectively, that they are forgetting about the role that care plays."[21]

The accuracy of the digitized data may also be unreliable. We heard from health care workers that they cannot possibly capture the detailed information requested, such as how many ounces of water a resident drank at a meal, and they are often too rushed to accurately enter the data they do have. They often feel they have to document whatever is expected of them, however impossible the demands are, in order to protect themselves from discipline for not meeting the expectations. As a result, we do not have a clear picture of the level of care patients or residents are truly receiving or of the conditions that lead to violence. These missing pieces of information present yet another hurdle to change.

Hierarchy

Workers' efforts to achieve needed protections are also hindered by the hierarchy that is endemic to health care culture. Hospital administrators tend to be more responsive to the needs and demands of staff who are higher up in the hierarchy, such as doctors. Author Robert W. Fuller argues that what he calls "'rankism' in workplaces can lead to mistreatment based on people's education, social class or job function. . . . No one deserves condescension or the indignity of not being acknowledged and recognized by others."[22] That is not to say that doctors are fully protected from violence. They, too, are often subjected to verbal and physical assault, especially in ERs.

Public is kept in the dark

Silencing, which we highlighted as an individual-level hurdle, is rooted in organizational practices. It is one of the more insidious obstacles to prevention because it means the public is left largely unaware of just how severe and widespread violence is. Yet public demand and lobbying for change depend on awareness. The 2019 federal parliamentary report acknowledged the lack of public awareness of this growing problem.[23] Health care workers agree.

> I think it would make a difference if it was out in the public. I think I should be able to stand up there and tell the stories that have to be told because a lot of people don't realize what's happening. And I think that's tragic.

> I wish the public were better educated as to what really happens in a long-term care facility. The public needs to know the reality—our reality. You know what? They really only get a bath once every two or three weeks. I know some that just got a bed bath every eight or nine weeks. But you are not allowed to tell the family.

The fear-generated reluctance to speak out has fuelled a culture of silence about the day-to-day experience of health care staff. This was graphically highlighted in 2017 when *Time* magazine designated "The Silence Breakers" as Person of the Year. The story was written in response to the growing #MeToo movement that challenged the silencing of women who had been abused. The cover photo shows five women who played a significant role in bringing sexual harassment and violence to the public's attention. There was to be a sixth person on the cover, but only her shoulder and arm are visible. They belong to a nurse who had requested that her identify not be revealed because she feared being fired for bringing workplace violence into the public eye.

The colleges that regulate registered staff also play a role, however well-intentioned, in the problem of silencing. A nurse explained to us that, because of the need to protect patient confidentiality, silencing is not just an administrative practice. She said, "The College of Nurses doesn't want you to [publicly talk about assaults]. You're accountable and that would be grounds for disciplinary action." Even physicians are hesitant to report. An ER doctor told *Maclean's*, "There's this culture of acceptance, this culture of being afraid to make a complaint or ask for help because we could lose our licence to practise medicine."[24] In 2020, the *Ontario Medical Review* explained that doctors were generally unprotected by labour laws and had little recourse when it comes to violence.

> Aside from unclear rights and protection after a workplace violence event, physicians are often subjected to threats or actual disciplinary complaints to their regulatory colleges by the perpetrators of violence, further re-victimizing the physician victim and perpetuating the initial trauma impact.[25]

There is certainly value in maintaining a professional code of conduct. But when it comes to violence, a balance must be found that does not leave workers without a voice when it comes to exposing the problem and seeking support.

Democratic institutional governance

Hospital boards are setting priorities and making budgetary decisions without input from staff or the general public. In order to reflect the true wishes and needs of the public, hospital boards need to be publicly elected, just as school boards and public utilities are. Health care workers, the true experts, need to be represented on the boards, as they, better than anyone, know what is needed to enable them to provide the care their patients deserve.

Societal and cultural

The next ring outward in our slice of tree trunk would be the societal and cultural level—culture, customs, and beliefs. We raised earlier the normalization of violence as a risk factor. It is also a significant hurdle. Health care workers told us that violence has, in practical terms, become accepted in many of their workplaces. Some feel that it is being increasingly viewed by management and even their co-workers as part of the job. The normalization of violence has significant consequences for the well-being of health care workers and for the quality of care that the public receives. It is part of a broader phenomenon of social tolerance for involuntary risks to well-being.

Occupational and environmental hazards have become so commonplace they are now a way of life. We continue to overlook chemical exposures in our workplaces or accept the risks as the price we pay to earn a living, despite increasing evidence that many cancers and other diseases are work-related. We begrudgingly accept guidelines for fish consumption, hardly questioning why the fish are contaminated with mercury and other persistent toxins in the first place. We half listen to the smog alerts on the morning newscasts that caution vulnerable people to remain indoors to protect themselves from air pollutants related to the poorly regulated burning of fossil fuels. We put up with beach closings, grumbling more about the inconvenience than the environmental impacts. We accept blame for our own skin cancers, forgetting it was the pollutant-related destruction of the earth's protective ozone layer that increased the levels of ultraviolet radiation beaming down with the summer sunshine. We attend the funerals of miners and insulators, residents of First Nations reserves, and university professors who have died from asbestos-related diseases, all the while ignoring Canada's legacy of mining and exporting asbestos for decades after it was known to be harmful. We dutifully buy our carrots at the grocery store after being warned not to eat root vegetables from our own urban gardens, the soil having been contaminated by years of leaded gasoline use. It has taken us forty years to finally pay attention to the dire climate change predictions of scientists. Still, there are industry-orchestrated deniers who turn red in the face trying to convince us that human-induced climate change is a hoax.

Why are we seemingly so complacent about being denied the basic right to safe workplaces, and to clean air, water, soil, food, and sunlight? Perhaps our innate trusting nature stands in the way of protecting ourselves. Our ancient collective social and economic systems depended heavily on trust. Those simple collective systems have long since evolved into today's colossal global economic systems. Yet most people, to their credit, continue to exhibit a high degree of trust. At a basic level, we feel safe eating a can of chicken noodle soup that strangers have prepared for us. We drive down the road having faith that the cars in the oncoming traffic are not going to suddenly veer into our lane. And many people accept assurances that the work they do or the air they breathe won't do them harm—that the government is carrying out its mandated role of protecting them.

There are powerful outside forces shaping our beliefs and actions. We have been lulled into a level of complacency, self-blame, and inertia by our schools, the powerful commercial mass media, and societal institutions whose main function seems to be to put out incipient fires of discontent. Have you ever asked your local chief medical officer of health, for example, about environmental health concerns in your area? Chances are you will hear nothing about possible connections between air pollution and community disease rates or about emissions from the local plastics plant. You will most likely be told about the health unit's diligent monitoring of vaccination rates or their efforts to promote workplace and community personal wellness programs.

Violence against health care staff has to a certain extent become normalized. It is not simply an occasional aberration, in which an individual patient assaults an individual staff person. It is widespread and out of control. Nor does violence occur in a void. As stated in a report jointly released by a coalition that includes the ILO and WHO:

> There is growing awareness that confronting stress and violence requires a comprehensive approach. Instead of searching for a single solution good for any problem and situation, the full range of causes which generate stress and violence should be analysed and a variety of intervention strategies adopted. There is also growing awareness that stress and violence at work is not merely an episodic, individual problem but a structural, strategic problem rooted in wider social, economic, organizational and cultural factors.[26]

Violence within health care settings reflects broader cultural violence as well as structural violence emanating from economic and political factors.[27]

Sexism

Because women make up most of the health care workforce (in 2018, over 90 per cent of the 431,769 nurses in Canada were women[28]), sexism increases the ways they are exploited as workers. Dr. Bill Whitehead, a nursing educator in the U.K., has studied oppression among workers in the nursing profession. Whitehead holds that, "traditionally, [oppression] refers to the unfair use of power by a ruling group over another group within a social situation." He concludes:

> The nursing profession is oppressed on two social fronts. Nurses are overwhelmingly female and as such—in line with feminist theory— the entire profession (including the men within it) is subjugated in the same unjust way that women are within society.
>
> The majority of nurses identify themselves as being working class and the ONS [Office for National Statistics] categorises them below doctors and pharmacists in its social stratification. This posi-

tion in the social hierarchy leads to unfair discrimination and the injustice of oppression by the more powerful groups. Consequently, nurses are oppressed in the same way as other working class professions as part of the economic and social structure of society.[29]

Nurses' roles have changed dramatically over the past half century. Gone are the crisp white uniforms and caps. In discussions we had with a group of retired RNs several years ago, we were horrified to hear how in the 1950s, 1960s, and even into the 1970s nurses were expected to stand up when a doctor passed the nursing station or entered a room; they also had to step off the elevator to allow a doctor to enter.

In an article outlining the often troubled partnership between doctors and nurses, Dr. Lazar Greenfield wrote: "Much of the conflict is rooted in the historical dominant role of the physician and subservient role of the nurse as envisioned by [Florence] Nightingale. This relationship has continued to be reinforced by gender, education, and remuneration."[30] Nurses' professional responsibilities have moved far beyond the function of doctors' subordinates. Today they play a much larger role as medical practitioners. However, along with the respect they now experience as professionals, they suffer the effects of overwork, high demand, and burnout.

PSWs emerged as another important health care occupational group. Their ranks grew dramatically in the 1990s when governmental efforts to trim health care budgets were underway. PSWs replaced many of the more skilled and costly nurses.[31] They now provide much of the hands-on work in long-term care and home care. The overwhelming majority of Ontario's approximately one hundred thousand PSWs are women, and many are racialized.[32]

Occupational health and safety hazards in workplaces that have predominantly women employees have not received the same attention as those traditionally employing mostly men. Dr. Messing, who has creatively studied women and work using techniques she and her colleagues have pioneered, writes, "Women's health, women's work, and the occupational health of male workers are all extensively studied, but occupational health has not usually been analyzed by gender."[33] Violence against health care workers has been largely unaddressed.[34] As Dr. A. Banerjee and colleagues suggest:

> The failure to adequately address ongoing risk, the normalization of violence and the blaming of victims is characteristic of violence against women. We therefore question why gender has typically been absent in analyses of health-sector violence.[35]

Gender-based violence continues to thrive in our patriarchal society. Violence against health care workers is part of that overall social dynamic. The media, for example, often either depicts these workers as sexy and open to sexual exploitation, like the female nurses on *Grey's Anatomy* that are more than happy to sleep with the male doctors, or as miserable shrews, like Nurse Ratched in the Netflix series by that name, who is presented as a sociopathic tyrant who deserves to be maligned or assaulted. You may have seen the revealing, come-hither, sexy nurse costumes available at Halloween or for masquerade parties. If you search online, you'll find hundreds of styles, complete with plunging necklines, short skirts, and fishnet stockings. Ask a nurse who has spent the day fending off unwanted advances, groping hands, and verbal sexual abuse if they find such a portrayal entertaining or funny.

Women in general are no strangers to violence. Here are some alarming facts: half of all women in Canada have experienced at least one incident of physical or sexual violence since the age of sixteen; about every six days, a woman in Canada is killed by her intimate partner; and of the 83 police-reported intimate partner homicides in 2014, 67 of the victims—over 80 per cent—were women.[36] Now women increasingly face violence on the job. Dr. Robert Storey, the former head of labour studies at McMaster University, observed:

> Women workers are getting injured at ever-higher rates where their numbers are growing, and perhaps more importantly, women work-

ers in health care and education occupations area being subjected to forms of violence, e.g., assaults and other forms of attacks, that heretofore have been restricted to other occupations such as police officers.[37]

When you add sexism into the mix, you end up with an alienating working environment. And, as happens in broader society, women are seen as nurturers and self-sacrificing caregivers, or even more odiously, somehow responsible for or deserving of the abuse they endure. A nurse told us:

> It's part of an overall societal thing of violence against women because it does appear that management tends to victimize or put the blame on the victim. But when you're assaulted, it's not your fault, right?

Somehow many women have learned to normalize and to internalize discrimination and the threat of violence. Without much thought, almost as second nature, women will avoid situations that might put them in harm's way. For example, if they pull into a parking lot and notice a man sitting alone watching them from a parked car, they will automatically decide to park farther away—under the bright lights. Women will often avoid making eye contact with a group of men on a sidewalk or change their route. It is just a fact of life for women—they know at some gut level that they are at a higher risk because of their gender. But they pay a price for this caution, for the deeply ingrained awareness of their vulnerability and the coping mechanisms they rely on. Not only is their freedom of movement affected, along with their choices and sense of themselves, but they quietly live with the stress of that underlying element of fear and hypervigilance.

An intersectional lens

Structural and cultural violence can manifest as discrimination and disregard for many vulnerable, oppressed, or marginalized groups besides women. It can target particular sexual orientations or gender identities, immigrants, Black, Indigenous, or other racialized people, people with disabilities or health challenges, or with characteristics of physical appearance, belief or religion, personal practices, or occupational or socio-economic status. Discrimination and violence are deeply entrenched in our culture, organizations, relationships, and even in our feelings and beliefs as individuals. Discrimination is like an invasive cancer. The fact is, despite progress in some areas of human social organization, we live and work in a world that continues to be patriarchal, racist, colonialist, and stratified.

Viewing the issues health care workers described to us—psychological distress, inadequate protection, inconsistent policies, government failings, barriers to achieving needed changes, and the need to exercise their own agency—through an intersectional lens may provide clearer insights into the challenges workers face in overcoming them. Intersectionality acknowledges that gender, sexuality, race, and class intersect in ways that affect people's life experiences in the broader society and at work.

Health care worker exploitation can also be better understood when viewed through the lens of feminist political economy. Dr. Pat Armstrong and colleagues contend that health is "fundamentally related to the distribution of resources and power, which in turn are linked to gender and race—in short, to the political economy."[38] The prevalent social, political, and economic climate propagates inequalities related to gender, sexuality, racial identity, and social class.

Anti-gay prejudice

Violence against LBGTQ+ people is also rampant in society and, by extension, the health care workplace. A 2018 report from Statistics Canada states:

> Excluding violence committed by an intimate partner, sexual
> minority Canadians were more likely to have experienced physical

or sexual assault both since age 15 and in the past 12 months than heterosexual Canadians. Violence targeting sexual minority Canadians was also more likely to result in injuries than violence committed against heterosexual Canadians. . . .

Transgender Canadians were more likely to have experienced violence since age 15, and also more likely to experience inappropriate behaviours in public, online and at work than cisgender Canadians.[39]

A nurse told us how hard it is to be constantly harassed by patients and even some of his co-workers because he is gay. He said he often feels threatened. He even feared that he might be recognized and targeted by a patient on his own time away from work.

We live in a building; a quiet life. I walk my dogs and am kind of sporty. I have this feeling that somebody [from my job] is going to try to approach me in my personal life and maybe harm me or my husband or my pets in some way.

This nurse was seriously injured by a patient who was under the influence of drugs, and believes his sexuality was factor. "That's how I think the violence began with the patient that attacked me."

Racism

We were unable to find accurate current statistics about the racial make-up of the overall health care workforce in Canada. But we do know that racism in health care has deep roots. Black people, for example, were barred from nursing training in Canada until the 1940s and continue to suffer inequalities. Keisha Jefferies, a PhD candidate in Nursing at Dalhousie University, wrote in an article for The Conversation:

Overall, Black nurses are largely absent from leadership positions and specialty practice areas such as intensive care. Instead, Black nurses are often streamlined into areas that are more physically demanding and strenuous. At the same time, Black people are concentrated in entry-level positions, non-specialty roles or in non-licensed clinical roles such as personal care workers.[40]

In 2009, 42 per cent of the PSWs surveyed in Ontario self-identified as visible minority.[41] The COVID-19 crisis in long-term care shone light on the workforce caring for residents, many of whom are PSWs or aides. It has been reported that "racialized women make up 13 per cent of the total [overall] workforce, but 25 per cent of workers in nursing and residential care facilities."[42] In greater Montreal, which was especially hard hit by the virus, "up to 80 percent of the aides in long term care facilities are racialized women, mostly Black and Maghrebi."[43]

During interviews with researchers, many health care staff said they were regularly subjected to racist taunts and insults. A Chinese Canadian nurse interviewed for a *Toronto Star* story about racism against health care workers estimates that about 40 to 50 per cent of staff in her Vancouver hospital are of "ethnic minorities." A Black health care aide who was interviewed said she was shocked and upset by the treatment she was sometimes subjected to and recalled an incident in which a resident used the N-word in reciting the "Eeny, meeny, miny, moe" nursery rhyme.[44] Indigenous people, on the other hand, are under-represented among registered health care professions, which makes the provision of care to their communities more challenging.[45] And as the OCHU-CUPE poll revealed, a substantial majority of staff who are racialized, Indigenous, visible minority, or recently immigrated said they had experienced abuse related to their race or immigration status.

We all have a responsibility to challenge and eliminate racism at a broad societal level. But this is going to take time. The government and employers have an ethical obligation to protect all of their staff now. Studies show that racism has a serious impact on both the mental health and physical health of people of colour.

Dr. Abe Reinhartz, a colleague and physician with decades of experience working in occupational health, described an experience he'd had in a large urban hospital. A racialized nurse came to him, very upset, after being repeatedly insulted, harassed, and threatened by a patient. Dr. Reinhartz quickly intervened, telling the patient her behaviour was completely unacceptable and demanding that she apologize to the nurse or be "immediately discharged from the hospital."

As we heard from the health care workers we spoke with, not everyone is fortunate enough to have a compassionate professional to assist them. A racialized long-term care worker told us she is regularly physically and verbally abused because of her race. "I've gotten nails dug into my hands, I've gotten my glasses hit off my face, kicked in the stomach as well as racist comments, big time." She was being especially targeted by an individual who required a significant level of physical care, putting the caregiver at risk of injury. She said she finally called the Ministry of Labour after receiving no help from her employer. "They did come in and do an investigation, but really they did nothing for me."

Class prejudice

Another form of discrimination that isn't talked about as much is class prejudice or classism, which may be more at play than we consciously realize. In her book about working-class life, Sarah Smarsh writes:

> The person who drives a garbage truck may himself be viewed as trash. The worse danger is not the job itself but the devaluing of those who do it. A society that considers your body dispensable will inflict a violence upon you.[46]

Those who provide patients' most basic personal care—bathing, dressing, changing wet or soiled incontinence products, delivering meals and spoon feeding, cleaning rooms, administering medicine or physiotherapy, lifting and transporting—may be viewed by some as mere servants whose own lives and well-being don't really matter. This seems to be especially the case for those at the lower end of the medical occupational hierarchy.

The intersections of race, gender, class, and other societal and structural dysfunctions may not be at the root of all violence against health care staff, but they are formidable and complex hurdles that need to be addressed at many levels. A Black woman, for example, experiences not just sexism, but a racist form of sexism that is used against Black women. If she is also working as a health care aide or cleaner, she may experience class prejudice as well, being seen as "just the help," as one Black health care aide described it.[47]

Policy and governance

The outer layer of our tree trunk slice, out by the bark, is the policy and governance level. The health care staff we interviewed and the statistics available from various sources, including surveys and compensation records, indicate that existing regulatory, legislative, and budgetary protections are inadequate to prevent violence. In other words, the problems go well beyond individual workplaces. As a nurse told us, "I am not only pointing fingers at my employer. I believe it's a systemic problem." It is understandable why staff feel a sense of powerlessness as they watch the health care system being eroded.

The pending Ontario Time to Care Act, if passed, would improve staffing levels in long-term care. Unfortunately, shortly after the second reading of the bill, the government, while claiming to be committed to the goal of four hours of care per resident per day, announced that the increases would be phased in gradually and would not be fully in effect until 2025.[48] The Registered Nurses' Association of Ontario issued a statement saying it is "shocked by the lack of urgency" in the roll-out of the changes.[49]

Unforeseen effects of some policies

Managerial policies and government regulatory decisions are sometimes made that benefit one party while putting another at risk. For example, there is an apparent conflict between patient rights and worker rights related to the controversial practice of using restraints. Staff we interviewed explained that, since 2001, they have been required to minimize the use of restraints, which can be physical, chemical (pharmaceutical), or environmental. This is a laudable policy. Restraints can be physically and psychological harmful to patients, but the patients themselves—or the staff caring or them—can be hurt if patients are in the midst of a psychotic episode, raging, or out of control. Since the standard of care limiting the use of restraints has come into effect, no comparable protections against violence have been put into practice to accommodate this principle.

> So, they came out with the Patients' Bill of Rights. It's this pendulum of "this isn't working anymore, so we've got to try something else," but there's no medium. The pendulum doesn't stop. It swings way to the opposite end. All *we* have is a Code of Conduct.

PSW Heather Neiser believes that patients and residents deserve protection and respect. She also believes workers are equally deserving of protection. She explained:

> I understand we work where our residents live. I understand their rights. But what about our rights as workers? Do we not have the right to a safe workplace, the right to go to work and come home in one piece, the right to be treated with respect from families and our employer?

Study participants did express dismay that, in some cases, due largely to understaffing, the use of physical and chemical restraints seems to be increasing again.

> Now we're going back to all the restraints, because there's not enough staff. And now, I think that's in every part of the hospital. Like look at emerg. I had never seen anybody tied to a stretcher in my day ever. Now it's there every day.

The application of physical restraints must be done in such a manner that the health care workers doing the restraining are protected. It's essential to have enough staff to help manage an out-of-control patient. Specialized training is also crucial. But Scott Sharp, who was the go-to person for restraining violent patients, largely because of his strength and stature, was given only minimal training.

> They gave you a one-day course on restraining and how to handle people and they checked off the box . . . No offence to the people teaching the course, but they never even worked in the health care field before. So they would be going on about something irrelevant and we'd be going, "That never happens! What are you talking about?"

Scott is a real-life example of the harm that can arise when restraints are not utilized in a timely manner. Even though he was with an experienced team of co-workers the night he was assaulted, the patient was able to break free of their grasp, resulting in Scott's life-changing injuries.

In 2018, endeavouring to protect health care workers from violence, London Health Sciences established a new flagging policy whereby patients, after being screened and deemed potentially aggressive, were required to wear purple arm bands. Nearly ten thousand patients were flagged in the first year. The effort, however, was met with a considerable number of complaints.

> Advocates say the practice unfairly targets people who have a mental illness and infringes on patients' human rights.
>
> In fact, about a dozen human rights complaints have been filed against the hospital and 150 patients have appealed their "violent" designation.[50]

One of the psychiatric nurses we spoke with talked about the problem of doctors taking patients off medications without considering the safety of the hands-on caregivers.

We had to give him some medication to really calm him down because he actually was getting sexually aggressive . . . This one doctor usually comes in and takes them off all their medication—this is where the violence starts. So he just happened to be in on this one weekend covering and I thought, if he changes one single medication on this patient, I am going to lose my mind. Because we finally got him at a level where he wasn't aggressive anymore. And the doctor opened the patient's door and said, "Oh, hello." He was kind of talking to him and he kicked him in the shin. And this doctor closed the door; he turned and looked at me and said, "He just kicked me." I said, "Good. Now you know how we feel." And he just kind of looked at me and then left. Didn't touch his chart, didn't change any medication.

Minimal legal rights and protections

Health care workers have fewer legal rights than many other workers. Their collective bargaining rights are legally restricted. They cannot strike to demand improvements in their working conditions. In addition, under Ontario law, health care workers have only a limited right to refuse work they believe to be unsafe. As one of the nurses we talked to told us, "The patients at the hospital, they have a patient advocate. There's no advocate for the nurse, is there, really? No." In reference to the right of a patient not to be restrained, she added, "We don't have the right not to be punched."

Many health care workers said they feel frustrated with their joint union-management health and safety committees. Challenging the current paralysis in the committees' function should become a priority for every local union. Health and safety committee members should prioritize the issue of violence and ensure that all union members are made aware of it. Local union meeting time should be set aside for dissecting violent incidents— examining their immediate and root causes, needed changes, whether the incidents were formally reported, and whether they were adequately addressed by the workplace joint committee. If management fails to appropriately respond to violations, complaints should be filed with the Ministry of Labour. If a sufficient number of local unions undertook such actions, the pressure would begin to mount for ministry engagement.

Workers are also feeling frustrated with the police and the labour ministry. Law enforcement, government agencies, and judicial systems provide few safeguards. During a conference presentation, PSW Heather Neiser expressed her annoyance with existing regulatory safeguards:

> When police are called, they talk employees out of charging residents . . . Management doesn't follow their own policies, and the Ministry of Labour is employer-friendly and does not protect the worker. We need to come up with ways to challenge the [ministry] inspectors.

There is currently no legislative protection for workers who choose to break the silence and speak out about violence. France Gélinas, an Ontario NDP member of provincial parliament, introduced a private member's bill in 2017 that, if passed, would provide protection for health care workers who speak out about violence. She explained to the Sudbury media:

> Workers in Ontario hospitals have been clear that they want protection from workplace violence and their employers have ignored them. When they speak out about violence or harassment, they are putting themselves at risk of reprisal from their employer. . . . The bill I'm introducing . . . will protect workers in all settings from reprisal for speaking out against violence or harassment. No one should head to work worried about being assaulted. Even more so, no one's career should be negatively affected for raising concerns about their personal safety or dignity.[51]

Gélinas introduced an updated bill in 2019 entitled Speaking Out About Workplace Violence and Workplace Harassment Act.[52] It passed first reading but, at the time of writing, continues to await further readings and assent.[53]

A possible deterrent to committing violence against staff might be the laying of criminal charges. However, according to several of the research participants we interviewed, patients with dementia or mental health issues are often considered by law to be not criminally responsible for their acts of aggression. While understandable, this designation hinders workers' efforts for protection as it sends a signal to patients that violence will have no consequences. It also eliminates some of the validation that might be needed by an assaulted person, which might help lead to healing and closure. While we were interviewing a health care worker who had sustained a serious head injury at the hands of an irate patient, he was informed that the criminal charge he had attempted to file had been dropped. He was shattered by the news.

> You feel so defeated through the process. He also pulverized the security guard that was monitoring him. What was used in the patient's defence was his medical status—an acquired brain injury.

The issue of charging mentally ill or challenged patients remains controversial. While health care workers are asking the criminal justice system to help to curb the inexcusable violence against them, social justice and human rights groups are calling for a more nuanced approach.

When we raised the idea at an OCHU-CUPE workshop that the law be changed to increase the repercussions for patients who perpetrate violence, a health care worker, who self-identified as First Nations, said she was not supportive of leaving such matters to the whims and prejudices of the legal and criminal justice systems. She said she feared Indigenous or other racialized patients or residents might be unfairly treated due to systemic racism. Others said extenuating circumstances must be taken into account when patients are being aggressive, such as the stress caused by one's illness, mental health problems, or dementia and that mentally vulnerable patients or residents might be unfairly charged.

Several health care workers said, while it's not ideal, laying criminal charges was necessary for their own protection. They suggested that the courts should be capable of sorting out who should be held criminally responsible, yet police and the courts are being publicly called out for heavy-handedness against people with mental health or addiction problems and for the inequitable treatment of Indigenous people, Black people, and people of colour. An organization that has emerged in Canada called Doctors for Defunding the Police wants spending on law enforcement reduced and instead applied to services that might help to support those who could otherwise end up in the criminal justice system. Following several deaths that occurred in police custody, the group stated: "These deadly tragedies highlight concerns around police response to individuals in distress or experiencing mental health crises and the use of lethal force against Black and Indigenous people."[54] The Canadian Cultural Mosaic Foundation proposes, rather than using law enforcement to deal with social and mental health crises, that society instead "address the root causes of crime" by investing in "education, mental health supports, affordable housing, youth programs, accessible transit and employment opportunities."[55]

Michael Hurley, president of OCHU-CUPE, which strongly supports the amendment to allow charges, admits the amendment itself is not the cure for violence against health care workers, saying it is "a complex issue."

> It is rooted in society's attitude towards violence against women; the impact that cuts to services like mental health and addictions are having; increased drug use; public impatience with longer waits within institutions for attention and the way in which work is managed within health care. The problem of violence won't go away just with this amendment to the Criminal Code. But talking about the problem, exposing it and working for change will turn this problem around.[56]

Most health care workers we spoke with say holding accountable aggressors who are deemed to be mentally competent is not too much to expect.

If I walked into a police station and slapped the first officer I saw, I'd be charged. I'd be thrown in jail and they'd probably throw away the key. However, if someone walks into our emergency department and slaps us upside the head or spits at us or sexually assaults us—it's okay, because they're our client, they're our patient. They don't get charged with assault; they don't get charged with a criminal offence, even though that's what it is.

Suffice to say, the issue is contentious and would require a much more in-depth discussion than we can offer here.

In 2019, an amendment to the federal Criminal Code was introduced by Don Davies, a federal member of Parliament and vice-chair of the Standing Committee on Health. When introducing his proposed amendment, he told the House of Commons:

This legislation would amend the Criminal Code to require a court to consider that if the victim of an assault is a health care sector worker, this fact would be an aggravating circumstance for the purposes of sentencing. . . . This bill sends a strong message that those who provide such critical services must be treated with respect and security . . . and we must take care of theirs.[57]

The 2019 federal parliamentary report, *Violence Facing Health Care Workers in Canada,* acknowledged the need for judicial engagement, but to date this bill has not been passed into law.

So, whom can health care workers go to? According a nurse we interviewed:

What I think there needs to be is a system in place, a neutral system, outside of Human Resources, because [workers are] afraid for their employment if they go to HR. But if there was a third party that was arm's length, like some sort of ombudsman, an advocate, an independent third party, that people could deal with when racial issues come up or violence in the workplace.

Protective legislation needs to be enacted and adequate

financial resources allocated to ensure safety for all health care workers. Until such time, those who are in unions or associations can use the collective bargaining process to negotiate protective language. The Canadian Federation of Nurses Unions produced a "Workplace Violence Toolkit" that includes tips for negotiations and links to model language provided by other unions.[58] Unions and associations have achieved success in many jurisdictions. In 2018, Unifor, CUPE, and Service Employees International Union (SEIU), for example, joined forces in an Ontario-based campaign under the banner Together For Respect. After organizing rallies and workplace actions, they succeeded in negotiating a settlement that included new language on workplace violence.[59] The Ontario Nurses Association also won language "cementing agreement to a safe workplace free of violence and harassment."[60]

Neoliberalism

There are many flaws in Ontario's health care system and its public health approaches, which are being eroded by a series of governments that have been following the dogma of neoliberal capitalism. As Dr. Kean Birch, an associate professor at York University and co-editor of *Science as Culture*, explains, under neoliberalism the goal is to create an

> economic system in which the "free" market is extended to every part of our public and personal worlds. The transformation of the state from a provider of public welfare to a promoter of markets and competition helps to enable this shift.
>
> Neoliberalism is generally associated with policies like cutting trade tariffs and barriers. Its influence has liberalized the international movement of capital, and limited the power of trade unions. It's broken up state-owned enterprises, sold off public assets and generally opened up our lives to dominance by market thinking.[61]

Neoliberalism blossomed under Premier Mike Harris in the 1990s and its resulting austerity-driven cuts have shattered the social safety net. The Liberal McGuinty and Wynne years continued the trend. The Doug Ford populist Conservatives then unabashedly escalated the attacks on social democratic ideals with drastic reductions in spending on "basic liberal democratic protections," placing more emphasis on the "free market" and so-called efficient government.[62]

The ideas of individual choice and responsibility dominate neoliberal arguments and health policies. By focusing on individually modifiable personal behaviours, neoliberal ideas omit primary prevention of systemic risks and structurally influenced factors through regulation, policy, economic decisions, and cultural values. George Monbiot, a British writer and environmental and political activist, describes how neoliberalism limits the power of ordinary citizens and, of course, workers.

> Freedom from trade unions and collective bargaining means the freedom to suppress wages. Freedom from regulation means the freedom to poison rivers, endanger workers, [and so on].[63]

Privatization or, as Monbiot calls it, the "marketisation" of such public services as health care, commodifies what rightfully belongs to us as citizens. In other words, these services become money-making enterprises. Perhaps it is not coincidental that, at the same time as our universal publicly funded system is being eroded, for-profit health care is on the rise, resulting in increased financial responsibility on the individual. It is an alarming divergence from the raison d'être for Canada's medicare system. Retired nurse Linda Clayborne told us:

> I don't think that anyone could tell you today what our health care system is anymore. I don't know what it is. Everything's being privatized. Services are being taken away, especially from seniors and the most vulnerable people in society.

Increasing privatization of health care also impedes the allocation of resources towards the enhancements that are needed to protect workers from violence. The public-private partnerships that are now the norm in Ontario in the development of new hospital facilities should be disallowed. Bonnie Lysyk, the auditor general of Ontario, examined seventy-four such P3 projects and concluded that the province had paid $8 billion more than if they had been publicly built. Randy Robinson from the Canadian Centre for Policy Alternatives explains:

> P3s can offer a political benefit to governments, who can take on large debt repayment obligations without those debts appearing on their books. Public-private partnerships also deliver economic benefits to corporate law firms and financiers, who earn high fees arranging complex contracts and lending money to government at rates higher than government normally pays.
>
> But for the people who actually pay for P3s—like the people of Ontario—they are costly disasters that drag on for decades.[64]

Likewise, privatization of long-term care facilities should not be permitted. Their track record makes it clear they need to be placed within the sphere of our universal public system. The Canadian Medical Association has been advocating for this since 1984.[65] After extensively studying the problems in long-term care, Dr. Pat Armstrong and her co-researchers have called for an end to privatization.

> Private, for-profit services are necessarily more fragmented, more prone to closure and focused on making a profit. The research demonstrates that homes run on a for-profit basis tend to have lower staffing levels, more verified complaints, and more transfers to hospitals, as well as higher rates for both ulcers and morbidity. Moreover, managerial practices taken from the business sector are designed for just enough labour and for making a profit, rather than for providing good care.[66]

The COVID-19 pandemic has further brought the negative effects of privatization to light. A study published in August

2020 found more serious outbreaks and higher rates of death in Ontario's private long-term care homes than in not-for-profit homes. The authors concluded, "The COVID-19 pandemic has laid bare long-standing issues in how [long-term care] homes are financed, operated and regulated."[67] Dr. Nathan Stall, a member of the science table advising Ontario premier Doug Ford, told the *Toronto Star* in January 2021 that a report on COVID-19 related infections and deaths in long-term care had found "homes with for-profit status had outbreaks with nearly twice as many residents infected . . . and 78 per cent more resident deaths . . . compared with non-profit homes."[68]

The provision of quality health and medical care must become the priority, rather than an insatiable appetite for profit that is driven by the market economy.

What all this means for health care workers is that they are left working within institutions that have been systematically under-funded and understaffed in order to save money. As more services become part of the private domain, in which the return of profit is the primary motive, health care workers pay the price in terms of their safety and well-being, as does the public. Canada's health care system is becoming uncomfortably influenced by the U.S. model. As Dr. Craig Slatin has observed, these decisions can be directly correlated with the increasing incidence of violence.

> In the 1980s efforts abounded in the U.S. to make hospitals function more like a business than a critical health service. This led to understaffing and de-skilling, and by the mid-1990s nurses and aides had back injury rates that exceeded some mining and manufacturing sectors—and that has not been resolved. As health care workers were made to "do more with less"—the neoliberal credo that helped shift financial health care resources to upper management, owners, and in some cases shareholders (the groups who were given the privilege of doing less with more—money and wealth, that is)—vio-lence became a regular and constant workplace exposure. It didn't take long for the new U.S. model to be taken up throughout North America and much of the world.

Our public health care system has been eroded at the hand of governments, which provide funding and set standards and regulations. We must go back to the roots of medicare and eliminate the profit motive in health care. More public money needs to be put into the system, but beyond that, there needs to be increased democratization of health care services. Chronic underfunding is a significant hurdle to implementing protections. National and provincial standards for funding, staffing, and beds are needed. So are national and provincial standards for staff protections. Many of the protections that are now on the books are piecemeal, inconsistent, and not necessarily enforced.

Pulitzer Prize winning journalist Chris Hedges uses the phrase "sacrifice zones" to describe communities that have been polluted by industry, callously subjecting residents to increased risk of illness and death.[69] The affected people are left to fight for their own protection, rather than being able to count on government. We were struck by the similarities to the situation in health care facilities, which are in their own way sacrifice zones. Many health care workers feel like they are being left to their own devices when it comes to protection from violence.

Compensation system

It was also the research participants' experience that the WSIB did not compensate many of the physical and psychological effects of violence. Such serious conditions as PTSD, cumulative stress, and long-term effects of concussion are not uniformly recognized. As one health care worker said, "What's the point of filing a claim? They don't do anything about it anyway." The lack of recognition of work-relatedness by the WSIB presents a hurdle to protection against further harm—psychological and economic—related to the violence that caused the injury in the first place. It also forces injured workers back to work before they are ready. According to Dr. Robert Storey, the WSIB in Ontario is a neoliberal institution par excellence—and by this, I mean its administrative policies, programs and organizational structure are right out of the new public management manuals where the thrust toward efficiency, effectiveness and financial accountability—often caught and promoted in the supremely corporate phrase "best practices"—supersede all other organizational objectives. I mean as well that that the joined-at-the-hip neoliberal ethos of individualism/responsibilization is an integral part of its disciplinary rationality with regard to its "clients"—injured workers.[70]

Getting the authorities to act

Fixing the health care system so that it provides the care the public expects and deserves while protecting those who provide that care is going require some fancy footwork. Those who have the power to make changes—by passing protective legislation, providing appropriate funding, designing safe facilities, establishing safe staffing levels, offering appropriate emotional and mental health supports, instituting protective policies, and making the compensation system more equitable—can no longer pretend they know nothing about the problem of violence against health care staff. The question remains: How do we get them to act on that knowledge?

8.

Collective Quest for the Cure

What we have learned—in a nutshell

With the invaluable contributions of health care workers—their voices—we have learned that violence against health care staff is essentially out of control. Besides experiencing physical and verbal assaults, they are being sexually harassed and assaulted, hassled and groped, and worse. And they are left feeling degraded and traumatized. Many victims feel they are being blamed for the assaults against them. To add further to the harm that is done by the violence itself, many staff find themselves without adequate post-incident supports, leaving them to suffer emotionally, physically, and financially. And to keep this immense problem hidden from view, health care staff are essentially barred by their employers from speaking publicly about violence.

We have learned that there are workable solutions, many based on health care workers' own experiences and ideas. They range from the simplifying of incident reporting procedures to reimagined building redesign, with adequate funding and staffing emerging as paramount. We have outlined the complex and interrelated hurdles health care workers face in attempting to gain needed protections.

How might health care workers overcome those daunting hurdles and achieve the protections, respect, support, and rights that they deserve? This, we believe, will require the energy and power of a broadly based social movement. As an exasperated hospital clerical worker told us:

> There comes a time when you've got to say, "Enough is enough."
> I think this is what we're trying to do now, to fight back. And to say,
> "Hell no! It's not part of our job. Never has been. Shouldn't be." We
> need to get the message out.

Getting from here to there

Clearly, the status quo is not working—in health care or in the wider world. We all need to learn that, in spite of messages to the contrary, it is okay to think critically, to question authority, to be skeptical about pseudo-scientific facts, misleading statistics, or insincere assurances. As civil rights leader Ms. Ella Baker once said, although in the context of police and state-sponsored racism, "My basic sense of it has always been to get people to understand that in the long run they themselves are the only protection they have against violence or injustice."[1]

Too often we are grateful for a few nods towards protection from the government or employers. But unfortunately, these are often just words or nice-sounding plans without real implementation strategies or adequate resources. We may be happy for signage that is placed in the ER stating that health care staff are to be respected or a refresher course in de-escalation. We are grateful for whatever gains we can get. These small or token improvements may move in the right direction, but they often seem to be meant more to placate those demanding protection than to truly address the problem. Another prominent civil rights leader, Dr. Martin Luther King, cautioned against "the tranquilizing drug of gradualism." Similarly, health care workers today need deep, system-wide, sweeping changes, not little crumbs that cost almost nothing—and do very little.

Many articles and books have been written about social movements. We won't try to replicate their insights here, but it's fair to say that they broadly agree that we need each other in order to push the boulder up the hill. It's never straightforward and it's never easy. There is a saying, "If you want to go fast, go alone. If you want to go far, go together." In a *Harvard Business Review* article written about being a good ally to movements such as #MeToo and Black Lives Matter, the authors state:

> We view allyship as a *strategic* mechanism used by individuals to become *collaborators, accomplices,* and *coconspirators* who fight injustice and promote equity in the workplace through supportive personal relationships and public acts of sponsorship and advocacy. Allies endeavor to drive systemic improvements to workplace policies, practices, and culture.[2]

The media can even be allies when it comes to publicizing the issue at hand.

Unions and federations that represent health care workers, other than one's own, are sometimes viewed as competition, but they can be natural allies around specific issues. Health care unions across the U.S., for example, collaborated in a campaign led by the AFL-CIO (American Federation of Labor and Congress of Industrial Organizations) in support of federal legislation to compel the national Occupational Safety and Health Administration to "to issue a workplace violence prevention standard requiring employers in the health care and social service sectors to develop and implement a plan to protect their employees from workplace violence."[3] Occasions such as the April 28 Day of Mourning, Injured Workers Day, International Women's Day, and National Day of Remembrance and Action on Violence against Women are ready-made for campaigning with other unions or community groups around the issue of violence. The same is true for incidents of violence against health care workers that catch the attention of the public.

Other allies might include health care worker organizations, whose members, such as doctors and other professionals, might be willing to join with the unions to promote a common message or campaign. In Canada, many professional organizations have been publicly advocating for an end to health care violence, including, among others, various provincial nurses' associations, Canadian Federation of Nurses Unions, Canadian Medical Association, Canadian Association of Emergency Physicians, and provincial doctors' associations. Health care workers might find common cause with citizens groups, sexual assault centres, supportive researchers and academics, and such organizations as the Canadian Health Coalition and provincial health coalitions. Robert DeMatteo, former senior health and safety officer for the Ontario Public Service Employees Union, advises that, because of the global nature of our economy, unions also need to reach out beyond their own jurisdictions to the broader international occupational health movement:

> Workers and unions around the world are struggling with the same forces that keep us weak and unable to fight for improvements in health and safety. We must join with other struggles, both to assist and learn.[4]

We are gratified that as researchers we have been able to play a small role in the unions' efforts to bring violence against health care workers to light. We have watched primarily from the sidelines as various campaigns have unfolded. We presented our research findings and recommendations at a health care workers' conference in 2019 sponsored by OCHU-CUPE. We asked the delegates what strategies might be employed by their union to bring about the recommended changes. While some issues, such as staffing levels and legislative protections, were given higher priority than others, it was decided that a multi-pronged campaign would be launched to promote *all* of the preventative measures brought forward in our research, as outlined at the end of chapter 6. OCHU-CUPE launched media blitzes, rallies, poster and button campaigns, legal actions, government lobbying, contract negotiations, and broad dissemination of information.

For our part, we set out with Michael Hurley on province-wide media tours in 2017 and 2019 to release our research results and to help build public support and pressure. The various media conferences received wide coverage, internationally, nationally, provincially, and locally. We held a press conference at Queen's Park and also presented to members of provincial parliament at a members' breakfast. A 2017 episode of TVO's *The Agenda* was dedicated to an in-depth discussion of the issue. The host, Steve Paikin, criticized the Ministries of Health and Labour for declining his invitation to come on the show with us.

OCHU-CUPE also forged alliances with other unions, greatly increasing their power, influence, and reach. They continue to collaborate in joint legal actions and campaigns, such as a drive-by rally at Queen's Park organized by CUPE, SEIU, and Unifor in March 2021 demanding "No more temporary fixes" and that the provincial budget to be announced the following day "include respect, protection and pay for dedicated front-line staff."[5] The various joint actions and negotiations have met with some success. More protective contract language has been negotiated but there is still much to be done. Worker protection needs to be legislated, not left to the vagaries of the collective bargaining process.

Perhaps the most important alliance the health care workers in Ontario have forged is with the public. Citizens have an important role to play in supporting health care workers and advocating for improvements to the system itself. Natalie Mehra, executive director of the Ontario Health Coalition, explains that, although her group primarily advocates on behalf of patients, she recognizes there are common interests with respect to violence in health care settings. She believes "the conditions of care are the conditions of work."[6] The coalition is actively committed to resurrecting our health care system. In 2019, for example:

In an unprecedented show of unity, more than 150,000 health professionals and workers and tens of thousands of patient advocates wore a sticker that said "Stop Health Privatization" and distributed leaflets warning about the Ford government's radical healthcare restructuring plans. . . . The Coalition has vowed to fight to protect local healthcare services from cuts, privatization, and mergers.[7]

Sharon Richer, secretary-treasurer of OCHU-CUPE, said her union is determined to address system issues within the health care system. For that to happen the public needs to be made aware of the problems. Richer said:

We continue to remind them [governments] that hospitals that are dangerous for staff to work in are also dangerous for patients. Increased staffing, in areas like psychiatry, and improved alarm, flagging and reporting systems, are all needed.[8]

The health care system belongs to everyone. We have the right to health care that is timely, comprehensive, and safe. It is dehumanizing to wait for care, suffer neglect, and experience disrespect. We have to demand a return to the dream that the creators of Canada's universal health care system followed. At the same time, we must be careful not to take out our frustrations on the front-line workers who are caught in a system that limits their ability to perform their duties.

A social movement adage promises, "If we fight, we win." There is no sure-fire recipe for success. There are, however, many inspiring examples of people who have dared to challenge the status quo. We need look no further than the women's movement for examples of courageous individuals collectively challenging their oppression under the patriarchal thumb of a society that cheats them of their basic rights. Women hold up half the sky. They also make up over 85 per cent of health care workers. Together, women are a force to reckon with, as are racialized, Black, brown, Indigenous, LBGTQ+, non-binary, environmental, social justice, and labour activists.

Solidarity is a key component for change. Women, as an example, have gained considerable experience over the past decades in getting beyond their differences and working together towards common goals as they challenge a system that attempts to control them by eroding their sense of self-worth. As Dr. Karen Messing says in her book about women and solidarity, "Working women need to get together to insist on changes. Once women stop feeling ashamed of being women, we can start to defend our interests. If we can do it through a union, we get more protection and safety in numbers."[9] And, we would add, working together—especially within a union or community group—brings a richness of capabilities, knowledge, and experiences.

In our various adventures with grassroots action research, we have seen the sparks ignite and the energy explode in people who have begun to challenge the powers that be. And we believe that if enough activists can light enough sparks, regulations will be enacted and laws will be enforced, environments will be cleaned up, and people will be compensated for harms done to them. Occupational and environmental health research will be funded, harmful substances will be banned, jobs will be protected and lives will be saved, and the future will be more secure for our children and their children and beyond—across the globe. You see, it just so happens that the same characteristic that can make us act like lemmings jumping over a cliff, can, with some fine-tuning, empower us instead to move mountains. To end the unacceptable injustice of unfettered violence against health care workers, we need to wholeheartedly embrace trust in each other and trust in the awesome power of collective action.

Afterword

Health Care Workers during COVID-19

Silenced and sacrificed

The COVID-19 pandemic has reached its tentacles into almost all aspects of our personal, social, economic, and political lives. We believe a discussion about how it has been handled, or rather mishandled, belongs squarely in a book about violence against health care workers. The catastrophic rate of infection and death that hospital and long-term care workers have been experiencing is an expression of violence in itself. However, we had carried out this research and most of the writing before the pandemic took hold, so we will discuss this occupational health disaster separately here.

We knew instinctively that, as the scourge of the coronavirus began to spread, there would be severe consequences for health care workers. In Ontario, despite persistent assurances from the government that health care workers were adequately protected under its guidelines, these workers made up a disproportionate number of the infections in the first year of the pandemic. Sharon Richer of OCHU-CUPE reported in March 2021, which would be about one year in, "Nearly 20,000 [Ontario] health care workers have contracted COVID-19 at work and 20 have died."[1] The same month, Amnesty International reported that globally, at least seventeen thousand health workers had died from COVID-19 over the past year. Amnesty's Steve Cockburn elaborated:

> For one health worker to die from COVID-19 every 30 minutes is both a tragedy and an injustice. Health workers all over the world have put their lives on the line to try and keep people safe from COVID-19, yet far too many have been left unprotected and paid the ultimate price.[2]

Health care workers were facing many challenges before the pandemic was declared. We were particularly concerned about what would happen to the precarious staff in long-term care facilities, a marginalized workforce that was already overwhelmed with work. Because of the institutional practice of silencing staff, the voices of long-term care workers were not the first to bring the crisis to the public's attention. We heard about it from the young, scandalized Canadian military personnel who were conscripted to replace infected care providers in several Ontario and Quebec facilities.[3] The soldiers described finding appalling conditions and heart-breaking neglect, substantiating the stories health care staff had been telling us in our research. Jaw-dropping media stories were met with a swift response from such groups as the Ontario Health Coalition, health care unions, and outraged family members. The Council of Canadians launched a petition campaign in support of long-term care residents.

> Cockroach and bug infestations, seniors calling out repeatedly for help, rotting food, COVID-19-infected patients put in the same room with those who are healthy, missed meals, seniors left in soiled diapers and linens—these are just some of the things Canadian Armed Forces (CAF) personnel have seen while helping in five long-term care homes in Ontario.[4]

As the pandemic raged, more and more residents were infected and perished. In Ontario alone, almost four thousand died in the first year.[5] Paul Webster, an award-winning journalist, wrote an article for *The Lancet* in which he stated:

> When Canada's national health data agency reported in June, 2020, that Canada had the worst record among wealthy nations for COVID-19-related deaths in long-term care facilities for older people, many observers referred to it as a "national disgrace."[6]

Private facilities were especially hard hit.[7]

Hospitals were similarly caught off-guard. Resources were hastily redirected as unprepared governments and administrators stumbled, seemingly lost, through the early weeks and months. For many health care unions, medical professionals, researchers, and advocacy groups in Ontario, the crisis in health care generated by the pandemic was no surprise. These groups were all too aware of the slow-moving deterioration of the system, the decades-long but consistent process of defunding, understaffing, deregulating, privatization, and trading of efficiencies for care.[8] The full consequences of these governmental decisions were being exposed for all to see.[9] Although there has been a lot of bluster from the current provincial government about ending "hallway medicine," the required policies have not been put into place and the money is not being directed where it is needed. The government's laissez-faire approach to hospital overcrowding, already a shameful breach of its duty to provide equitable, respectful, quality health care to the public, was now resulting in an unimaginable nightmare, as field hospitals were set up in parking lots and patients were being transported out of their home districts.[10]

The decades-long decline in health care that rendered workers vulnerable to exploitation and violence likely contributed to the high rates of COVID-19 infection among staff, patients, and residents. The public reacted with sufficient outrage to the news of the disproportionate incidence of infection and death among elderly residents to force all levels of government to at least acknowledge there was a serious problem.

Already overworked, and now surrounded by disease and death, while working in constant fear that they themselves would be infected, health care staff suffered even greater levels of stress, burnout, and unrelenting anxiety. Their working conditions began to take a tremendous toll on their health and well-being.

Researching the effects

Our research into the physical and psychological effects of COVID-19 on health care workers began in the first weeks of the pandemic. Michael Hurley shared with us the results of a poll that OCHU-CUPE had commissioned, in which over three thousand union members participated. An overwhelming majority indicated they did not believe they were being adequately protected from infection. Eighty-seven per cent said there was not enough personal protective equipment (PPE) on hand to keep them safe, and 91 per cent responded that they felt abandoned by the provincial government.[11]

Michael asked us to collect and review the emerging scientific literature about how the virus was spread and what protections were needed. Evidence was emerging that it was being transmitted in very small droplets carried through the air, that is, aerosolized. Despite mounting evidence of such potential for airborne transmission, many health officials, including those making decisions about worker protection, emphatically denied that the pathogen could be spread through the air, arguing it was transmitted through surface contact and via droplets created during such "aerosolizing" medical procedures as intubation, manual ventilation, and continuous positive airway pressure (CPAP) ventilation.[12] Health care workers in Ontario were assured that wearing gowns, face shields, and surgical masks, maintaining a distance of two metres, and careful handwashing would provide sufficient protection.[13] Yet, within weeks of the pandemic being declared, research had determined that coughing and sneezing can transmit tiny droplets several metres. Furthermore, numerous studies had concluded that COVID-19 can be spread before it causes symptoms. Studies have now found that even singing, speaking, or breathing can aerosolize the virus.[14] Increasingly, virologists and occupational disease experts recommended airborne virus protection, such as N95 respirators (a "respiratory protective device designed to achieve a very close facial fit and very efficient filtration of airborne particles"[15]) or, better yet, elastomeric or powered air-purifying respirators.[16]

The official recommendations for health care worker protection took an irregular path. Until early March 2020, the U.S. Centers for Disease Control and Prevention was recommending that all personnel potentially coming into contact with COVID-19 patients be provided with N95s.[17] Suddenly the agency changed its guidelines to recommend only surgical masks for non-aerosolizing care. We learned that these compromises were almost surely based on a severe shortage of supplies, rather than on science.[18] The World Health Organization similarly failed to recommend adequate airborne protection. Rory O'Neill, editor of *Hazards*, an occupational health and safety journal in the U.K., criticized the WHO for its handling of worker protection, as did the International Trade Union Confederation, which demanded that the WHO change its stance.

> The unions were supported by the science and many scientists. On 6 July 2020, a letter endorsed by 241 scientists urged the WHO to recognize that COVID-19 can be spread by "aerosol" or "airborne" transmission and revise its guidance.[19]

Dr. David Michaels, former head of the U.S. Occupational Safety and Health Administration, told the *New York Times*:

> It's been disappointing that both the W.H.O. and the C.D.C. [Centers for Disease Control] have suggested that surgical masks are adequate.... Reliance on surgical masks has no doubt led to many workers being infected.[20]

Dr. Lisa Brosseau, a University of Illinois expert on respiratory protection for infectious disease, wrote about the limitations of surgical masks. She said, in light of recent scientific findings, that "healthcare organizations must return to using respirators for confirmed and suspected COVID-19 patients when supply chain problems are resolved."[21]

Government science panel

Michael invited us to present the literature we had gathered on COVID-19 transmission and on the recommended PPE to a government panel in April 2020 that was setting guidelines for health care worker protection in Ontario. During these consultations, spokespersons for various unions representing health care workers argued for abiding by the recommendations of the 2006 Ontario SARS Royal Commission. They reminded the panel of the significance of the SARS inquiry, which had offered a roadmap for handling future outbreaks. One of the key recommendations the commission made was to abide by the precautionary principle, which advises that, "during a healthcare crisis, policy makers cannot wait for scientific certainty to make decisions."[22] In other words, if we are going to err, it must be on the side of caution. It also recommended "listening to front-line health workers" and

> That in any future infectious disease crisis, directives involving worker safety be prepared with input from the workplace parties who have to implement them, including employers, health worker representatives and Joint Health and Safety Committees.[23]

Yet, despite the admonishments of the SARS Commission and the presentation of plentiful emerging evidence of airborne transmission, there was no changing the government's position. In direct defiance of the precautionary principle, government representatives on the panel insisted that the science regarding airborne transmission was not well enough established to act upon. When challenged about the climbing rates of health care worker infections, their response was either silence or, as one panel member told us, "They likely contracted it riding home on the bus, not at work." There was no evidence to support such an outlandish contention. The meetings ended abruptly in June 2020, and the guidelines remained unchanged.

When viewed through the experiences of those on the front lines, the coronavirus response has been a series of failures: failure to apply the precautionary principle that is fundamental to public health, failure to provide proper protections for workers, and failure to place human health before the economy.[24] Over the first year of the pandemic, numerous revisions of the guidelines for health care worker protection have been issued. But until the unions collectively exercised agency and launched a court action, the Ontario government continued to limit the use of N95s primarily to those conducting aerosolizing procedures on COVID-19 patients. While certainly a welcome development, the negotiated agreement reached in October 2020 with the province to make N95s mandatory when requested[25] still left many health care staff, particularly those in long-term care and home care, without N95s. Furthermore, it has not reduced heavy workloads, understaffing, or other structural factors that were already problematic before being exacerbated by the additional challenges of the pandemic.

In November 2020, Sharleen Stewart, president of SEIU Healthcare, issued a statement calling for a "rethink and a reset" and demanding that health care workers to be listened to. She said, "SEIU Healthcare and our union partners have pragmatic solutions—derived directly from the voices of those fighting the battle on the frontline."[26]

A closer look

In April and May 2020, as the pandemic was unfolding, we undertook a research study to explore the day-to-day realities of front-line staff within hospitals and long-term care. We conducted in-depth anonymous interviews with ten health care workers from facilities across the province. We talked to nurses, PSWs, clerical staff, and cleaners about their experiences and concerns. Words on a page cannot convey the level of emotion we heard in the voices of the individuals we interviewed. We did not expect such intense distress. All of the health care workers we interviewed expressed feelings of anxiety, stress, anger, and fear. There was an overarching sense of being disrespected, neglected, and exploited.

There is very little trust in the government's decisions and policies regarding the level of protection health care workers are being granted. A long-term care PSW explained that she believes that often the decisions about their safety aren't truly based on "best practice" but are really the "bare minimum." She had read the Ministry of Health guidelines that said she only needs an N95 when involved with aerosol applications. "Yet, we're looking at other countries and we're thinking, 'They're treating this as airborne. They're wearing N95 masks with suspected or presumed or positive COVID patients and we're wearing surgical masks.' That's unacceptable."

Many workers told us they had requested N95s when coming into contact with a suspected or confirmed case. Most were denied. A hospital cleaner described an incident in which she was told she was only entitled to a surgical mask, leaving her feeling vulnerable and frustrated.

> They say that a cough doesn't cause it to be aerosolized. I know the large droplets drop down, but how do you know there's not micro-organisms when I'm cleaning the bedside, the railing, the table, under the bed, mopping it. I'm working a foot away from the patient, and they're saying, "No, you're not allowed to wear an N95" . . . I asked for one with a suspected case . . . I didn't get it.

One interviewee told the story of a co-worker—a nurse—who was sent in without proper protection to care for a patient suspected of being infected. Though the patient was shortly confirmed to be positive, the nurse was not considered to have been sufficiently exposed to be allowed to self-isolate for the fourteen days required under government guidelines. She was told she must continue to come to work. After several days, she developed symptoms and became very ill and subsequently tested positive, requiring hospitalization. The entire experience has deeply affected her emotional well-being. The interviewee, who regularly communicates with her affected colleague, said, "She's physically okay now, but mentally, I don't think she'll ever be the same. And she's a young nurse starting out. I hope she will be able to one day tell her story, but she's not there yet."

Health care workers' family relationships are also strained as a result of the measures they are taking in order not to transmit the virus. A PSW described maintaining a separate bedroom and bathroom from her husband in order to protect him. She broke down crying, recounting how she has completely avoided seeing her young grandchildren because she can never be certain she isn't infectious.

Adding insult to injury is the stigma that has developed around those working in health care. They may be seen as a danger to others, intensifying an already stressful experience.

My husband doesn't want to tell his co-workers what his wife is going through because then they think my husband has the virus and treat him like he's a threat to them. It has gotten to the point that I don't want to tell anybody I'm a nurse. And I don't really blame them because, if I were in their shoes, I'd be thinking, "Oh my god, she's a nurse."

Some of the staff also believed that because the overwhelming majority of health care workers are women, they were particularly vulnerable to exploitation from their employers and the government. As one of the nurses told us, "Many of us are single parents. We're looking after elderly parents. We have other responsibilities, and we are being put at risk. And I honestly think that if these were male-dominated jobs, we would be looked after differently."

We were told that some of them had tried to exercise their

legal right to refuse work they believed to be unsafe. Ministry of Labour inspectors dismissed their concerns, deeming that the employer was abiding by government-issued guidelines, and ordered the concerned individuals to return to work without any further protections.

In November 2020 our study, entitled "Sacrificed: Ontario Healthcare Workers in the Time of COVID-19," was published in the journal *New Solutions*.[27] There are striking commonalities in the findings of our previous studies about the issue of violence and this research on health care workers' experience during the pandemic. Both sets of studies demonstrate systemic shortcomings. According to the health care workers:

- They do not receive the support they require
- Joint occupational health and safety committees and the Ministry of Labour are not functioning as mandated
- Health care workers fear reprisal if they speak up about their concerns
- They feel anxious, sad, abandoned, and vulnerable
- Emotional injuries, such as PTSD, are compounded by the lack of institutional acknowledgement of their suffering
- Women and racialized people feel undervalued
- The limited health and safety legal and bargaining rights of health care workers inhibit them from exercising agency over their working conditions

A monumental failure

In the interviews we conducted, it emerged that the primary concern for health care workers, and by extension, their families, was that they were inadequately protected—and they were angry about it. Many were aware that Canadian federal and provincial ministries of health had not heeded the recommendations of the SARS Commission, including the need to stockpile N95s, and of several reports warning about the inadequacies of the country's outbreak preparedness.[28] Furthermore, Canada was slow to respond to the inevitable demand for supplies. Canadian National Emergency Strategic Stockpile personnel had issued a warning in February 2020 that supplies of PPE, including N95s, were too low to "weather a pandemic," but the federal government failed to order needed PPE until mid-March.[29] In April 2020, Dr. Sandy Buchman, president of the Canadian Medical Association, commented that governments were "caught flat-footed.... All we have seen are cutbacks. We haven't seen adequate resources allocated to health care."[30]

Health care workers find it ironic that, at the same time that they are being lauded as heroes, their safety and mental well-being are being sacrificed.[31] They, like many workers during the pandemic, have been deemed essential, but, in terms of protection, seem not to be valued as such. Harry Glasbeek, Osgoode Hall Law School professor emeritus, asserted:

> This is an arresting public acknowledgment of the state of play under contemporary capitalism, which its cheerleaders like to label liberal democratic capitalism. While our history books, our media, and our cultural institutions mostly tell the story of our lives by focusing on—and frequently celebrating—important, wealthy and powerful people . . . it turns out that, when things need to be done, unheralded, unsung, unnoticed workers are crucial to social wellbeing. Indeed, all too often, as is the case during the crisis created by COVID-19, it is the least admired, the least respected workers, to whom we turn to maintain our health, security and welfare.[32]

Linda Silas, president of the Canadian Federation of Nurses Unions, stated, "As a society we must respect the safety of all workers, just as we respect the safety of patients and the public. This pandemic is having life-and-death impacts on frontline workers, and we must learn from our mistakes and do better."[33]

The findings of our research are very consistent with those published in other studies and reports. A Canadian study of nurses who regularly cross the border into the U.S. to treat COVID-19 patients found they were experiencing "increased mental health concerns."[34] An editorial published in a Canadian newspaper highlighted the emotional toll COVID-19 is taking on physicians.[35] A report sponsored by the CFNU expressed nurses' dismay about "their employers' seeming disregard for their health and safety concerns. And they worry about the unknown."[36] In a study from Australia, doctors and nurses reported that they felt unprotected and abandoned.

> Deficiencies in work health and safety, respiratory protection, personal protective equipment and workplace culture have resulted in a loss of psychological and physical safety at work associated with an occupational moral injury. The challenge for healthcare leaders is to repair trust by addressing HCW [health care worker] concerns and fast track solutions in collaboration with them.[37]

Amnesty International issued another report in May 2020 that outlined the failure of governments across the globe to protect health care workers, resulting in of thousands of deaths, with little recourse.

> They have further faced reprisals from the authorities and their employers for raising safety concerns, including arrests and dismissals, and even in some cases been subjected to violence and stigma from members of the public.[38]

Takeaways

The findings from our study on health care workers during the pandemic engender a number of recommendations, many of which mirror those from our violence studies.

Staffing levels and capacities in Ontario's hospitals and long-term care must be increased, at least to the level of the rest of Canada. This would not only improve health care for the public, but it would, in turn, reduce workers' stress related to staggering workloads.

There also needs to be a change in workplace culture, in which staff's concerns are heard, respected, and addressed. Studies of health care workers' psychological well-being during a viral outbreak have found that strong management support can help to mitigate mental distress.[39] While caring supervisors and such outpourings of community support as pot banging, social media messages, posters, and billboards might help to bolster morale, what health care workers truly need is improved working conditions, protection, and more power to shape their work environment.

Adequate PPE and protective administrative and engineering controls would reduce fear and anxiety related to the risk of becoming infected.[40]

The immediate requirements of health care staff for mental health supports must be addressed to mitigate the psychological effects of working during the pandemic.[41] Specialized counselling and accommodations must be readily available for those who need them. As a hospital nurse indicated, the inadequacies of the health care system, perhaps most poignantly within the long-term care system, have been exposed like never before.

> At the end of the day, the silver lining of this pandemic is that it has brought to light the dismal condition that health care is actually in. It has shone a light on it, not only for the government, but also the public to actually see what is happening in hospitals and long-term care. Hopefully after this pandemic is over, [we] will fix what is broken, and move forward and build on that so the next time—because there will be a next time—we're ready for it, and we won't be in an unsafe situation like this ever again.

The government needs to substantially reinvest in the weakened public health care system and halt the current trend towards increased privatization, including stopping private ownership in long-term care and reclaiming the sector as part of our universal public system. Structural violence that is embedded in health care institutions must be addressed. Appropriate preparations must be put into place for future viral outbreaks. Researcher and sociologist Dr. Jane McArthur advocates, "As governments and public health officials prepare for a return to normal, the precautionary principle should be front and centre."[42] A revamping of priorities, away from the profit motive and towards the health and well-being of persons, mandates investment in preparations that would mitigate risks and improve the lives of everyone.

The failure to meet the challenges presented by the pandemic underscores the consequences of chronic under-resourcing and deregulation. There will be enduring repercussions related to the failings and floundering of governments and public health agencies to protect health care workers and the public during the pandemic. The healing process is likely to continue long after COVID-19 has been contained.

The crisis experienced during the pandemic provokes a number of questions. What will the world look like after it's over? Will we be better prepared for the next one? Will health care workers be better protected? Will there be a reinvestment to remedy the weakened public health care systems? Are there lessons for broader precautionary measures for other critical health threats, such as climate change? Sam Gindin, a long-time labour analyst and activist, submits that the pandemic has brought about the urgent need for action on many fronts, including climate change.

Though largely pushed to the side during the pandemic, COVID-19 served as the canary-in-the-mine for capitalism's general unpreparedness for not only future health pandemics but also the infinitely greater environmental crisis already enveloping us. Unlike health pandemics, the environmental crisis can't be resolved through lockdowns, social distancing, and vaccines. It demands a radical restructuring of how society is organized, what we value, and how we relate to each other—issues that dwarf the already traumatic experiences with COVID-19.[43]

We need a systems approach that sees beyond the individual to the collective nature of how we live, work, and play. Respect and equity for health care workers will be central to realizing this goal.

Notes

Preface

1   J. T. Brophy, M. M. Keith, and M. Hurley, "Assaulted and Unheard: Violence Against Healthcare Staff," *New Solutions: A Journal of Environmental and Occupational Health Policy* 27 no. 4 (1987): 581–606; J. T. Brophy, M. M. Keith, and M. Hurley, "Breaking Point: Violence Against Long-Term Care Staff," *New Solutions: A Journal of Environmental and Occupational Health Policy* 29 no. 1 (2019): 10–35; and J. E. McArthur et al, "Novel Virus, Old Story: Governments Failings Put Health Care Workers at Risk," in *Sick of the System: Why the COVID-19 Recovery Must Be Revolutionary*, ed. BTL Editorial Committee (Toronto: Between the Lines, 2020), 39–58.

Chapter 1. Drawing Back the Curtain

1   E. A. Stanko, "Violence," in *The Sage Dictionary of Criminology*, ed. E. McLaughton and J. Munie (London: Sage, 2001), 316.

2   *Working for Change: Ten Years of Health and Safety Activism in Windsor, Ontario,* produced by M. Keith et al (Windsor, ON: Bird Dog Productions, 1992).

3   M. Milczarek, *Workplace Violence and Harassment: A European Picture*

(Luxembourg: European Agency for Safety and Health at Work (EU-OSHA), 2010), https://osha.europa.eu/.

4   "Workplace Violence," American Academy of Experts in Traumatic Stress' website, 2014, www.aaets.org/.

5   K. Messing, *One-Eyed Science: Occupational Health and Women Workers* (Philadelphia: Temple University Press, 1998); International Labour Organization, *Providing Safe and Healthy Workplaces for Both Women and Men* (Geneva: ILO, n.d.), www.ilo.org/.

6   Canadian Union of Public Employees, "Nurse Fired for Speaking Up about Patient Violence to Make First Public Statement Wednesday in North Bay," news release, 16 February 2016, https://cupe.ca/.

7   Ontario Council of Hospital Unions–Canadian Union of Public Employees (OCHU-CUPE), *Voices: Hospital Workers Talk about Violence in the Workplace* (Toronto: OCHU-CUPE, 2017), https://ochu.on.ca/.

8   C. Thompson, "Nurses Say Little Has Changed Since Dupont Death," *Windsor Star*, 12 November 2015, https://windsorstar.com/.

9   "Workplace Violence—Complying with the OHS Act," Public Services Health & Safety Association's website, www.pshsa.ca/.

10 *Occupational Hazards in Hospitals*, EURO Reports and Studies 1068 (The Hague: World Health Organization, 1983).

11 L. A. Stokowski, "Step Away from That Nurse! Violence in Healthcare Continues Unabated," Medscape, 19 November 2014, www.medscape.com/.

12 Canadian Nurses Association, *Fact Sheet: Violence in the Workplace* (Ottawa: Canadian Nurses Association, 2005), www.cna-aiic.ca.

13 B.J. Sibbald, "Workplace Violence Is Not Part of a Doctor's Job," *CMAJ* 189 no. 5 (2017): E184; W. Eriksen, K. Tambs, and S. Knardahl, "Work Factors and Psychological Distress in Nurses' Aides: A Prospective Cohort Study," *BMC Public Health* 6 (2006): 290; L. A. Snyder, P. Y. Chen, and T. Vacha-Haase, "The Underreporting Gap in Aggressive Incidents from Geriatric Patients Against Certified Nursing Assistants," *Violence and Victims* 22 no. 3 (2007): 367–79; C. M. B. Fernandes et al, "Violence in the Emergency Department: A Survey of Health Care Workers," *CMAJ* 161 no. 10 (1999): 1245–48. Out of 3,802 Canadian family physicians surveyed for one study, "98% had experienced at least one incident of minor abuse, 75% had experienced at least one incident of major abuse, and 39% had experienced at least one incident of severe abuse." B. Miedem et al, "Prevalence of Abusive

Encounters in the Workplace of Family Physicians: A Minor, Major, or Severe Problem?" *Canadian Family Physician* 56 no. 3 (2010): e101–e108. A survey of paramedics in Ontario and Nova Scotia found that 75 per cent had experienced violence in the previous year, 67 per cent were verbally assaulted, and 26 per cent had been subjected to physical assault. B. L. Bigham et al, "Paramedic Self-Reported Exposure to Violence in the Emergency Medical Services (EMS) Workplace," *Prehospital Emergency Care* 18 no. 4 (2014): 489–94.

14 A. Kumari et al, "Workplace Violence Against Doctors: Characteristics, Risk Factors, and Mitigation Strategies," *Journal of Postgraduate Medicine* 66 no. 3 (2020):149–54.

15 V. Hackethal and C. P. Vega, "Workplace Violence in Healthcare Major Problem, Unrecognized," Medscape, 3 June 2016, www.medscape.org/; J. P. Phillips, "Workplace Violence Against Health Care Workers in the United States," *New England Journal of Medicine* 374 (2016): 1661–69, https://doi.org/10.1056/NEJMra1501998.

16 Phillips, "Workplace Violence Against Health Care Workers."

17 A. Escrig-Pinol, "The Risk of Workplace Violence for Home Care Providers," Healthy Debate, July 2019, https://healthydebate.ca/.

18 National Center for the Analysis of Violent Crime, *Workplace Violence: Issues in Response* (Quantico: FBI Academy, 2003), www.fbi.gov/; Sylvain de Léséleuc, *Criminal Victimization in the Workplace*, Canadian Centre for Justice Statistics Profile Series, no. 13 (Ottawa: Statistics Canada, 2004), www.statcan.gc.ca/; National Institute for Occupational Safety and Health, *Violence: Occupational Hazards in Hospitals*, DHHS (NIOSH) publication no. 2002–101 (Cincinnati: NIOSH, 2002), www.cdc.gov/niosh/.

19 Canadian Federation of Nurses Unions, "CFNU President Unveils New Survey Results and Report Showing Safe Patient Care Declining, Workplace Violence Increasing—Many Nurses Considering Leaving Their Jobs," news release, 8 June 2017, https://nursesunions.ca/.

20 *Workplace Violence in Healthcare* (U.S. Occupational Safety and Health Administration, 2015), www.osha.gov/.

21 "Protect Workers from Violence," AFL-CIO website, https://aflcio.org/.

22 Canadian Centre for Occupational Health and Safety, "Violence Against Healthcare Workers: It's Not 'Part of the Job,'" *Health and Safety Report* 13 no. 9, www.ccohs.ca/.

23 "Workplace Violence Against Women Rising, Driven By Growing Rates in Education Sector," Institute for Work and Health's website, 12 April 2019, www.iwh.on.ca/.

24 D. Hango and M. Moyser, *Harassment in Canadian Workplaces* (Ottawa: Statistics Canada, 2018), www.statcan.gc.ca/.

25 "Workplace Violence Against Women Rising."

26 Between 2006 and 2015, there were 16,617 violence-related lost-time injuries among Canadian health care workers compared to 7,517 among those in all non-health care occupations combined. Canadian Federation of Nurses Unions, *Enough Is Enough: Putting a Stop to Violence in the Health Care Sector—A Discussion Paper* (Ottawa: CFNU, 2017), https://nursesunions.ca/.

27 Sara Mojtehedzadeh, "Violence Against Health-Care Workers 'Out of Control,' Survey Finds," *Toronto Star*, 5 November 2017, www.thestar.com/.

28 Mojtehedzadeh, "Violence Against Health-Care Workers." In comparison, consider a 2018 Statistics Canada report that found that in Canadian workplaces overall a much smaller number of employees had experienced harassment on the job in the past year: 19 per cent of women employees and 13 per cent of men. Hango and Moyser, *Harassment in Canadian Workplaces.*

29 *Workplace Violence and Harassment: A Guide for ONA members* (Ontario Nurses Association, 2019), www.ona.org/.

30 B. Sibbald, "Workplace Violence Is Not Part of a Doctor's Job," *CMAJ* 189, no. 5 (2017): E184, https://doi.org/10.1503/cmaj.170086.

31 "Male Patient Charged after B.C. Nurse Badly Beaten on the Job," CBC News, 26 September 2019, www.cbc.ca.

32 "Bloodied, Broken and Burned Out: 88% of Long-Term Care Staff Experience Violence," Cision, 8 April 2019, https://newswire.ca; J. T. Brophy, M. M. Keith, and M. Hurley, "Breaking Point: Violence Against Long-Term Care Staff," *New Solutions* 29 no. 1 (2019): 10–35.

33 "Nearly 9 in 10 Long-Term Care Staff Experience Violence," *Canadian Occupational Safety,* 15 April 2019, www.thesafetymag.com/.

34 A. Banerjee et al, "Structural Violence in Long-Term, Residential Care for Older People: Comparing Canada and Scandinavia," *Social Science & Medicine* 74 (2012): 390–98.

35 *This Is Long-Term Care* (Ontario Long Term Care Association, 2018), www.oltca.com/.

Chapter 2. Under the Scope

1   J. T. Brophy, M. M. Keith, and M. Hurley, "Assaulted and Unheard: Violence Against Healthcare Staff," *New Solutions: A Journal of Environmental and Occupational Health Policy* 27 no. 4 (2018): 581–606; J. T. Brophy, M. M. Keith, and M. Hurley, "Breaking Point."

2   M. Keith, "Workplace Health and Safety Mapping: The Why and How of Body Mapping," *Occupational Health Review* 102 (March/April 2003): 31–33; M. Keith et al, "Identifying and Prioritizing Gaming Workers' Health and Safety Concerns Using Mapping for Data Collection," *American Journal of Industrial Medicine* 39 (2001): 42–51; M. Keith et al, *Barefoot Research: A Work Security Manual for Workers* (Geneva: International Labour Organization, 2002).

3   "What Is a Concussion?" Centers for Disease Control's website, www.cdc.gov/.

4   "Traumatic Brain Injury Information Page," National Institutes of Health's website, www.ninds.nih.gov/.

5   A. Colantonio, "Beyond Football: Intimate Partner Violence and Concussion/Brain Injury," *Canadian Psychology/Psychologie canadienne* 61, no. 2 (2020): 163–66, https://doi.org/10.1037/cap0000208.

6   S. Smarsh, *Heartland: A Memoir of Working Hard and Being Broke in the Richest Country on Earth* (New York: Scribner, 2018), 74.

7   *Post-Traumatic Stress Disorder (PTSD) in the Nursing Profession: Helping Manitoba's Wounded Healers* (Manitoba Nurses Union, 2014), https://manitobanurses.ca/.

8   "Mental Health Disorders Common Following Mild Head Injury," Science Daily, 30 January 2019, www.sciencedaily.com/.

9   "Facts about Women and Trauma," American Psychological Association's website, 2017, www.apa.org/.

10 "Workplace Violence," American Academy of Experts in Traumatic Stress' website, 2020, www.aaets.org/.

11 "Candace Rennick's Remarks—Ottawa Press Conference on Breaking Point," Canadian Union of Public Employees, 2 April 2019, https://cupe.on.ca/.

12 M. O. Schroeder, "The Psychological Impact of Victim-Blaming—and How to Stop It," *US News & World Report*, 19 April 2016, https://health.usnews.com/.

13 B. Zhou, S. Guay, and A. Marchand, "I See So I Feel: Coping with

Workplace Violence Among Victims and Witnesses," *Work* 57 no. 1 (2017): 125–35.

14 V. Di Martino, *Workplace Violence in the Health Sector: Relationship Between Work Stress and Workplace Violence in the Health Sector* (Geneva: ILO/ICN/WHO/PSI, 2003), www.who.int/.

15 K. L. McSteen, "Cumulative Stress," Oncology Nurse Advisor, 23 March 2012, https://oncologynurseadvisor.com/.

16 D. Hango and M. Moyser, *Harassment in Canadian Workplaces* (Ottawa: Statistics Canada, 2018), www.statcan.gc.ca/.

17 L. Young "'It's a Traumatic Moment': How Everyday Racism Can Impact Mental Health," Global News, 3 April 2018, https://globalnews.ca/.

18 R. K. Timothy, "Racism Impacts Your Health," The Conversation, 28 February 2018, https://theconversation.com/; M. Omole, "How Racism Affects Your Health," *The Walrus,* March 2018, https://thewalrus.ca/.

19 I. Olson, "Quebec Temp Agency Head Says Provincial Health Network Often Requests White Personnel," CBC News, 17 March 2021, www.cbc.ca/.

20 "The Facts about Gender-Based Violence," Canadian Women's Foundation's website, www.canadianwomen.org/.

21 "Intersectionality," website of the Sexual Violence Prevention and Response Office, McMaster University, 2021, https://svpro.mcmaster.ca/.

22 G. C. Hansen et al, "Workplace Violence Against Homecare Workers and Its Relationship with Workers Health Outcomes: A Cross-sectional Study," *BMC Public Health* 15 (2015): 11, https://doi.org/10.1186/s12889-014-1340-7.

23 "Risks of Violence in the Field: Taking Care of Healthcare Worker Safety," Guardian Mobile Personal Safety's website, 9 April 2015, www.guardianmps.com/.

Chapter 3. Finding an Abnormality

1 Di Martino, *Workplace Violence in the Health Sector.*

2 D. Hartley et al, "Workplace Violence Prevention for Nurses On-Line Course: Program Development," *Work* 51 no. 1 (2015): 79–89, https://doi.org/10.3233/WOR-141891.

3 Hartley et al, "Workplace Violence Prevention."

4 W. Kuhn, "Dealing with Violence in the Emergency Department," website of the Medical College of Georgia, Augusta University, www.augusta.edu/.

5 Hartley et al, "Workplace Violence Prevention."

6 H. Chaudhury et al, "The Influence of the Physical Environment on Residents with Dementia in Long-Term Care Settings: A Review of the Empirical Literature," *Gerontologist* 58 no. 5 (October 2018): e325–e337, https://doi.org/10.1093/geront/gnw259.

7 U. H. Granheim, A. Horsten, and U. Isaksson, "Female Caregivers' Perceptions of Reasons for Violent Behaviour Among Nursing Home Residents," *Journal of Psychiatric and Mental Health Nursing* 19 (2012): 154–161, https://doi.org/10.1111/j.1365-2850.2011.01768.x.

8 Hartley et al, "Workplace Violence Prevention."

9 Di Martino, *Workplace Violence in the Health Sector.*

10 B. K. Fasanya and E. A. Dada, "Workplace Violence and Safety Issues in Long-Term Medical Care Facilities: Nurses' Perspectives," *Safety and Health at Work* 7 (2016): 97–101, https://doi.org/10.1016/j.shaw.2015.11.002.

11 D. A. Rastegar, "Health Care Becomes an Industry," *Annals of Family Medicine* 2 no. 1 (2004): 79–83.

12 A. Banerjee et al, "'Careworkers Don't Have a Voice': Epistemological Violence in Residential Care for Older People," *Journal of Aging Studies* 33 (2015): 28–36; T. Daly et al, "Lifting the 'Violence Veil': Examining Working Conditions in Long-Term Care Facilities Using Iterative Mixed Methods," *Canadian Journal of Aging* 30, no. 2 (2011): 271–84.

13 *This Is Long-Term Care 2016* (Toronto: Ontario Long Term Care Association, 2016), www.oltca.com/.

14 Hartley et al, "Workplace Violence Prevention."

15 Hartley et al, "Workplace Violence Prevention."

16 *Workers' Comp Is a Right* (Ontario Network of Injured Workers' Groups, 2017), https://injuredworkersonline.org/.

Chapter 4. Birth and Decline of the Health Care System

1 C. Sismondo, "The History of Why Canada's Health Care System Falls Short," *Maclean's*, 23 May 2018, www.macleans.ca/.

2   "Milestones: Universal Policies," Canadian Public Health Association's website, www.cpha.ca/.

3   L. Brown and D. Taylor, "The Birth of Medicare: From Saskatchewan's Breakthrough to Canada-Wide Coverage," *Canadian Dimension*, 3 July 2012, https://canadiandimension.com/.

4   Brown and Taylor, "The Birth of Medicare."

5   Government of Canada, Royal Commission on Health Services, 1961–1964, www.canada.ca/.

6   "Making Medicare: The Second Hall Commission, 1979–1980," Canadian Museum of History's website, 2010, www.historymuseum.ca/.

7   Brown and Taylor, "The Birth of Medicare."

8   C. Simpson et al, "How Healthy Is the Canadian Health-Care System?" The Conversation, 24 September 2017, http://theconversation.com/.

9   P. Armstrong and H. Armstrong, "Contradictions at Work: Struggles for Control in Canadian Health Care," *Socialist Register* (2010): 145–67.

10 Armstrong and Armstrong, "Contradictions at Work."

11 "Commission on the Future of Health Care in Canada: The Romanow Commission," Government of Canada's website, www.canada.ca/.

12 "Health—Hospital Beds Per 1,000 People—Countries Compared," Nationmaster, www.nationmaster.com/.

13 "OECD Countries by Hospital Beds," World Atlas, 2017, www.worldatlas.com/.

14 OCHU-CUPE, *Pre-budget Submission by the Ontario Council of Hospital Unions/Canadian Union of Public Employees to the Standing Committee on Finance and Economic Affairs of the Ontario Legislature* (CUPE Research, 17 January 2019), https://ochu.on.ca/.

15 Ontario Health Coalition, "Hospital Overload: Ford Government Begins Its Assault on Ontario Hospitals," *The Bullet*, 5 February 2019, https://socialistproject.ca/.

16 Canadian Union of Public Employees, *Fewer Hands, Less Hospital Care* (CUPE, 2016); Stella Yeadon, "Ontario Lags Provinces in Hospital Care, Funding," *Counterpoint*, 20 October 2016, https://cupe.ca/.

17 One of the significant impacts of the inadequate funding was the reduction in the number of hospital beds and the staff to needed to attend to the patients in the beds. "Nursing in Canada, 2019," Canadian Institute for Health Information's website, 30 July 2020, www.cihi.ca/.

18 *Ontario Hospitals: Leaders in Efficiency* (Toronto: Ontario Hospital Association, 2019), www.oha.com/.

19 "Premier Ford Can't Wish Hallway Medicine Away and Cut Millions of Dollars from Hospitals, Long-Term Care, Public Health and EMS in 2019," Ontario Health Coalition, 25 July 2019, www.ontariohealthcoalition.ca/.

20 G. Albo, "Divided Province: Democracy and the Politics of State Restructuring in Ontario," in *Divided Province: Ontario Politics in the Age of Neoliberalism*, ed. G. Albo and B. M. Evans (Montreal: McGill-Queen's University Press, 2019).

21 D. Allan, "Medicare: The Privatization of Healthcare in Canada," *Global Research*, 5 October 2011, www.globalresearch.ca/.

22 "$22 Billion in Cuts to Funding for Public Services Planned By Mr. Ford," Ontario Health Coalition's website, 3 June 2018, www.ontariohealthcoalition.ca/.

23 B. Murnigham, *Selling Ontario's Health Care: The Real Story on Government Spending and Public Relations*, The Ontario Alternative Budget, Technical Paper no. 11 (Ottawa: Canadian Centre for Policy Alternatives, 2001), www.policyalternatives.ca/.

24 C. Fanelli and M. P. Thomas, "Austerity, Competitiveness, and Neoliberalism Redux: Ontario Responds to the Great Recession," *Socialist Studies* 7 no. 1/2 (2001): 141–70.

25 Albo, "Divided Province."

26 Allan, "Medicare."

27 Fanelli and Thomas, "Austerity, Competitiveness, and Neoliberalism."

28 "When It Comes to Hospitals It's 'Hacksaw Kathleen,'" Ontario Health Coalition's website, 28 May 2016, www.ontariohealthcoalition.ca/.

29 "Everything Doug Ford Cut or Cancelled during His First Year as Premier," Flare News, 7 June 2019, www.flare.com/.

30 J. Frketich and G. LaFletche, "Introducing Ontario's New Health Care Super Power," *Hamilton Spectator*, 22 July 2019, www.thespec.com/.

31 E. C. Schneider et al, "Mirror, Mirror 2017: International Comparison Reflects Flaws and Opportunities for Better US Health," The Commonwealth Fund, July 2017, www.commonwealthfund.org/.

32 In fact, the wait time increased in 2016–17 by 11 per cent over the previous year. CIHI statistics show that "90% of visits were completed within 32.6 hours—a significant increase from 29.3 hours the year before and 28.3 hours in 2012–2013. Every jurisdiction saw an increase in ED length of stay for admitted patients." "Emergency Department Wait Times in Canada Continuing to Rise," CIHI's website, November 2017, www.cihi.ca/.

33 W. Watson, "Why Canada's 'Best' Health-Care System Just Got Ranked Last—Again," *Financial Post*, 11 October 2017.

34 A. Drummond, "Why Hospital ERs Are So Overcrowded—It's Not Patients' Fault," *Ottawa Citizen*, 4 December 2017.

35 M. Vigliotti, "Emergency Department Wait Times on the Rise in Canada: CIHI Data," iPolitics, 28 November 2019, https://ipolitics.ca/.

36 "Primary Health Care Providers, 2016," Health Fact Sheet, Statistics Canada's website, 27 September 2017, www.statcan.gc.ca/.

37 Drummond, "Why Hospital ERs Are So Overcrowded."

38 *Hallway Health Care: A System Under Strain, 1st Interim Report from the Premier's Council on Improving Healthcare and Ending Hallway Medicine* (Toronto: Government of Ontario, January 2019), www.health.gov.on.ca/.

39 A. Picard, "'Tis the Season for Hospital Overcrowding—But the Flu Isn't to Blame," *Globe and Mail*, 7 January 2019.

40 N. Macdonald, "Canada's Health Care System Is Hopelessly Sclerotic," CBC News, 12 June 2019, www.cbc.ca/.

41 P. Daflos, "NDP Plans Underway for Big Changes to Health-Care System," CTV News, 30 Nov 2017, https://bc.ctvnews.ca/.

42 "Wait Times for Priority Procedures in Canada," CIHI's website, 9 July 2020, www.cihi.ca/.

43 "Hospital Overload: Backgrounder on Ontario's Hospital Bed Shortage," Ontario Health Coalition's website, 2015, www.ontariohealthcoalition.ca/.

44 Health Quality Ontario, *Measuring Up, 2018* (Toronto: Queen's Printer for Ontario, 2018), www.hqontario.ca/.

45 Canadian Mental Health Association, *Mental Health in the Balance: Ending the Health Care Disparity in Canada* (CMHA, 2018), www.cmha.ca/.

46 Auditor General of Ontario, "Specialty Psychiatric Hospital Services," chapter 3, section 3.12 in 2016 *Annual Report of the Office of the Auditor General of Ontario*, www.auditor.on.ca/.

47 G. M. Liss and L. McCaskell, "Injuries Due to Violence: Workers' Compensation Claims Among Nurses in Ontario," *AAOHN Journal* 42, no. 8 (1994): 384–90.

48 Liss and McCaskell, "Injuries Due to Violence."

49 "Health Care Sector Trends," Ontario Ministry of Labour's website, 2018, www.ontario.ca/.

50 "Inside a Nurse's World: Where Stress Is Status Quo," CBC News, 19 April 2017, www.cbc.ca/.

51 A. Jameton, *Nursing Practice: The Ethical Issues* (New Jersey: Prentice-Hall, 1984).

52 A. Jameton, "What Moral Distress in Nursing History Could Suggest about the Future of Health Care," *AMA Journal of Ethics* 19 no. 6 (2017): 617–28.

53 D. Martin, "Ontario's Nurses Are Facing Unprecedented Levels of Stress," *Ottawa Citizen*, 6 June 2019.

54 Canadian Nurses Association, *Position Statement: Taking Action on Nurse Fatigue* (Ottawa: CNA, 2010), www.cna-aiic.ca/.

Chapter 5.
Birth and Decline of the Long-Term Care System

1 J. Struthers, "Home, Hotel, Hospital, Hospice: Conflicting Images of Long-Term Residential Care," in *Care Home Stories: Aging, Disability, and Long-Term Residential Care*, ed. S. Chivers and U. Kriebernegg (Bielefeld, DE: transcript, 2017), https://library.oapen.org/.

2 Struthers, "Home, Hotel, Hospital, Hospice."

3 Struthers, "Home, Hotel, Hospital, Hospice."

4 J. Struthers, "Reluctant Partners: State Regulation of Private Nursing Home Ontario, 1941–1972," in *The Welfare State in Canada: Past, Present, and Future,* ed. Raymond Blake et al (Irwin Publishing, 1997), 171–92.

5 T. Daly, "Dancing the Two-Step in Ontario's Long-Term Care Sector: More Deterrence-Oriented Regulation = Ownership and Management Consolidation," *Studies in Political Economy* 95 no. 1 (2015): 29–58, https://doi.org/10.1080/19187033.2015.11674945.

6 N. M. Stall et al, "For-Profit Long-Term Care Homes and the Risk of COVID-19 Outbreaks and Resident Deaths," *CMAJ* 192 no. 33 (2020), https://doi.org/10.1503/cmaj.201197.

7 "About Long-Term Care in Ontario: Facts and Figures, 2019," Ontario Long Term Care Association's website, www.oltca.com/.

8 C. Simpson et al, "How Healthy Is the Canadian Health-Care System?" The Conversation, 24 September 2017, http://theconversation.com/.

9 Auditor General of Ontario, "After Admission, Patients Experiencing Long Waits at Large Community Hospitals for In-Patient Beds and Surgery," news release, 30 November 2016, www.auditor.on.ca/.

10 *This Is Long-Term Care 2019* (Toronto: Ontario Long Term Care Association, 2019), www.oltca.com/.

11 A. Jones, "There Were 29 Homicides in Ontario Long-Term Care Homes in the Past Six Years, Report Says," *Toronto Star,* 21 January 2019.

12 *This Is Long-Term Care 2019.*

13 *This Is Long-Term Care 2019.*

14 Ontario Long Term Care Association, *More Care, Better Care: 2018 Budget Submission* (Toronto: OLTCA, 2018), www.oltca.com/.

15 S. Sharkey, *People Caring for People: Impacting the Quality of Life and Care of Residents of Long-Term Care Homes—A Report of the Independent Review of Staffing and Care Standards for Long-Term Care Homes in Ontario* (Toronto: Government of Ontario, 2008), www.hhr-rhs.ca/.

16 "Bill 13, Time to Care Act (Long-Term Care Homes Amendment, Minimum Standard of Daily Care), 2020," Legislative Assembly of Ontario's website, www.ola.org/.

17 *Situation Critical: Planning, Access, Levels of Care and Violence in Ontario's Long-Term Care* (Toronto: Ontario Health Coalition, 2019), www.ontariohealthcoalition.ca/.

18 J. Struthers, interview with James Brophy and Margaret Keith, 18 September 2019.

19 R. Lowndes and J. Struthers, "Changes and Continuities in the Workplace of Long-Term Residential Care in Canada, 1970–2015," *Journal of Canadian Studies* 50 no. 2 (2016): 368–95.

20 D. Martin, "Ontario's Nurses Are Facing Unprecedented Levels of Stress," *Ottawa Citizen,* 6 June 2019.

21 Lowndes and Struthers, "Changes and Continuities."

22 J. McKenzie, "Round Table Discussions Hope to Resolve PSW Crisis in Sudbury," CBC News, 6 June 2019, www.cbc.ca/.

23 Chaudhury et al, "The Influence of the Physical Environment."

24 J. Cohen-Mansfield, "Nonpharmacologic Interventions for Inappropriate Behaviors in Dementia: A Review, Summary, and Critique," *American Journal of Geriatric Psychiatry* 9 no. 4 (2001): 361–81; Neena Chappell, Stephen Bornstein, and Rob Kean, *Agitation and Aggression in Long-Term Care Residents with Dementia in Newfoundland and Labrador* (St. John's, NL: Newfoundland & Labrador Centre for Applied Health Research, Memorial University, 2014), www.nlcahr.mun.ca/.

25 "About Long-Term Care in Ontario, 2019."

26 P. Armstrong, "When Choosing a Nursing Home, Check the Clothing and Laundry," The Conversation, 14 August 2018, www.theconversation.com/.

27 T. Carabino, "I Will Not Let My Father's Death Be in Vain," Canadian Association of Retired Persons' website, 5 October 2017, www.carp.ca/.

28 Jones, "There Were 29 Homicides."

29 M. Mancini, "At Least 29 Ontario Long-Term Care Residents Killed By Fellow Residents in 6 Years," CBC News, 20 January 2019, www.cbc.ca/.

30 Mancini, "At Least 29."

31 A. Banerjee and P. Armstrong, "Centring Care: Explaining Regulatory Tensions in Residential Care for Older Persons," *Studies in Political Economy* 95 (Spring 2015): 7–28.

32 Y. Song et al, "Factors Associated with the Responsive Behaviours of Older Adults Living in Long-Term Care Homes Towards Staff: A Systematic Review Protocol," *BMJ Open* 9:e028416 (2019), https://doi.org/10.1136/bmjopen-2018-028416.

Chapter 6. Treatment Strategies

1   E. Brohman, "Nurse Assaulted By Patient At HSC Suffering Long Term Effects," CBC News, 29 July 2019, www.cbc.ca/.

2   Phillips, "Workplace Violence Against Health Care Workers"; National Institute for Occupational Safety and Health, *Violence: Occupational Hazards in Hospitals*, DHHS (NIOSH) publication no. 2002–101 (Cincinnati: NIOSH, 2002), www.cdc.gov/niosh/; and T. Lowe, "Violence: Shift Work, Stress, and Violence," *New Solutions* 23, supplement (2013): 1–167.

3   G. Karakurt and K. E. Silver, "Emotional Abuse in Intimate Relationships: The Role of Gender and Age," *Violence and Victims* 28 no. 5 (2013): 804–21, https://doi.org/10.1891/0886-6708.vv-d-12-00041.

4   Phillips, "Workplace Violence Against Health Care Workers."

5   "A Matter That Concerns Us All," Preventing Interpersonal Violence in the Workplace, website of the Institute de recherche Robert-Sauvé en santé et en sécurité du travail, 2014, www.irsst.qc.ca/.

6   B. Strachan, "Kamloops Nurse Attacked By Mentally Ill Patient," CBC News, 9 December 2013, www.cbc.ca/.

7   Phillips, "Workplace Violence Against Health Care Workers."

8   Brohman, "Nurse Assaulted by Patient."

9   H. Ulrichsen, "'Happens Too Often': Stabbing of HSN Nurse By Patient Highlights Pervasive Violence in Health Care Sector," Sudbury.com, 25 October 2019, www.sudbury.com/.

10 J. Bieman, "London Hospital Reviewing Violent Patient-Flagging Amid Backlash," *London Free Press*, 21 February 2019, https://lfpress.com/.

11 K. Lippel, "Conceptualising Violence at Work Through a Gender Lens: Regulation and Strategies for Prevention and Redress," *University of Oxford Human Rights Hub Journal* 1 (2018): 142–66.

12 N. R. Collins and B. Rogers, "Growing Concerns with Workplace Incivility," *Workplace Health and Safety* 65 no. 11 (2017): 564, https://doi.org/10.1177/2165079917719468.

13 "Incivility, Bullying, and Workplace Violence: ANA Position Statement," 22 July 2015, American Nurses Association website, www.nursingworld.org/.

14 Di Martino, *Workplace Violence in the Health Sector.*

15 A. Schablon et al, "Frequency and Consequences of Violence and Aggression Towards Employees in the German Healthcare and Welfare System: A Cross-Sectional Study," *BMJ Open* 2:e001420 (2012), https://doi.org/10.1136/bmjopen-2012-001420.

16 Canadian Press, "Patients Lacking English Need Equal Access to Interpreters across Canada: Doctor," *Victoria News*, 4 November 2019, www.vicnews.com/.

17 R. Steele and K. Linsley, "Relieving In-Patient Boredom in General Hospitals: The Evidence for Intervention and Practical Ideas," *BJPsych Advances* 21 (2015): 63–70.

18 C. Arik, R. Anat, and E. Arie, "Encountering Anger in the Emergency Department: Identification, Evaluations and Responses of Staff Members to Anger Displays," *Emergency Medicine International* (2012), https://doi.org/10.1155/2012/603215.

19 "Physician Billing Codes in Response to COVID-19," Canadian Institute for Health Information's website, 8 April 2020, www.cihi.ca/.

20 R. H. Glazier et al, "Shifts in Office and Virtual Primary Care during the Early COVID-19 Pandemic in Ontario, Canada," *CMAJ* 193 no. 6 (February 2021): E200–E210, https://doi.org/10.1503/cmaj.202303.

21 *Gardens That Care: Planning Outdoor Environments for People with Dementia* (Glenside, AU: Alzheimer's Australia SA, 2010), www.enablingenvironments.com.au/.

22 Ontario Long Term Care Association, *More Care, Better Care: 2018 Budget Submission* (Toronto: OLTCA, 2018), www.oltca.com/.

23 A. Sagan, "Canada's Version of Hogewey Dementia Village Recreates 'Normal' Life," CBC News, 3 May 2015, www.cbc.ca/.

24 Sagan, "Canada's Version."

25 D. Farsetta, "Being Mortal: Nursing and What Matters in the End," Center for Aging Research and Education, newsletter, Issue 6, 11 February 2015, https://care.nursing.wisc.edu/.

26 M. Marychuk, "Malton Village Workers Say Butterfly Care Model Is Taking a Toll on Their Health," Mississauga.com, 1 May 2019, www.mississauga.com/.

27 Marychuk, "Malton Village Workers."

28 M. Welsh, "The Fix," *Toronto Star*, 20 June 2018, https://projects.thestar.com/.

29 P. Armstrong et al, *Models for Long-Term Residential Care: A Summary of the Consultants' Report to Long-Term Care Homes and Services, City of Toronto*, 15 April 2019, www.toronto.ca/.

30 M. Welsh, "Nursing Homes Could Get Big Benefit from Emotion-Focused Care Models, Says New Report Commissioned by Toronto," *Toronto Star,* 8 March 2019.

31 Ontario Ministry of Labour and Ministry of Health and Long-Term Care, "Preventing Workplace Violence in the Health Care Sector," Government of Ontario's website, 15 May 2017, www.ontario.ca/.

32 R. Devitt, I. Andress, and K. Edmonson, "Zero Tolerance for Workplace Violence in Health Care: A Call to Action," Healthy Debate, 16 March 2015, www.healthydebate.ca/.

33 *Violence Facing Health Care Workers in Canada: Report of the Standing Committee on Health* (Ottawa: House of Commons, 2019), www.ourcommons.ca/.

34 Phillips, "Workplace Violence Against Health Care Workers."

35 "Quality Improvement Plan Guidance: Workplace Violence Prevention," Health Quality Ontario's website, revised February 2019, www.hqontario.ca/.

36 Brohman, "Nurse Assaulted by Patient."

37 D. M. Gates, G. L. Gillespie, and P. Succop, "Violence Against Nurses and Its Impact on Stress and Productivity," *Nursing Economics* 29 no. 2 (March–April 2011): 59–66.

38 Phillips, "Workplace Violence Against Health Care Workers."

39 Gates, Gillespie, and Succop, "Violence Against Nurses."

40 Occupational Safety and Health Administration, *Guidelines for Preventing Workplace Violence for Healthcare and Social Service Workers*, OSHA report no. 3148-04R (U.S. Department of Labor, 2016), www.osha.gov/.

41 S. Zhao et al, "Coping with Workplace Violence in Healthcare Settings: Social Support and Strategies," *International Journal of Environmental Research and Public Health* 12 no. 11 (2015): 14429–44, https://doi.org/10.3390/ijerph121114429.

42 "CUPE Ontario's Communities Not Cuts Campaign Rallies at Doug Ford's Office," Canadian Union of Public Employees' website, 14 November 2019, https://cupe.ca/.

43 Government of Ontario, *Workplace Safety and Insurance Act*, 1997, S.O. 1997, c. 16, Sched. A, www.ontario.ca/.

44 Steve Mantis, ONIWG Research Committee Chair, to Premier Kathleen Wynne, "WSIB's Principle of 'Better at Work' Contravenes 'Time to Heal' and WSI Legislation," Kaministiquia, ON, 21 July 2016, Ontario Network of Injured Workers' Groups' website, https://injuredworkersonline.org/.

45 Ontario Network of Injured Workers' Groups, *Phantom Jobs & Empty Pockets: What Really Happens to Workers with Work Acquired Disabilities?* (ONIWG, May 2019), https://injuredworkersonline.org/.

46 Brohman, "Nurse Assaulted by Patient."

47 Devitt, Andress, and Edmonson, "Zero Tolerance."

48 "Stop the Violence Rally," Canadian Union of Public Employees Local 1974's website, 9 March 2018, https://cupe1974.ca/.

Chapter 7. Rocky Road to Recovery

1 L. L. Heise, "Violence Against Women: An Integrated, Ecological Framework," *Violence Against Women* 4 no. 3 (1998): 262–90, https://doi.org/10.1177/1077801298004003002.

2 "The Ecological Framework," Violence Prevention Alliance, World Health Organization's website, 2021, www.who.int/.

3 T. Chamorro-Premuzic and D. Lusk, "The Dark Side of Resilience," *Harvard Business Review*, 16 August 2017, https://hbr.org/.

4 T. Sierra, "The Problem with Using Words Like 'Grit' and 'Resilience' to Describe Burnout," Op-Med, 6 June 2019, https://opmed.doximity.com/.

5 Z. Villines, "Battered Woman Syndrome and Intimate

Partner Violence," Medical News Today, 3 December 2018, www.medicalnewstoday.com/.

6 J. Huizen, "What Is Gaslighting?" Medical News Today, 14 July 2020, www.medicalnewstoday.com/.

7 *Violence Facing Health Care Workers in Canada.*

8 C. Criado Perez, *Invisible Women: Data Bias in a World Designed for Men* (New York: Abrams Press, 2019), 139.

9 K. Messing, *Bent Out of Shape: Shame, Solidarity, and Women's Bodies at Work* (Toronto: Between the Lines, 2021).

10 D. Nelkin and M. Brown, *Workers at Risk: Voices from the Workplace* (Chicago: University of Chicago Press, 1984), 181.

11 Noam Chomsky, *Understanding Power: The Indispensable Chomsky,* ed. P. R. Mitchell and J. Schoeffel (New York: The New Press, 2002), 250.

12 M. E. Seligman, "Learned Helplessness," *Annual Review of Medicine* 23 no. 1 (1972): 407–12.

13 *APA Dictionary of Psychology,* s.v. "Learned Helplessness," https://dictionary.apa.org/.

14 Michael Lerner, *Surplus Powerlessness: The Psychodynamics of Everyday Life and the Psychology of Individual and Social Transformation* (Humanities Press International, 1991).

15 Lerner, *Surplus Powerlessness.*

16 Rebecca Solnit, "Silence and Powerlessness Go Hand in Hand—Women's Voices Must Be Heard," *The Guardian,* 8 March 2017, www.theguardian.com/.

17 G. B. Adams and D. L. Balfour, "Public Service Ethics and Administrative Evil: Prospects and Problems," September 2003, https://udayton.edu/.

18 Adams and Balfour, "Public Service Ethics."

19 Lippel, "Conceptualising Violence at Work." See also A. Banerjee et al, "Structural Violence," *Social Science & Medicine.*

20 P. Hartzband and J. Groopman, "Medical Taylorism," *New England Journal of Medicine* 324 (2016): 106–9.

21 E. J. Topol, A. Verghese, and A. M. Kleinman, "Caregiving and the Soul of Medicine," Medscape, 1 November 2019, www.medscape.com/.

22 P. Battah, "Workplace Class System Impacts on Morale, Productivity," CBC News, 22 November 2015, www.cbc.ca/.

23 *Violence Facing Health Care Workers in Canada.*

24 A. Tanner, "The Gruesome Killing of An Alberta GP Puts a Spotlight on Physician Abuse," *Maclean's*, 11 November 2020, www.macleans.ca/.

25 M. Mammoliti, "Violence Against Physicians," *Ontario Medical Review*, 24 November 2020, www.oma.org/.

26 Di Martino, *Workplace Violence in the Health Sector.*

27 Banerjee et al, "Structural Violence," *Social Science & Medicine*; J. Galtung, "Violence, Peace, and Peace Research," *Journal of Peace Research* 6 (1969): 167–91; J. Galtung, "Cultural Violence," *Journal of Peace Research* 27 (1999): 291–305; R. J. Howerton Child and J. C. Mentes, "Violence Against Women: The Phenomenon of Workplace Violence Against Nurses," *Issues in Mental Health Nursing* 31 no. 2 (2010), https://doi.org/10.3109/01612840903267638; Pat Armstrong et al, "Structural Violence in Long-Term Residential Care," *Women's Health & Urban Life* 10 (2011): 111–29.

28 Nursing Statistics, Canadian Nurses Association's website, www.cna-aiic.ca.

29 B. Whitehead, "Will Graduate Entry Free Nursing from the Shackles of Class and Gender Oppression?" *Nursing Times* 106 no. 21 (2010): 19–22.

30 L. J. Greenfield, "Doctors and Nurses: A Troubled Partnership," *Annals of Surgery* 230 no. 3 (September 1999): 279–88, https://doi.org/10.1097/00000658-199909000-00001.

31 S. Torres, S. Parniak, and C. Kelly, "Community Health Workers and Personal Support Workers," from *Introduction to the Health Workforce in Canada*, n.d., www.hhr-rhs.ca/.

32 D. Izenberg and M. Taylor, "Who Are Ontario's Personal Support Workers?" Healthy Debate, 1 March 2018, https://healthydebate.ca.

33 Messing, *One-Eyed Science.*

34 Armstrong et al, "Structural Violence," *Women's Health & Urban Life.*

35 Banerjee et al, "Structural Violence," *Social Science & Medicine.*

36 Canadian Women's Foundation, *Fact Sheet: Moving Women Out of Violence,* August 2016, https://canadianwomen.org/.

37 R. Storey, "By the Numbers: Workers' Compensation and the (Further) Conventionalization of Workplace Violence," in *The Violence of Work: New Essays in Canadian and US Labour History*, ed. Jeremy Milloy and Joan Sangster (Toronto: University of Toronto Press, 2021), 160–83.

38 P. Armstrong, H. Armstrong, and C. Fuller, *Health Care, Limited* (Ottawa: Canadian Centre for Policy Alternatives, 2000), 39, www.policyalternatives.ca/.

39 B. Jaffray, "Experiences of Violent Victimization and Unwanted Sexual Behaviours Among Gay, Lesbian, Bisexual and Other Sexual Minority People, and the Transgender Population, in Canada, 2018," Statistics Canada's website, 9 September 2020, https://www150.statcan.gc.ca/.

40 K. Jefferies, "Recognizing History of Black Nurses a First Step to Addressing Racism and Discrimination in Nursing," The Conversation, 11 May 2020, https://theconversation.com/.

41 Canadian Research Network for Care in the Community, *Ontario Personal Support Workers in Home and Community Care: CRNCC/ PSNO Survey Results*, In Focus Backgrounder, 2010, www.ryerson.ca/.

42 B. Sethi, "Personal Support Workers Are the Backbone of Health Care but the Bottom of the Power Structure," The Conversation, 2 September 2020, https://theconversation.com/.

43 A.-A. Bouka and Y. Bouka, "Canada's COVID-19 Blind Spots on Race, Immigration and Labour," Policy Options, 19 May 2020, https:// policyoptions.irpp.org/.

44 O. Mosleh, "Front-Line Health-Care Workers Speak Up about Racism At Work," *Toronto Star,* 31 May 2020, https://thestar.com/.

45 In 2016, there were 9,695 Indigenous nurses in Canada. While making up 4.9 per cent of the Canadian population, they represented only 3 per cent of registered nurses. *Aboriginal Nursing in Canada,* Professional Occupations in Nursing NOC 2016-301 (Saskatoon: University of Saskatchewan College of Nursing, [2016]), https://nursing.usask.ca/.

46 Smarsh, *Heartland,* 45.

47 Mosleh, "Front-Line Health-Care Workers."

48 C. Appia, "Ontario Long-Term Care Residents to Get 4 Hours of Direct Care Daily By 2025," Toronto.com, 3 November 2020, https:// toronto.com/.

49 "RNAO Statement in Response to the Government's Announcement on Increasing Direct Care for Long-Term Care Resident to Four Hours Per Day," Cision, 3 November 2020, www.newswire.ca/.

50 K. Dubinski, "Almost 10,000 Patients Have Been Flagged as 'Potentially Violent' in LHSC in the Last Year," CBC News, 3 June 2019, www.cbc.ca/.

51 "NDP Legislation Looks to Protect Workers Who Speak Up about Workplace Violence," Sudbury.com, 13 December 2017, www.sudbury.com/.

52 "Gélinas' Bill Would Ban Reprisals Against Health-Care Workers Reporting Violence," Sudbury.com, 9 May 2019, www.sudbury.com/.

53 "Bill 111, Speaking Out about Workplace Violence and Workplace Harassment Act, 2019," Legislative Assembly of Ontario's website, www.ola.org/; F. Gélinas, "Bill 111: An Act to Amend the Occupational Health and Safety Act to Protect Workers Who Speak Out about Workplace Violence and Workplace Harassment," Legislative Assembly of Ontario's website, 2019, www.ola.org/.

54 W. Glauser, "Why Some Doctors Want to Defund the Police," *CMAJ* 192 no. 48 (2020): E1644–45, https://doi.org/10.1503/cmaj.1095905.

55 "Let's Talk Defunding the Police in Canadian Context," Canadian Cultural Mosaic Foundation's website, 6 July 2020, www.canadian culturalmosaicfoundation.com/.

56 Canadian Union of Public Employees, "'Help Discourage Violent Attacks on Health Staff': Nurses Ask MPPs to Support Change to Criminal Code for Nurses Week," news release, 2 May 2017, https://cupe.ca/.

57 "Don Davies on Criminal Code," OpenParliament.ca, 28 February 2019, https://openparliament.ca/

58 "Workplace Violence Toolkit," Canadian Federation of Nurses Unions' website, https://nursesunions.ca/violence/.

59 "Northern Ontario Hospital Workers Win New Contract," UNIFOR's website, 23 April 2018, www.unifor.org/.

60 "Workplace Violence Toolkit."

61 K. Birch, "What Exactly Is Neoliberalism?" The Conversation, 2 November 2017, https://theconversation.com/.

62 R. Keplin, "Doug Ford and Neoliberalism: 'Opening Ontario' by Shutting Down Democratic Process," *Canadian Dimension*, 31 August 2020, https://canadiandimension.com/.

63 G. Monbiot, "Neoliberalism: The Ideology at the Root of All Our Problems," *The Guardian*, 15 April 2016, www.theguardian.com/.

64 R. Robinson, "At What Cost? Ontario Pushes Ahead with P3s," The Monitor, 17 September 2019, https://monitormag.ca/.

65 A. Wherry, "Leaving Out Long-Term Care Was Medicare's Original Sin—and We're Paying for It Now," CBC News, 28 May 2020, www.cbc.ca/.

66 P. Armstrong et al, *Re-imagining Long-Term Residential Care in the COVID-19 Crisis* (Ottawa: Canadian Centre for Policy Alternatives, 2020), www.policyalternatives.ca/.

67 N. M. Stall et al, "For-Profit Long-Term Care Homes and the Risk of

COVID-19 Outbreaks and Resident Deaths," *CMAJ* 192 no. 33 (2020): E946–55, https://doi.org/10.1503/cmaj.201197.

68 R. Ferguson, "Ontario's For-Profit Nursing Homes Have 78% More COVID-19 Deaths Than Non-Profits, Report Finds," *Toronto Star*, 20 January 2021, www.thestar.com/.

69 C. Hedges and J. Sacco, *Days of Destruction, Days of Revolt* (Nation Books, 2012).

70 Storey, "By the Numbers."

Chapter 8. Collective Quest for the Cure

1 J. Birnbaum, *Civil Rights since 1787: A Reader on the Black Struggle* (New York: NYU Press, 2000), 468.

2 T. M. Melaku et al, "Be a Better Ally," *Harvard Business Review*, November–December 2020, https://hbr.org/.

3 K. Quinnell, "New Bill Seeks to Protect Health Care and Social Service Workers from Workplace Violence," Workplace Fairness' website, 19 November 2018, www.workplacefairness.org/.

4 R. DeMatteo, "Grassroots Activism Is the Key to Worker Health and Safety," Diablogue, 10 January 2017, https://diablogue.org/.

5 "Health Care Workers Rally At Queen's Park Drive-By Action," Cision, 23 March 2021, www.newswire.ca/.

6 "Natalie Mehra (Ontario Health Coalition) on How the Conditions of Work Are the Conditions of Care," excerpt of the Nippissing NDP's Economic Recovery Health Readiness webinar, 29 April 2020, YouTube video posted 2 May 2020, 0:25, https://youtu.be/SW5LVrg_tfU.

7 Ontario Health Coalition, "Day of Action Against Healthcare Cuts and Privatization," *The Bullet*, April 2019, https://socialistproject.ca/.

8 "Stop the Violence Rally," Canadian Union of Public Employees Local 1974's website, 9 March 2018, https://cupe1974.ca/.

9 Messing, *Bent Out of Shape.*

Afterword

1 OCHU–CUPE, "Healthcare Workers Launch International Women's Day Actions with Message to Premier Ford: 'Respect Us, Protect Us, Pay Us,'" news release, 7 March 2021, https://ochu.on.ca/.

2 "COVID-19: Health Worker Death Toll Rises to at Least 17000 as Organizations Call for Rapid Vaccine Rollout," Amnesty International's website, 5 March 2021, www.amnesty.org/.

3   M. Stephenson. S. Bell, and A. Russell, "Military Teams Raise Concerns about Conditions at Ontario Care Homes," Global News, 26 May 2020, www.globalnews.ca/.

4   Jan Malek, "Military Report on Long-Term Care Homes Reveals Long-Known Truths," Council of Canadians' website, 2020, https://canadians.org/.

5   Ontario Health Coalition, "Almost 4,000 Dead in Long-Term Care as We Approach End of Wave 2: Wave 2 Deaths Exceed Wave 1," news release, 12 March 2021, www.ontariohealthcoalition.ca/.

6   P. Webster, "COVID-19 Highlights Canada's Care Home Crisis," *The Lancet* 397 no. 10270 (2021): 183, https://doi.org/10.1016/S0140-6736(21)00083-0.

7   E. Tubb, K. Wallace, and B. Kennedy, "For-Profit Nursing Homes in Ontario Say Ownership Has Nothing to Do with Their Higher COVID-19 Death Rates," *Toronto Star*, 26 February 2021, www.thestar.com/.

8   P. Armstrong and H. Armstrong, "Contradictions at Work: Struggles for Control in Canadian Health Care," *Socialist Register* 46 (2010): 145–67.

9   McArthur et al, "Novel Virus, Old Story."

10 "Ontario Says a COVID-19 Field Hospital Is Expected to Take Patients This Month," CTV News, 15 April 2021, https://toronto.ctvnews.ca/; M. Crawley and S. Jonas, "Ontario Hospitals Allowed to Transfer Patients without Consent," CBC News, 9 April 2021, www.cbc.ca/.

11 "Ontario Health Minister Misinformed: 87 Per Cent of Province's Health Care Staff Polled Say Not Enough PPE on Hand to Keep Them Safe," Canadian Union of Public Employees' website, 30 March 2020, https://cupe.ca/.

12 Public Health Ontario, *Technical Brief: IPAC Recommendations for Use of Personal Protective Equipment for Care of Individuals with Suspect or Confirmed COVID-19*, fourth revision, 30 May 2020, www.publichealthontario.ca/.

13 Ontario Health, *Personal Protective Equipment (PPE) Use during the COVID-19 Pandemic*, 11 Aug 2020, www.ontariohealth.ca/.

14 J. Schijven et al, "Quantitative Microbial Risk Assessment for Airborne Transmission of SARS-CoV-2 via Breathing, Speaking, Singing, Coughing, and Sneezing," *Environmental Health Perspectives* 129 no. 4 (2021), https://doi.org/10.1289/EHP7886.

15 "N95 Respirators, Surgical Masks, and Face Masks," U.S. Food and Drug Administration's website, 9 April 2021, www.fda.gov/.

16 C. R. MacIntyre and Q. Wang, "Physical Distancing, Face Masks, and Eye Protection for Prevention of COVID-19," *The Lancet* 395 no. 10242 (2020): 1973–87, https://doi.org/10.1016/S0140-6736(20)31142-9; E. L. Petsonk and P. Harber, "Respiratory Protection for Health Care Workers: A 2020 COVID-19 Perspective," *American Journal of Industrial Medicine* 63 no. 8 (2020): 655–58, https://doi.org/10.1002/ajim.23144; D. De Chang et al, "Protecting Health-Care Workers from Subclinical Coronavirus Infection," *Lancet: Respiratory Medicine* 8 no. 3 (2020): E13, https://doi.org/10.1016/S2213-2600(20)30066-7.

17 J. Gollan and E. Shogren, "31,000 and Counting," Reveal, 12 May 2020, https://revealnews.org/.

18 S. Soucheray, "Unmasked: Experts Explain Necessary Respiratory Protection for COVID-19," *News and Perspective*, website of the Center for Infectious Disease Research and Policy (CIDRAP), University of Minnesota, 13 February 2020, www.cidrap.umn.edu/.

19 R. O'Neill, "WHO Knew: How the World Health Organization (WHO) Became a Dangerous Interloper on Workplace Health and Safety and COVID-19," *New Solutions: A Journal of Environmental and Occupational Health Policy* 30 no. 3 (2020): 237–48, https://doi.org/10.1177/1048291120961337.

20 A. Mandavilli, "Medical Workers Should Use Respirator Masks, Not Surgical Masks," *New York Times*, 1 June 2020, www.nytimes.com/.

21 L. Brosseau, "COVID-19 Transmission Messages Should Hinge on Science," *News and Perspective*, CIDRAP website, 16 March 2020, www.cidrap.umn.edu/.

22 C. Lauren and E. Crosby, "Applying the Precautionary Principle to Personal Protective Equipment (PPE) Guidance during the COVID-19 Pandemic: Did We Learn the Lessons of SARS?" *Canadian Journal of Anaesthesia* 67 (2020): 1327–32, https://doi.org/10.1007/s12630-020-01760-y.

23 Justice Archie Campbell, *Executive Summary*, vol. 1 of *Spring of Fear: The SARS Commission Final Report* (Toronto: SARS Commission, 2006), www.archives.gov.on.ca/.

24 McArthur et al, "Novel Virus, Old Story."

25 UNIFOR, "Health Care Unions Welcome Significantly Improved COVID-19 Protections for 400,000 Health Care Workers," news release, 5 October 2020, https://unifor.org/.

26 "SEIU Healthcare Response to Rising COVID-19 Cases," Cision, 12 November 2020, www.newswire.ca/.

27 J. T. Brophy et al, "Sacrificed: Ontario Healthcare Workers in the Time of COVID-19," *New Solutions* 30 no. 4 (2020): 267–81, https://doi.org/10.1177/1048291120974358.

28 K. Tomlinson and G. Robertson, "Ottawa Had a Playbook for a Coronavirus-Like Pandemic 14 Years Ago: What Went Wrong?" *Globe and Mail,* 9 April 2020, www.theglobeandmail.com/.

29 J. P. Tasker, "Ottawa Slow to Respond to PPE Shortages Flagged in February," CBC News, 14 August 2020, www.cbc.ca/.

30 K. Tomlinson et al, "Canadian Medical Association Pushes Ottawa to Explain Lack of Preparation Ahead of Pandemic's Arrival," *Globe and Mail,* 9 April 2020, www.theglobeandmail.com/. Lack of preparedness is not unique to Canada. According to Professor Andrew Watterson in the U.K., "missed opportunities" to implement proactive measures have left health care agencies scrambling to deal reactively with equipment shortages and to devise plans and protocols under duress. A. Watterson, "COVID-19 in the UK and Occupational Health and Safety: Predictable Not Inevitable Failures by Government, and Trade Union and Nongovernmental Organization Responses," *New Solutions* 30 no. 2 (2020): 86–94, https://doi.org/10.1177/1048291120929763.

31 C. Slatin, "Under the Knee of Jim Crow and Neoliberalism," *New Solutions* 30 no. 2 (2020): 80–82, https://doi.org/10.1177/1048291120938232.

32 H. Glasbeek, "The Pandemic and Capitalism's Essential Workers," *Canadian Dimension,* 9 March 2021, https://canadiandimension.com/.

33 Canadian Federation of Nurses Unions, "Nurses Launch Investigation into Canada's Failure to Protect Health Care Workers from COVID-19," news release, 22 June 2020, https://nursesunions.ca/.

34 J. Ralph et al, "Heroes, or Just Doing Our Job? The Impact of COVID-19 on Registered Nurses in a Border City," The Conversation, 21 August 2020, www.theconversation.com/.

35 J. Horton, "Doctors' Disorders: After COVID-19, Physicians Will Have to Face a Crisis of Another Sort," *Globe and Mail*, 8 May 2020, www.theglobeandmail.com/.

36 Mario Possamai, *A Time of Fear: How Canada Failed Our Health Care Workers and Mismanaged COVID-19* (Ottawa: Canadian Federation of Nurses Unions, 2020), https://nursesunions.ca/.

37 M. Ananda-Rajah et al, "Hearing the Voices of Australian Healthcare Workers during the COVID-19 Pandemic," *BMJ Leader* 5 (2021): 31–35, https://doi.org/10.1136/leader-2020-000386.

38 Amnesty International, *Exposed, Silenced, Attacked: Failures to Protect*

Health and Essential Workers during the COVID-19 Pandemic (London: Amnesty International, 2020), https://amnesty.ca/.

39 S. K. Brooks et al, "A Systematic, Thematic Review of Social and Occupational Factors Associated with Psychological Outcomes in Healthcare Employees during an Infectious Disease Outbreak," *Journal of Occupational and Environmental Medicine* 60 no. 3 (2018): 248–57, https://doi.org/10.1097/JOM.0000000000001235.

40 P. M. Smith et al, "The Association Between the Perceived Adequacy of Workplace Infection Control Procedures and Personal Protective Equipment with Mental Health Symptoms: A Cross-Sectional Survey of Canadian Health-Care Workers during the COVID-19 Pandemic," *Canadian Journal of Psychiatry* 66 no. 1 (2021): 17–24, https://doi.org/10.1177/0706743720961729; Brooks et al, "A Systematic, Thematic Review."

41 M. D. Braquehais et al, "The Impact of the COVID-19 Pandemic on the Mental Health of Healthcare Professionals," *QJM: An International Journal of Medicine* 113 no. 9 (2020): 613–17, https://doi.org/10.1093/qjmed/hcaa207.

42 J. E. McArthur, "How Governments Can Make Public Health Decisions When Some Information about Coronavirus Is Missing," The Conversation, 4 May 2020, https://theconversation.com/.

43 S. Gindin, "Political Openings: Class Struggle during and after the Pandemic," *New Solutions* 30 no. 4 (2021): 260–66, https://doi.org/10.1177/1048291120974422.

Index

battered person syndrome, 162–63

B.C. Nurses' Union, 125

bed shortages: "bed blockers," 103–4; hospital, 47–49, 84–85, 86, 231n17; long-term care, 103–4, 105–6; Ontario per capita, 85; psychiatric and addiction units, 95, 142; staff cuts and workload demands, 67–69, 92–93. *see also* wait times

Behavioural Supports Ontario (BSO), 62–63, 137

Belgium, 174

Bent Out of Shape (Messing), 164

Beth Israel Deaconess Medical Center (Boston), 127

"Better at Work" (WSIB), 153

Bianchi, Andria (bioethicist), 130

Bill 13/Time to Care Act (Ontario), 107, 188

Birch, Kean, 196

Black Lives Matter, 204. *see also* social movements

blaming the victim. *see* victim-blaming

body mapping technique, 26–32. *see also* injuries (workplace)

British Medical Association, 134

British National Health Service, 80

Brosseau, Lisa, 214

Brown, Lorne, 81

Brown, Michael, 165

Buchman, Sandy, 219

building design/features, 51–56, 96, 128–29, 134, 136

Bulmer, Laura (nurse), 13

burnout: "compassion fatigue," 33; COVID-19, 212; leaving careers, 43–44, 111; "resilience," 162;

sick calls, 68–69, 93. *see also* understaffing

Butterfly model (Canada), 139–40

Canada Health Act (1984), 82

Canada Health and Social Transfer (1995), 83

Canadian Armed Forces (CAF), 210

Canadian Association of Emergency Physicians, 205

Canadian Association of Retired Persons, 116–17

Canadian Centre for Policy Alternatives, 198

Canadian Cultural Mosaic Foundation, 194

Canadian Federation of Nurses Unions (CFNU), 13, 196, 205, 219–20

Canadian Health Coalition, 205

Canadian Institute for Health Information (CIHI), 84, 94, 232n32

Canadian Medical Association (CMA), 80, 82, 104, 136, 198, 205, 219

Canadian Medical Association Journal, 15

Canadian Mental Health Association (CMHA), 94

Canadian National Emergency Stockpile, 219

Canadian Nurses Association (CNA), 99

Canadian Union of Public Employees. *see* CUPE

Canadian Women's Foundation, 42

capitalism. *see* neoliberalism

family physicians, 225n13

feminist political economy, 184

Financial Post, 88

flagging: human rights issues, 130, 190; policies, 34, 57–58, 129–30; prevention strategy, 156, 207

Flint, Michigan, 172

Ford, Doug/Ford government, 87, 197, 199, 207

forensic units, 96, 149

for-profit care. *see* privatization

France, 37, 84

Fuller, Robert W., 176

funding. *see* underfunding

gaslighting, 163, 167. *see also* normalization of violence

Gates, Donna, 150, 151

Gélinas, France, 192

Gentle Persuasion approach, 140

George, Dudley (Ipperwash), 86

George Brown College, 13

Germany, 133

Gindin, Sam, 222–23

Glasbeek, Harry, 219

global justice movements, xiii, 204–5

Globe and Mail, x

governance. *see* policy and governance issues

Grassy Narrows First Nation, 172–73

Great Depression (1930s), 79

Green House Model, 139–40

Greenfield, Lazar, 181

Grey's Anatomy (television show), 182

Groopman, Jerome, 174–75

Guelph General Hospital, 16, 154

Hahn, Fred, 152

Hall, Emmett (Justice), 81–82

Hall Commission (1961), 81

hallway medicine, 90–92, 211. *see also* overcrowding

Harris, Mike/Harris government, 85–86, 196–97

Hartzband, Pamela, 174–75

Harvard Business Review, 204

Haslam-Stroud, Linda, 11, 87

Hazards (U.K.), 213

health care violence, overview, 11–16, 17–18

health insurance, public. *see* medicare

Health Quality Ontario, 94, 146, 147

Heartland: A Memoir of Working Hard and Being Broke in the Richest Country on Earth (Smarsh), 33

Hedges, Chris, 200

Hogewey dementia village (Holland), 138

home care workers, 13, 44–45

Homes for the Aged (1940s), 102–3

Homes for the Aged Act (1949), 102–3

Hospital Restructuring Act (2019) Ontario, 87

Hôtel-Dieu Hospital (Windsor), 11

House of Commons, federal, 82, 164, 195

housekeeping/cleaners, 38, 57, 65, 188

Houses of Refuge/"poor houses," 101–2

hurdles: ecological framework, 160; individual/personal, 160–61; interpersonal, 169–71;

psychological hurdle, 161–62; under-reporting, 147–48

North Bay Regional Health Centre, 7

North Carolina, 60

Norway, 128

Nurse Ratched stereotype (Netflix), 182

nurses: burnout and moral distress, 98–99; defunding and erosion of care, 97; female as most vulnerable, 12; ratios in Ontario, 84; sexism and gender-based violence, 180–83; systemic racism, 185–86. *see also individual nurses*

O. Reg. 187/15 Amendment (2017), 146

occupational health and safety. *see* clinical risk factors; normalization of violence; prevention strategies; social movements

Occupational Health and Safety Act, 146–47, 157; definition of workplace violence (Type II), 11

OCHU-CUPE: advocacy, 7, 206, 207; and COVID-19 pandemic, 209–10, 212; on criminal code amendments, 193, 194; health care workers' conference, 130, 205; hospital violence statistics, 14–15, 97; long-term care statistics, 17–18, 110; racialized workers, 41, 186; research collaboration, xv; *Voices,* 9, 24, 92, 148–49

OECD, 127

Oncology Nurse Advisor, 39

O'Neill, Rory, 213

ONS (Office for National Statistics U.K.), 180–81

Ontario: health care system decline, 84; hospital bed capacity lowest per capita, 84

Ontario Council of Hospital Unions–Canadian Union of Public Employees. *see* OCHU-CUPE

Ontario Health Coalition: advocacy work, 84, 85, 87, 105, 107, 206–7; executive members, 111, 117; response to COVID-19, 210; *Situation Critical* (2019), 107

Ontario Health Insurance Plan (OHIP), 86–87

Ontario Hospital Association, 85

Ontario Hospitals: Leaders in Efficiency (2019, OHA report), 85

Ontario Long Term Care Association (OLTCA), 18–19, 105, 137

Ontario Medical Review, 177

Ontario Network of Injured Workers Groups (ONIWG), 153–55

Ontario Nurses Association (ONA), 11, 87, 196; survey (2012), 15

Ontario Premier's Council, 90

Ontario Provincial Police, 86

Ontario Public Service Employees Union (OPSEU), 205

Ontario Workplace Safety and Insurance Board (WSIB). *see* WSIB (Ontario)

organizational risk factors/hur-

Margaret M. Keith is an occupational and environmental health advocate and researcher, focusing particularly on women and work. She earned a PhD from the University of Stirling. Margaret served as Executive Director of the Windsor Occupational Health Information Service before joining the Occupational Health Clinics for Ontario Workers in Sarnia. She and her partner, James Brophy, assisted the First Nation's community of Aamjiwnaang near Sarnia in exploring health problems related to environmental pollution from the adjacent petrochemical industry. Margaret was co-author of an internationally recognized research article documenting a skewed sex birth ratio uncovered after examining Aamjiwnaang birth records. She lives in Southwestern Ontario.

James T. Brophy is a career activist, researcher, and advocate focusing on occupational and environmental health. He received his doctorate from the University of Stirling on occupational risks for breast cancer. He is a former executive director of the Occupational Health Clinics for Ontario Workers (OCHOW) in Windsor and then Sarnia, where he and his partner, Margaret Keith, helped to document one of the largest cohorts of asbestos diseased workers in Canadian history. In recent years, he collaborated on research exploring violence against health care workers and on the lived experience of inadequately protected health care staff working during the pandemic. He lives in Southwestern Ontario.